1985

To Bobby —
Love,
Poppop & Granny
XXXX
OOOO

LIZARDS & LONGBOATS, PIRATES & PATRIOTS, CODES, CAVES & COVES...

LIZARDS & LONGBOATS, PIRATES & PATRIOTS, CODES, CAVES & COVES...

exploring the mysteries of yesterday

Jean Dorcy

Our Sunday Visitor, Inc.
Huntington, Indiana 46750

Scripture texts contained herein are taken from *The Jerusalem Bible*, copyright ©1966 by Darton, Longman & Todd, Ltd., London, and Doubleday & Company, Inc., New York, as well as from the *Revised Standard Version, Catholic Edition*, copyright ©1966 by the Division of Christian Education of the National Council of the Churches of Christ in the United States of America. The author and publisher are grateful to the aforementioned for the use of their material. If any protected materials in this work have been inadvertently used without permission, we apologize and request notification from the copyright holder.

Copyright ©1979 Our Sunday Visitor, Inc.
All rights reserved.

ISBN: 0-87973-635-6
Library of Congress Catalog Card Number: 79-53069

Cover design and illustrations by James E. McIlrath

Published, printed, and bound in the United States of America

To K, who taught me long ago that history is not stuffy;

to librarians, who have always been kind to me —

and especially to those at the Timberland Regional Libraries,

who all but flew pigeons to the moon to get me books;

and to my friends, who helped to make this book possible:

¡Mil gracias! — "A thousand thank-yous!"

Contents

Foreword... 11

[1]
The Talking Rocks... 13

[2]
Dinosaur Tracks... 25

[3]
The Rolling Worlds... 36

[4]
Happy Hunting Ground... 45

[5]
There Are Giants in Those Woods!... 56

[6]
Those Who Have Vanished... 67

[7]
Land Beyond the Sunset... 80

[8]
The Land of Sometime... 94

[9]
Frostie Seas With Myghty Yslands of Yce... 111

[10]
City in the Sky... 122

[11]
Gold, Frankincense, and Myrrh... 128

TABLE OF CONTENTS (continued)

[12]
Manila Galleon . . . 141

[13]
A New Mexico in the North . . . 162

[14]
Time Capsule . . . 179

[15]
The Great Land . . . 191

[16]
The Battle of Glorieta Pass . . . 202

[17]
The Beautiful Ships . . . 213

[18]
Horizons . . . 226

List of Things to Read, Do, See, and Discover . . . 237

Index . . . 248

Yahweh, you are the only one.
You made the heavens, the heaven of
    heavens, with all their array,
the earth and all it bears,
the seas and all they hold.
To all of these you give life
and the array of the heavens
    bows down before you.

— Nehemiah 9:6

Foreword

The author of this book does not believe in spontaneous generation, either of microbes or planets. She accepts the scriptural account of God creating the world in six days, though holding no set opinion about the length of these days. Where, or when, God took "dust from the ground, and breathed into his nostrils the breath of life; and man became a living being" (Genesis 2:7), we may know some day — and, then again, we may not. It has not yet been revealed to us, either by revelation or by science.

There have been, in the years of recorded history, a great many theories about the origin of the earth. A very long time ago it was believed that the world was built on the back of a huge turtle afloat in a great sea. Some of the modern theories are nearly as far out, including the suggestion that the world began when some atoms just got together *out there* and began making a world, which just kept tootling along by itself until it got to be the elaborate planet which we call home.

It is the fate of theories, good and bad, to be laughed at and fought over; if this happens when they are first suggested, it may mean that the inventor starves to death. Hundreds of years later, people are still laughing over the old theories and fighting over the reasonable ones; men feel very strongly about this subject. Today we have more theories than we know what to do with, with more appearing all the time.

A great deal of information has been quite literally dug up since Darwin's theory of evolution, which was supposed by many to be the last word in evolution a century ago. At this time we are just smart enough to know that we do not have the last word — yet.

We know that the rocks that make up our earth have evolved and that our material world has been formed by many powers that work upon each other. Hardly anyone believes that the world has always been here, just the way it is. That means that it had to start somewhere, sometime. One of the world's greatest astronomers has recently stated cautiously that it would all be quite a lot easier if one just believed in God.

It seems reasonable to believe that when one has traced back the causes behind the causes which gave us this star-spangled universe full of beautiful miniatures, one would find, not chaos — for chaos never created anything except more chaos — but God's fingerprint. In other words, no matter how much the universe evolved, it had to be God who pushed the button in the first place.

Chapter 1
The Talking Rocks

One of the biggest questions you will ever ask will come to your mind the day you first take a good look at the world around you and discover that it is very big and very beautiful. The question, of course, is: *How did it get here and why is it like this?*

The story of the making of our world can be read in two places: you can read it in the creation story in the Bible, where only an outline of the history is told. And you can read it from the books of stone from which the world is made. Only now, after all these centuries of study, are we beginning to understand both of these books. Neither Scripture nor science can be read off easily at first sight like an adventure story, though it really is the most exciting story ever told.

One of the best places to study about the making of the world is in caves. The rocks will talk, if we will listen, and caves are made of rock.

Caves are, sometimes, places for pirates to use for hiding treasure, or storage space for bats with hang-ups. Caves offer many dark corners where a mother wolf can raise her cubs, or a mother bobcat her kittens, or, for that matter, for a mother rattlesnake to keep her little rattlers. Caves were the homes, or camps, of long-forgotten hunters who painted mammoths or great wild bulls on the walls and ceilings, or very simply left handprints of the whole tribe on the cave wall. Campers and college students and fugitives from the law, pioneers, miners, and Indians made use of caves. Lost cows wander into them, setting up neighborhood rumors about moaning ghosts. The Cliff Dwellers of the dry Southwest lived in caves a thousand years ago, building apartment houses under the edges of the great mesas. Caves are good for lots of things. Above all, caves are history books, and they tell the story of how this world was made, billions of years before there was any man to write the story.

Going down into the caves beneath our world is like going into the basement of a house to see how the foundations were laid. Caves are mother earth's basement, full of treasures from long ago.

Speleologists are scientists who make a special study of caves. Spelunkers are amateur cave explorers who make it a hobby to find and study caves. You will notice that the first part of those words are the same: both involve caves. "Ologist" at the end of a word usually means that the person is a professor of some kind of science. Paleontologists study fossil remains in rocks; hydrologists, water; geologists, the history and structure of the earth. Since these all have something to do with caves, the experts often work together in working out a problem in science. They are like a group of detectives, each one at the top of his own subject, working to find the answers we need.

If you ever get worried about what holds up the mountains and all this vast world of farms and deserts and cities, set your mind at rest; it all has a very solid foundation that has been building for a long, long time. This foundation is made of stone of different kinds. Some of the stone is made by water, some by fire, some by both. It is the lifework of these scientists to find out all they can about the history of the earth. Both spelunkers and speleologists will tell you that the earth is not only old and solid, it is also very beautiful. They agree that there is nothing in the upstairs world to compare with the beauty they have seen underground, when the tiny beam of their lamp shows up a wall of glittering stone that has been hidden there in the dark since the world was finished.

One of the reasons that a cave is such a good place to study our planet's history is that caves often cut down through many layers of rock, like cutting into a cake with many layers. Usually the bottom layers of rock are the oldest, though sometimes an earthquake will mix up the layers and make it difficult to "read." Many of the oldest rocks were formed out of liquid like the molten steel in a mill. Others were laid down over billions of years by water. Limestone, which is quite young as rocks go (only about two hundred forty million years old), was made by the action of water on fossil shells in the early days of seashells.

Most caves are made of limestone and were formed in two separate actions. First, the caves were formed by volcano, by earthquake, or by rivers cutting down through the rock layers much in the way that the Colorado River is making the Grand Canyon. Then, over endless ages, they were decorated by dripping water, a process that is still going on and may last for millions of years yet.

Caves may be formed by some sudden volcanic upheaval or earthquake, but the decorations come about drop by drop. If you were to blow a soap bubble onto a dark tabletop, and you watched while the bubble burst, you would see — very faintly — a ring on the tabletop where the bubble had been. It is the soap in the bubble that you see; the soap is the "something else" mixed with the oxygen and hydrogen in the water. In the same way, a drop of water containing a weak acid acts on the limestone, and leaves a tiny ring. The acid is the "something else." As tens of thousands and millions of drops fall in the same place, they form a tiny tube, then a bump, then an icicle-shaped object hanging from the cave ceiling. Perhaps at the same time a tiny mound of limestone builds up from below. The hanging one is called a stalactite and the standing one a stalagmite. If they meet in the middle, they may form a column. Very sensibly, this is called dripstone, because that is what it does — it drips. This may be a very simple process, but it takes time: several million years, perhaps.

How many caves are there in the United States? Probably more than fifty thousand, including a great many public caves you can safely visit, and any number of "wild" caves that should be left to the experts. Some areas have many more than others; there are 437 known caves in Missouri, and more than 600 in Arkansas. The states of Virginia, Alabama, Tennessee, and Kentucky have great numbers, and practically every state in the Union has several. Tom Sawyer's cave and Cudjo's cave turn up in your reading, and perhaps you sing the sad song of Floyd Collins, who was trapped in a cave and died. You have also probably read many exciting stories about buried treasure in caves. Quite likely there is a public cave within fifty miles of where you live, which you might find much more exciting than stories.

Caves, like people, are very different from each other. There are the dry caves of the Southwest, carved by wind and sand and long-forgotten rivers, where the stone cities of the Cliff Dwellers still look out upon a landscape that was once green with gardens and busy with the people who farmed them. These caves sometimes run back for miles of twisting passages under the mesa, but most of them are shallow and cling to the cliff like swallows' nests. The best example of this kind of cave can be found on the banks of the Grand Canyon, very high up, by which we can tell that they have been there a long time. The Colorado, which is a hardworking river, moves enough silt to fill twelve thousand freight cars per day. It takes a while to dig a gorge that deep.

A fascinating study in rocks are the ocean caves, which most people call sea-lion caves. Here great colonies of sea creatures of many kinds live happily in huge flat rooms with watery floors. Because the sea level has changed so many times in the history of the earth — as ice was formed or melted at the poles, or as the great Ice Age glaciers came and went — the caves are sometimes found in surprising places. There must be many of them out on the continental shelf where no one but divers can see them.

In the northern states, in the area once covered by the ice sheets, there are caves formed of glacier ice. Some of the most beautiful of these are at Mount Rainier in Washington State — though these are not always open to the public because they change all the time and are not always safe for tourists. There is a crystal cave in Idaho with decorations of the most delicate icy lace, which stays frozen even when it is hot enough to fry hamburgers on the sidewalks above.

Deep in the badlands of the New Mexico desert are the famous ice caves that were a hideout for Geronimo a century ago.

An early explorer discovers one
of the many fascinating caves found
in the Southwest and other areas.

Waterless wastes surround the place, a terrible land with volcanic rocks like broken glass, a land of sure death to anyone who has run out of water, unless he knows about the caves. Here in this black hole in the ground the ice never melts unless you put it over a fire to melt for drinking. The walls are covered with icy lace "like egret feathers," someone said. Not a square yard of the floor is level, and it is as slippery as a skating rink. Next to the ice caves are loads of charcoal brought in by some careful outlaw.

Behind the ice cave there is pottery which can be dated nearly a thousand years ago. But the cave is far more famous for its outlaws than for its pottery. Geronimo made constant use of the place, baffling the American soldiers suffering out in the desert trying to find him. People with names like Pegleg Pete and Horned Toad Johnson and Pumphandle McClary, hunting gold and dodging Apaches, reported seeing the caves. This may have been the place where Jim Bridger, the famous mountain man, said he saw "puttrified birds a-settin' in puttrified trees a-singin' puttrified songs."

Lava caves that figure in history as a battlefield are the Lava Beds National Monument near Tule Lake in northern California. If you have read the story of the Modoc Indian subchief Captain Jack and his people, fighting a last-ditch battle to keep their homeland, you will remember his sad words, "Nobody will ever want these rocks! Give us a home here!" His tragic plea went unanswered and his people are gone now.

Caves are often full of mystery. One that has so far defied solution has the mold of a rhinoceros in the lava rocks of a cave in eastern Washington. There are a number of caves here; the mystery is, what is a rhinoceros doing in one of them? Or rather, what *was* he doing here — for there is nothing left of him but the mold, or impression, of a beast that has completely disappeared. The nearest rhinoceros, unless you look in the zoo, is in Africa. And this one is a real old-timer; scientists tell us that he is at least twenty million years old. What was he doing in the cave? It looks as if he was already dead when he went into the cave — died in a flood, perhaps — and there must have been a volcano erupting at the same time, because molten lava poured down around him and made a mold, as you might make a rubber mold to make plaster figures.

He is called the "Blue Lake Rhino" because he was found near Blue Lake. We can tell that he was a very special rhino because he had two horns. But all the relatives anyone can find are some distant cousins in Oregon who had only one horn. Where are his brothers, friends, classmates? And where, for that matter, is he, of whom all we have is an impression in the lava?

Aside from these special kinds of caves, the greater number of American caves are limestone, first made, then decorated, by water. In some of these the water is still there, in lakes deep underground, or lost rivers that keep appearing and disappearing.

Carlsbad Caverns, the largest and best known of American caves, is typical of most limestone caverns. It is located in desert country in southern New Mexico, not far from the Mexican border. This entire area, including the White Sands military proving ground and the saline (salt) lake country to the north, was once under water for a long time. Since the future United States has been under water at least twenty times while the earth was being made, this was not surprising. But, aeons ago and for a very long time, a great inland sea reached from the Gulf of California to the Rockies. There are fossil shells over the whole area, even on top of the Sandia Mountains, to show where it was. Shells from this great sea built the limestone caves at Carlsbad.

Indian legends say that the saline country was the "garden of Eden" of their creation story. Here, they say, was the world's most beautiful green valley, with sparkling lakes and streams. However, man sinned by breaking a rule his Creator had given him, and a great salt sea rolled in over the valley and stayed there until the land beneath it was nothing but desert. However much truth there is in this legend, this is almost exactly the way scientists have decided that this country became a desert. The waters of the great salt sea must have trickled down between the cracks in the rocks and carved away the enormous cave system, with its halls and giant rooms at different levels.

These caves were undiscovered for a long time. Sometime, a few hundred years ago, Indians camped in the outer cave. They drew pictures on the wall and left some of their gear behind. No one tried to go deep into the tunnels. A century ago, a few people went in a little way and came out telling spooky stories. Nobody really took time to explore it until, in 1901, a young man named Jim White was startled by what looked like a tornado roaring up out of the earth.

He went nearer and discovered that the dangerous-looking cone of the tornado was made up of bats — millions of them — and they were coming out of a hole in the ground. He came back again and again to see them. He found that the bats left the cave every evening at dusk to hunt, and that it took them three hours to get out because there were so many of them. Later, a scientific count showed that there were between five and eight million bats, and that they came out at the rate of one hundred per second. They made a roar like a river rushing through a rocky gorge (or like a subway train, perhaps) because of the beating of millions of wings. After a night's hunting, they came whirring back at daybreak and hung themselves neatly on their own little hangers on the cave roof, and slept all day.

It was years before Jim White could get anybody to believe the stories he told about the underground wonderland that he was the first man in all time to see. People said that the bats were smelly and probably dangerous, and who would believe things he told them about great halls with stone draperies that glittered like jewels? Finally, the National Geographic Society did a full-scale exploration, and the cave was opened to the public. In the years since, it has become one of New Mexico's favorite tourist attractions.

Carlsbad is not the most colorful among the big caves; Luray Caverns in Virginia claims that honor. But Carlsbad has almost all the things one ever finds in a limestone cave, and it is an ideal place to study and make tests on caves. Tourists have given most of the names to the Carlsbad formations: the American Eagle, the Three Little Monkeys, the Papoose Room, the Green Lake Room, the King's Palace, Rock of Ages, Hall of the Giants. Besides the great halls and enormous draperies of stone, there are tiny doll-sized halls and rooms which delight small children.

Not until after World War II and the advance of color photography could the great dark rooms be photographed in natural colors so that stay-at-homes could see them in books and magazines. Even so, it took a lot of camera equipment and thousands of specially made flashbulbs to do the job. People today are apt to think that every tourist has a motion-picture camera hanging from one shoulder and a Polaroid from the other. Photography has moved very fast in the past fifty years, and the men who first photographed the caverns in color have a place among the pioneers.

Limestone is ordinarily white. Minerals dissolved in the water during the stone's formation add blues, browns, and yellows. Colored lighting is now used to highlight the exhibits. The cavern has also been fitted with easy walkways, a lunchroom, and an elevator.

The water is long gone from Carlsbad, but many other caves still have the sunken lakes or rivers that helped to make them. Some have bottomless pits that no one has yet found a way to explore. Some have small green lakes that glitter in the lamplight, or black water talking to itself far down in the darkness. Kentucky's Mammoth Cave has a great deal of gypsum formation — puffy shapes like cotton balls, flowers spun from gypsum, or long, sharp needles like glass. Lewis and Clark Cave in Montana is a fairly small cave, but it has very rich decorations, and seems to have an example of everything that could possibly be made from limestone.

Something odd about caves is that they "breathe." This is not just a matter of wind blowing in one opening and out the other; the cave breathes with the barometric pressure — *in* when the barometer rises, *out* when it falls. Or it breathes in and out every eight minutes, or whatever its timing says. Some caves breathe with the season; *in* during summer, *out* in winter. Cave of the Winds, in the Black Hills of South Dakota, is a famous cave with a breathing problem. This was once the sacred cave of the Indians. It is a very beautiful and strange place, with neither stalactites nor stalagmites. Instead, it is nearly covered with delicate stone lacework, pinkish in color.

More than one cave has been discovered because some innocent bystander had his hat snatched off by a hole in the ground, which politely returned it twenty minutes later. There is a great deal that we do not know about caves yet.

Sometimes the name of a cave tells you what kind of place it is. Endless Caverns has miles of underground tunnels, many of which have never been explored. Cave of the Winding Stair in the Mojave Desert is very deep, and — like so many others in the Southwest — abounds in treasure legends. Spanish Cave, or Caverna del Oro ("Cavern of Gold"), is popularly supposed to have a sunken river with banks of gold-bearing sands. Echo River is a feature of Mammoth Cave that always interests visitors. The Lost Sea of Craighead Caverns is supposed to be the largest underground lake in the world.

A place in Florida with a real mouthful of name, Devil's Milhopper State Geological Site, is a good example of how thought and money can take a wild cave and turn it into an enjoyable and educational park. It started with a deep sink, a natural feature located north of Gainesville. A natural trail and steps now lead down into the sink, which is one hundred fourteen feet deep. Brooks flow down the sides of the sink in tiny waterfalls from natural springs. The walls have been planted with trees and ferns not usually found in Florida, and part of it is cut into the rocky soil, showing shells, bones, and teeth of long-ago animal visitors to the park. It is a pleasant green park, with many stories of the past that can be read from its rocks.

Probably everyone in America lives within reasonable distance of at least one public cave that he could visit. It is a simple thing to go to the library and find out what caves your state has to offer, and to write for information about whichever one you choose. Then you can make a school or family trip out of it and try your hand at reading the great stone books that tell us almost all we know about the years before man wrote history in words. You could call this "Experimental History" — something that you yourself experience.

Wild caves are tempting, but they are too dangerous for any but very experienced speleologists or spelunkers. A cave is not a place to play; it is a place to study. There is one rule that any sensible cave explorer keeps: No matter how experienced you are, *never* go into a cave alone — no matter how smart you are or who dared you to do it. None of us knows, until he lives through it himself, what effect absolute silence and absolute darkness will have on him. It is all too easy to drop your flashlight and panic. So leave the wild caves to the experts. But do, if you can, visit one of the big public caves and see how much you can read of the language of stone.

Chapter 2
Dinosaur Tracks

A few years ago, some fishermen off the coast of Africa caught a strange fish in their nets. It was six feet long, and when they first pulled it up from the depths it was bright blue, with white eyes. It was covered all over with scales so solid they looked like armor plate. From the size of the creature, they thought it must be some kind of a shark, but no one had ever seen a shark like this one, with a mouth four feet wide. Frightened as they were, they brought the strange fish in to shore to ask the scientists from the museum what it was.

The museum staff had no problem telling what kind of fish it was; there was a very good description of it in their books. But they simply did not believe their eyes. The blue fish was a coelacanth, an armored fish. His fossils were found in rocks millions of years old. He was supposed to have vanished from the earth seventy million years ago!

In the time when the coelacanth was an ordinary citizen of the ancient seas instead of a Johnny-come-lately in another age, he lived in a fearful world. True, there were no fishermen in it to catch him in a net, but fifty-foot sharks with six-inch teeth swam all around him looking for food. He needed those armored scales all over his body, or he would not have lasted one year, let alone seventy million. All his neighbors were savage and single-minded; what they wanted was *food*. His protection was the same as that adopted by some of the land animals of the time — tough plates that even a very sharp tooth could not bite through.

For this was the age of the dinosaurs, the "terrible lizards," the biggest creatures ever to live on land, and a frightening world it must have been. It seems a little rude to call it the age of the monsters, but some of them looked like the sort of thing they dream up in Hollywood to make "monster" movies. They lived in a world that did not look much like the one we are living in. For one thing, much of the earth was covered by water at the time. A great shallow sea lay across all the interior of North America. There were no finished mountains, but a great many of them were being built by active volcanoes, which filled the air with black smoke and gases. Few of the great rivers had yet started to flow, and the water was swampy and probably smelly.

All of the plants and trees alive at the time were green, and the whole landscape must have been very green, without a bird or flower or butterfly to add any other color. Some of the trees would look familiar to us; for example, there was an early sort of palm tree with scraggly brushes on the top, and tall spindly pine trees dotted the landscape here and there. The tree that was the most plentiful was an early form of our redwood, which has survived down to our times in some parts of the world. Also, the strange ginkgo, or maidenhair tree, with its leaves like maidenhair fern, can be found today as a tree. It grew as a great fern in the days when coal was being made; once in a while, a piece of coal turns up with the print of that unusual leaf. These, with the giant horsetail rushes, made up the greenery of the dinosaur world.

Wading around in the mud or swimming in the weedy lakes, or perhaps nibbling from the treetops, were the strangest animals that ever walked the earth. We call them dinosaurs ("terrible lizards") because they look to us more like lizards than anything else we know. They also looked somewhat like crocodiles and turtles, which is quite natural, because they were all reptiles. The ground shook when the big ones took a step; it was something like the First National Bank lifting up one corner of the building and starting to walk, very slowly, a corner at a time. They have been called "thunder lizards" because everything trembled when they moved. The very thought of anything that size coming after you is enough to give you a year's nightmares.

In the days of the silent pictures, someone made a movie of Sir Arthur Conan Doyle's story, "The Lost World." It had a very funny scene in it where a big dinosaur is brought to London, to give an idea what it might be like to have something that size in captivity. It was a very amusing movie, but of course that is not at all the way it happened. Man and dinosaur could not possibly live in the same sort of world. Even the "green jungle" of the Amazon is nothing in comparison to the savage, primitive world of seventy million years ago. The earth was not ready for man yet when the huge beasts had their day and moved on.

The "day" of the terrible lizards was one hundred twenty million years long, and in that time there were changes both in the creatures themselves and the land they lived on. Not all of the dinosaurs of which we have information lived at the same time. All dinosaurs were small in the beginning of their day. They grew and changed as time went by, and were modified by the kind of food they ate and the sort of enemies they had, or what the volcanoes in the neighborhood were doing at the time. The huge creatures we know the most about came toward the end of the dinosaur age, and they seemed to get more fantastic in design as they went along. Life must have been good for them to have lived so many millions of years before they disappeared.

Dinosaurs came in all sizes. Many were small, the size of chickens, and had to step lively if they wanted to stay alive. At the other end of the scale, *Brontosaurus* in the American Museum of Natural History is sixty-five feet long. He is roughly the weight of eight big elephants, which is a lot of lizard, and his head was about the size of yours. Big brother *Brachiosaurus* could be seventy-five feet long and a couple of elephants heavier. One *Diplodocus* skeleton is eighty-five feet long. Once grown to these impressive sizes, the big lizards were not easily damaged, though none of them ever got the best of an erupting volcano, and one could break a leg in an earthquake crack. They lived in herds, as peaceful animals usually do, and — barring accident — it is thought that they could live to be one hundred fifty to two hundred years old. However, dinosaur eggs and baby dinosaurs were a delicacy for their neighbors of all sizes, and it was hard to raise a family. The big meat eaters — savage *Allosaurus* and his cannibal cousin, *Tyrannosaurus* — kept clear of a wallop from *Brontosaurus's* tail, which could knock you clear across the lake. Everybody's enemy, they attacked smaller beasts or wounded dinosaurs, eating everything in sight, alive or dead.

It is just as well that man was not around to share this primitive world. Aside from the meat eaters, he would be perfectly safe from the dinosaurs, which were all staunch vegetarians and could hurt him only by stepping on him. However, there were fifty-foot crocodiles that hardly bear thinking about, and the only flying creatures of the time were big batlike horrors right out of a spook movie. There was even a dragonfly with wings a yard wide.

Elasmosaurus looked like a toothpaste ad, and, alas, his teeth were his only beauty. *Triceratops* was made for trouble; he had three great horns on his head and a wide, bony collar. Unless he was taken by surprise from behind, he looked pretty well able to take care of himself. *Stegosaurus* looked as if he had been put together out of junk; great plates of leathery material stuck up along his spine, and at best he must have tasted like an old suitcase. He was built to defend himself, not to go around picking fights. His head was so small that it was hard to tell which was the head and which the tail, a thing that would puzzle his enemies.

An up-to-date dinosaur was *Dimetrodon*, who had both heating and air conditioning built in at that early date. The first scientists to examine his remains were under the impression that he used his great sail to go skimming over the water, but it did not really seem likely. So they decided that it was an air-cooling (or heating) fan. One very ugly little dinosaur had nothing remarkable but a spiked war club on the end of his tail. All he had to do was reverse, and swing into action.

There were some very fancy models of dinosaurs, especially in the last few million years of their time on earth. Some of the later ones look as if they had been designed by Dr. Seuss. One, a member of *Stegocephalia*, had a third eye on top of his head, which must have been very handy at times. *Coelophysis*, eight or ten feet high and lightly built, ran about on two legs like a chicken. What lovely drumsticks! He also had a good, solid set of teeth,

"The tracks of Noah's raven" turn out to be footprints of a small dinosaur. *(See page 32.)*

with their edges serrated like a steak knife. There was a great assortment of duck-billed dinosaurs, called at times (but not very politely) boneheaded dinosaurs. Members of the *Ankylosauria* family took no chances; there wasn't a place on them that didn't have a horn, or at least a knob. Horns and knobs were high style at the end of the dinosaur age, and everybody who was anybody had them.

The story of these fascinating animals was not known until about one hundred years ago. We still do not know the whole story. Back in the Middle Ages, several dinosaur skeletons were discovered in Europe, but everyone thought they were dragons which had been killed by some brave prince not too long ago. Early church art showed St. George slaying a dragon, which was understood to be evil, and the battle was that fight between good and evil which always goes on in this world. (It is strange to Western man that the Chinese, who still represent the dragon in art, regard him as good, not evil.) People who did not believe in dragons mistook the great bones for the skeletons of Hannibal's war elephants, which had crossed the Alps six hundred years before the coming of Christ. Even today, though we know better than that, there is a lot we do not know about dinosaurs. Today there are great arguments going on among scientists about the big lizards: Were they, as we have believed for a long time, cold-blooded? Or were they warm-blooded? It will be very hard to get an answer to that question.

America in colonial times was a vast treasure box of unknowns to the young, brave men who set about exploring it. No one was ever more interested in the things of science than President Jefferson, who backed many expeditions with both money and enthusiasm, and who never ceased to study the world around him. During his lifetime, someone found a big skeleton in a cave. The head was missing, but the beast had great curved claws which were well preserved. We know now that it was a giant sloth from the Ice Age of some ten thousand years ago. No one in Jefferson's America had ever heard of dinosaurs. How fascinated he would have been to see a coelacanth, seventy million years old and still alive and well near Madagascar!

The day of the dinosaur — and the coelacanth — ran from roughly four hundred million years ago to about seventy million years ago, at which time our fish apparently missed the boat and was left behind. During all those millions of years, the so-called fossil fuel that runs our factories and heats our homes was laid away in stony beds, to be dug up by us and used as coal and petroleum. Coal is formed from fossil vegetation from which all the lighter elements are gone, leaving only carbon.

Like police detectives, scientists are always interested in evidence, especially footprints. In 1802 a Massachusetts boy found some footprints on stone, and it was agreed by all that they must be the tracks of Noah's raven. It was a hundred years before science was ready to say that they were the tracks of a small dinosaur. Near San Antonio, Texas, there is an exhibit of fossil tracks of a whole herd of dinosaurs that walked across the soft bed of a creek leaving their prints for us to see, millions of years later. We can even tell that the herd must have been followed by one of the big meat eaters trying to grab a meal; the tracks of the little dinosaurs are all in the middle of the group, surrounded by the big ones, in the way that buffalo will react in order to guard their calves from wolves.

There is plenty of mystery surrounding the last of these beasts. Most of them died, all at about the same time, from causes that we do not yet know. But, here and there, some of them must have lived on, at least for a while. There is a cave in Oregon which has a great lizard scratched on the wall; it looks very much like our unstylish friend, the stegosaur. But who was on hand to sketch a live stegosaur, unless he lived on long after his time? The people of Loch Ness in Scotland are using all the new tools of the U.S. Navy, including sonar, to try to find out something about the shy monster (or monsters — there would almost have to be several) said to live in their lake. They have quite a few odd bits of evidence, including a sonar tracing, to tell them there is *something* there. *Things.* From what they have seen, it looks like a plesiosaur. If a coelacanth, why not a plesiosaur? Nobody expected to find dinosaur eggs in the Gobi Desert after the winds of literally millions of years — and-who-knows-how-many camels — have passed over them; but they were found, complete with tiny dinosaurs coiled inside them.

Evidence for the plesiosaur comes not only from Scotland but from four rather unexpected places. In 1915 a German submarine sank a British freighter in the North Atlantic; while they were watching the ship go down, up from the depths came a fritter-shaped beast, wounded and struggling wildly. Two years later in the same part of the ocean, a British armed cruiser sighted a huge creature swimming beside them. They shot it — and lost it — but all agreed, it looked like a plesiosaur. One of the Grace liners struck and killed another big sea creature at about the same place. They must have a nest somewhere in the North Atlantic — and at least one wandering member who turned up in the nets of a Japanese fishing boat very recently. There are hundreds of exciting discoveries waiting for the next generation of scientists.

One of our country's most interesting places to study the dinosaurs and their world is the Dinosaur National Monument on the Utah-Colorado border. This area has produced some of the finest museum fossils, many of which are in the natural-history museums in the big cities of our country. But its main interest is that it can help us to picture that far-off world that no man ever saw.

Colorado-Utah scenery has changed since those days; now you see blazing red-gold cliffs, the changing desert, and the strange, twisted forms of the mountains surrounding the valleys where the fossils are found. There were no mountains when the dinosaurs lived there, and it was not a desert; it was low, marshy country with lots of water. It would be a mistake to look up at a rocky cliff and picture a dinosaur peeking around the corner at you. The cliffs were not made yet when the dinosaurs moved on. The Rocky Mountains, indeed all the western mountains, were just in the process of being made in the ages after the dinosaurs were gone. All that the great beasts left here were their huge skeletons, many of which sank into the mud and were petrified (made into rock) by chemical action of the water and the mud.

Some places have really too many dinosaurs to be comfortable; dead ones drifted down the rivers, grounded on sandbars, and piled up until their weight sank them deep in the mud. One fascinating exhibit at Dinosaur National Monument is a mountain made of dinosaur bones which have hardened together as if they were set in cement. Scientists who work on these fossils use dental tools or small brushes, so that they will not harm the bones. A good many dinosaurs seem to have left us nothing but their smile, like the Cheshire cat; scientists must learn an unbelievable number of things about teeth in order to identify what they find. Not all dinosaurs had teeth. Like chickens, which must swallow small gravel to use as a grinder for food in their gizzards, so also did some of the big lizards have gizzards, swallowing stones called gastroliths.

It takes an expert to identify fossils; but, oddly enough, it is usually an amateur who makes the important finds, quite by accident, like the fishermen who caught the coelacanth. Many an amateur has done great things for science, simply by having the good sense to take his find to somebody who might know what it is. Most of the discoveries that have sent scientists on their way rejoicing have been made by a tired cowboy out looking for strays, or a college boy on a hike, or a group of Boy Scouts who have both energy and curiosity to spend. The next bit of vital information, the piece of the puzzle that all the world's scientists are waiting for, may fall into your hands.

If ever you have the chance to see the Dinosaur National Monument at Vernal, Utah, by all means do so. It is a fantastic place for a vacation trip, surrounded by some of the country's finest scenery. And if your city is large enough to have a natural-history museum with one of those huge white skeletons in it, go and see it — again and again. Study it, and it will tell you a lot about the world you live in.

What made the great animals die? This is a question that nobody at the present time can answer. Today we see the damage man can do to the balance of nature; but man is innocent of killing off the dinosaurs — he was *not* there. So what brought about the great dying? Volcanic eruptions and poisonous gases? Tornadoes, earthquakes, fires? The tsetse fly? Floods? Meteorites or gaslike substances from outer space? And why, when all the big beasts died, did the alligators survive, and the turtles? And the snakes and scorpions that are still very much with us? We shall discuss this further in Chapter 4.

The Bible is a strange place to look for a story about a dragon, but there is a very lively one in the Book of Daniel, Chapter 14. Daniel lived around six hundred years before Christ, which is a long, long time from seventy million years ago. At any rate, here is the story:

> There was also a great dragon, which the Babylonians revered. And the king said to Daniel, "You cannot deny that this is a living god; so worship him." Daniel said, "I will worship the Lord my God, for he is the living God. But if you, O king, will give me permission, I will slay the dragon without sword or club." The king said, "I give you permission."
>
> Then Daniel took pitch, fat, and hair, and boiled them together and made cakes, which he fed to the dragon. The dragon ate them, and burst open. And Daniel said, "See what you have been worshiping!"

It doesn't sound as if he was much of a cook, but anybody who will hand-feed a dragon deserves our interest.

Chapter 3
The Rolling Worlds

God said, "Let there be lights in the vault of heaven to divide day from night, and let them indicate festivals, days and years. Let them be lights in the vault of heaven to shine on the earth." And so it was. God made the two great lights: the greater light to govern the day, the smaller light to govern the night, and the stars.

— *Genesis 1:14*

God — who gives its luster to the insect's wing, and wheels his throne upon the rolling worlds. . . .

— *William Cowper*

Earth — the blue planet — a beautiful jewel in space.

— *Neil Armstrong*

Pioneer 10 rocketed out of our solar system a few years ago, carrying a diagram with messages about Earth and its people, designed for "anybody out there." At a later date *Voyager* probes, headed for Jupiter and Saturn, carried a phonograph record with greetings in sixty languages, and an hour and a half of music ranging from Bach and Beethoven to hard rock. It may be forty thousand years before it reaches the nearest star. The device carries a complete set of directions on how to set it in motion, the true American touch.

In other words, Earth has reached that point in time where we are launching out into space — first of all, hoping to find out more about our own planet, and secondly, hoping to find some intelligent life out there among the stars.

This is not the first time in history that man has stepped off into the unknown. In the fourteenth century, missionaries were sent to the interior of China, which is a long walk from Italy. They carried the most modern equipment then known — a manual of directions telling them what kind of creatures to expect in the unknown lands. There would be men who had dogs' heads, who talked by barking, the manual explained; these were very intelligent creatures, and they had whole armies made up of fighting dogs.

There would be men with only one arm and one leg, who moved around by turning somersaults, the manual continued. Another kind had big floppy ears which could be wrapped around them for warmth at night. Some had mouths so small they could not eat, but fed by inhaling steam. If you look at a copy of a fifteenth-century map, you will probably see a border of these creatures around the edge of the map. The missionaries were advised how to behave toward these people, and to find out — if they could — whether or not they had souls and were really human, or just very talented animals. Today when we talk about "little men from Mars," we are apt to picture them like this, even though we know better.

People of the fourteenth century should have known better, too; they had the account of Marco Polo who had lived for twenty years at the court of Kublai Khan and had written the most famous travel book in history about his experiences, but no one would believe Marco Polo. When he was on his deathbed, his friends begged him to confess "all those terrible lies" he had told about Cathay (as China was then called), so that he would not lose his soul. It is a funny thing about people: they find it much easier to believe fantasy than truth.

Our planetary system centers on a small star on the edge of a galaxy that has perhaps a hundred billion stars. Within this one small galaxy there may be as many as a billion suns with their own planetary systems similar to ours. There may be a million of them which contain warm, habitable planets. We do not know. But we are trying hard to find out. We have made the trip to the moon, which is our nearest neighbor in the skies. This is where we have to begin.

A thousand scientists from fourteen countries are studying the samples of soil and the nearly nine hundred pounds of rock brought back from the moon. They have discovered, among other things, that the moon has many of the same elements that the earth has, but in different amounts. It has almost no carbon and very little iron, of which we have so much. Moon rocks look as if they were made of tiny beads of stained glass, colored by titanium and other elements.

The moon is now "bugged" so that we can watch her like a doctor with a very sick patient. We want to know if there is, or ever was, water there, and whether there is any life at all, even of a very simple kind. Covered with a thick, fine, clinging dust, the moon from up close looks like a long-dead cinder pile — but is it?

One of the most important aims of the moonflights was to discover, if possible, how old the moon is and how it was formed. The reason for this, of course, is to gain more knowledge about our own planet. The books from which we seek our answers are the rocks brought back by the astronauts. All this very precise scientific story is written in stone, if we can just manage to read it.

Scientists today have much better ways of studying the messages in the stones than anyone did a half century ago. Back in the 1920s a very clever man worked out a system of reading tree rings to discover the age of trees. You have probably seen a tree-ring calendar, a slice cut across the trunk of a big tree with the important dates in history marked on the rings. This was one of the first time measurements, and from it men learned to tell the age of other things besides trees, and to tell what the weather had been like when the tree rings were formed. Since man has been working with the atom, he has found new methods of dating bones, fossils, and other once-living things by what is called the carbon-14 method. Even newer systems can now date rocks, which have never been alive, by radiometric means. Radiometric measurements give the earth's age at about four billion years.

There are several theories about the age of the moon. Rocks from the surface of the moon were formed nearly four billion years ago. This would mean that it may have been formed at the same time as the earth. There is one theory that the moon was once part of the earth, whirled out of it by gigantic power like a boy making and throwing a snowball into orbit. They point out that perhaps (these scientific "perhapses" are sometimes pretty big ones) — that perhaps the moon came from that great hole where the Pacific Ocean is at the moment. The moon is certainly bound to the earth by strong ties — twice in every earthly day, it moves the great oceans in tides all around the world.

The moon is about one fourth as big as the earth. Astronauts tell us that earthshine from our planet is far brighter on the moon than even the brightest moonlight is on earth. Both planets have a core so hot that it is melted, like molten steel, or glass when it is being worked. Both planets have this core wrapped carefully in layers of rock, very hard rock in the middle and lighter, "floating" rock on top. The earth has a system of sliding plates of this floating rock (we think) which helps to release the heat from the center. The hot, liquid rock bubbles up through hundreds of miles of tiny cracks and explodes here and there in volcanoes, which may cause earthquakes.

If you look at an earthquake map of the Western Hemisphere, you will see little warning dots almost all around the Pacific coasts of the world, the so-called "ring of fire." We are told that all the nervous little earth wriggles that occur somewhere every day are a safety measure, like the whistling valve on a steam-pressure cooker blowing off steam to keep from exploding. There have been some very bad earthquakes in history, and some in the past few years, but most of the volcanic eruptions took place long before man lived on earth.

The theory of sliding plates that float on top of the heavier rocks below is very popular today; it is called the continental drift theory. The idea is that at one time, terribly long ago, the continents were all together in one huge landmass and all the rest was ocean. If you will look at a map of the world — especially if you are good at jigsaw puzzles — you will see where this theory first came from. With patience, and filling in a gap here and there, you could almost put it together again.

The idea is that the continents are on plates of rock which move when material from the earth's center bubbles up between them. When the plates bump into one another, the surface scuffs up into mountains like a small rug caught under a door, or your bedclothes when you push them down so you can get out of bed. Building on this theory, scientists say that the first big landmass, which they call by a Greek name meaning "all the land there is," divided first into two continents and drifted apart. The southern one, Gondwanaland, included Africa, South America, Australia, Antarctica, and India. The northern continent, Laurasia, was made up of North America and Eurasia.

A few years ago, nobody would believe it possible that continents could float, but a great deal of evidence has come to us in the past twenty years. For one thing, the theory of rock magnetism strongly supports this idea. When rocks are in the molten state, being formed by volcanic forces, their magnetic parts line up in relation to the north magnetic pole, and they harden that way. No matter how they are tumbled around by earthquake or water, they can always be put back in the same relationship with the magnetic pole, and it can be seen where they were to begin with.

A second bit of evidence is that of the fossil animals that have been found on what must have been matching seacoasts at one time. Mineral deposits check out as being the same, even with three thousand miles of ocean between them. And, probably the strongest argument of all, the continents are still moving — perhaps only an inch a year, but give it another million years and things will be quite different.

Even the dinosaurs did their part for the continental drift

theory. Fossils found in the past few years in Antarctica show that a small (and very ugly) dinosaur lived there some two hundred million years ago when it was a tropical land. He could not swim the ocean, and there is no evidence of any land bridge he might have crossed over. He — or his ancestors — must have been on board when Antarctica docked, millions of years ago.

In studying the way our earth is made up, we must not overlook the fact that our place in the solar system is very important to us. Our planet is set up for a twenty-four-hour day, with nights of almost equal length as days (changing with the season, but the same on an average). The earth rotates at a speed of one thousand miles per hour. If it were to slow down to one hundred miles an hour, days and nights would be ten times as long, the sun would burn off all the vegetation by day, and at night everything would freeze.

The sun is roughly ninety-three million miles from earth and has a surface temperature of 12,000 degrees F., which is exactly right for us. The tilt of the earth gives us our seasons; if we were tilted at a different angle, vapors would pile up and build great continents of ice at the poles. If the moon were 50,000 miles away instead of around 240,000, the tides would be so great that they would cover the continents twice a day. When you see how carefully all this has been arranged to fit our planet, you see that it could not all just be a happy accident.

The shoreline of our continents has been changing since long before man took any notice of it. A continental shelf extends out from the landmass, and this forms one of the greatest fishing grounds in the world. In some places the ocean shores have been sinking, which means that port cities will some day have to move inland. Through the clear waters of Florida and the West Indies, you can see the remains of docks and harbors from long ago, which now are lost under the sea.

For hundreds of years, many people have looked at the Bible story of the flood as a "parable," a lesson-giving story similar perhaps to the animal fables about the dog in the manger, or the fox and the goose. It was thought that probably there had been a flood in biblical times, and that someone by the name of Noah had come out of it a hero; perhaps the Tigris or the Euphrates had flooded and covered that whole valley. It was pointed out by practical people that keeping all those animals in a boat for forty days was just asking for trouble — the fierce ones would eat the timid ones and there would be nothing left to get off the boat but the lions and tigers and perhaps the skunks.

Now, after all this time, in an age where many people do not read the Bible at all, science has come up with a real flood, a very big one, covering a good part of the earth. By taking core samples of the ocean bottoms in many places, they have located a time — around eleven thousand years ago — when fresh water flooded the earth. This was very near the end of the last Ice Age, when Canada and some of the United States were covered by glacier ice. At this time, for some reason we do not yet know, the ice cap started to melt very fast, and a great flood of fresh water rushed down the rivers into the Gulf of Mexico and caused a rise in sea levels all over the world. Some of the Antarctic ice cap melted, too, and added to the flood of fresh water. Scientists have tested fossil shells from around the world, and there — almost like tree-ring markings — are the marks of the fresh-water flood. Core samples from the ocean floor tell the same story. Was this Noah's flood? We have so much to learn.

There are places on earth where land is still building, so we can see something of what it must have been like in the first billions of years of our planet. The Florida Keys show us one example of land growth: coral reefs, seaweed, floating bits of plant and animal matter cling together, and when it gets anchored to the bottom you have the beginning of another island. Near Iceland, the island of Surtsey shows us another method of land building: volcanic. It has been only a few years ago since the seas there began boiling violently; fishing boats watched while a hissing, fiery mass came up from the deep and blew out lava until it had built up a volcanic mountain from the ocean floor, which made a small black island. It was too hot to walk on for several years; the Icelandic fishermen named it and kept track of its growth. A few years later, tiny green plants sprouted, probably from seeds carried by birds or drifting on the ocean.

In the state of Nevada there is a unique park where you can go to study the strange and terrible processes that the world went through while it was being formed. It is called the Valley of Fire, and no place is better named. It looks as though it might still be on fire, burned down to giant coals for a giant barbecue. Looking at these fantastic rocks, you can see the way that volcanic heat melted and bubbled and hardened the rocks, like food forgotten over a hot fire. You can also see the work of the other great land maker, water, in the striped cliffs that have formed there over millions of years. This land, like the dinosaur land of Utah-Colorado (which is not far away from it) was once under water. A warm, shallow sea washed over it for uncounted centuries; you can still find fossils of ancient shellfish all over the place. Then, when four or five of our future states tipped up on edge and formed the Rocky Mountains, all the ancient seas drained away into the oceans.

When rain came, it came in deluges, washing down rocks and logs and adding layer after layer to the sand flats. Sandstone, formed by centuries of flooding by mud and water, became colored with iron and other minerals. Rocks tumbled about in time of earthquake, grinding each other and piling up in new heaps that changed with every flood. If you go today to visit this land, you have the feeling that all these things just happened last week.

The ice ages brought many changes to all of North America. Ice did not get as far south as Nevada, but the rivers are artists, and great waters came down from melting ice. When the last Ice Age was over, there was a whole new set of scenery. Sanded by the winds and baked by the sun, it is there for us to see, and the story told by these fantastic red rocks is as strange as they are.

The Valley of Fire not only looks like a great furnace, it sometimes feels like it, too. But, oddly enough, though you might not choose to live there yourself, this was one of the earliest sites in America where people lived and built homes. A local museum has a priceless collection of pottery, all found within a few miles of this park, made by a people so old we do not know their names. This is the place called the Lost City where people lived who had crossed over the land bridge from Asia across the Bering Sea before the end of the last Ice Age. It must have been pretty much of a desert by that time, but these people lived here long ago.

One strange effect that time, water, and chemicals have on living things is petrifying them, that is, turning them to stone. Petrified wood and bones are our best example. Many dinosaur bones at the Dinosaur National Monument have been petrified; the actual bone tissue has been completely replaced by stone. Bones and trees may fall to dust — but stone will not; so we have a lot of beautiful fossils, thanks to the action of water and chemicals.

There are examples of petrified wood all over the world, but surely the most spectacular is at the Petrified Forest National Park in Arizona, with its companion wonderland, the Painted Desert. One of the first things you will notice there is the great size of the tree trunks lying on the desert ground where hardly a knee-high bush grows today. They must have been huge trees when they were growing — huge trees in such a desert? The park ranger will tell you that of course some of them floated down the river in floodtime, thousands of years ago. But he will also point out to you that the copper-colored land around you was not always a desert. In their lifetime, these trees grew, as in all the dinosaur country, on the edge of shallow seas of seventy million years ago. Water, chemicals, and time have made the fallen giants into jewels; trees that grew beside them have vanished long ago.

Some petrified wood is used for jewelry, though it is against the law to take any from a public park like the Petrified Forest National Park. Some of this wood is semitransparent, like agate, or perhaps has little feathery pictures in it. Silica, iron, and manganese are the main elements that worked on these fossils. Iron makes the red, yellow, and brown colors; manganese and carbon bring out the black and purple hues. Sometimes copper or chromium are present, and these make blues and greens. The finished product is harder than either plastic or glass.

It is a long distance from a moonflight to the tiny, perfect cell patterns of a piece of petrified wood, but God's fingerprint can be found on all the beauty, great and small, that goes to make up our world.

Chapter 4
Happy Hunting Ground

When Peter the Great was czar of Russia, which was about three hundred years ago, there was a shortage of ivory with which to do the fine art carving so popular then. Russia was too cold for elephants, and the walrus ivory had nearly been used up. The czar had heard about graveyards in Siberia where great white tusks of the extinct mammoth stuck up out of the banks of the rivers, just for the taking. So he sent a party of explorers far into the wilderness to find this ivory.

There were very few people in Siberia who had not reached it the hard way — as convicts, sentenced to hard labor — and they were not very friendly. Few people from outside had ever been in the interior, and the peasants ran from them in terror. Finally, the czar's party found a village where the people admitted that they knew of such places where there were beasts, but they were deathly afraid to go there.

The whole place was haunted, they said; terrible things happened there. Forced at gunpoint, they led the czar's men to where they could point out the place. There in that valley where the great wall of ice showed against the mountain, they said, were horrible big red creatures — giant rats — under the ground. It was plain to see that these creatures lived under the snow and would die if the winds of the upper world blew on them. The less you knew about them, the peasants insisted, the better. They were terrible, terrible! Men had gone crazy just from seeing them!

The peasants ran back to safety and the explorers went on to find the terrible creatures — fixed in a wall of ice, dead, but looking very much alive. They were not skeletons, but whole great bodies covered with reddish hair — mammoths, quick-frozen, just as an avalanche had caught them, thirty thousand years ago! Nature's deep freeze had kept them perfectly; scientists sent back by the czar discovered that the leaves of the last meal the mammoths had eaten were still green. One of them had made his last meal of buttercups! Also, the meat was still good to eat — if you like mammoth.

Thanks to this discovery and others like it, we know quite a lot about the great red beasts under the snow, and about the time known as the Ice Age of our planet, when they were walking around in the happy hunting ground created by the melting ice.

It is only in the past hundred years or so that we have known much about the ice ages, or the animals that were living at that time. In the past fifty years, scientists have discovered that there were several ice ages, spread over many thousands of years. Only in the past few years has it been known that man was living on the earth at the end of the last Ice Age, which was from ten thousand to fifteen thousand years ago. Some of the ancient cave paintings indicate that he was here twenty-five thousand years ago. We do not know yet, for sure. But when the last great glaciers were dying and the ice drew away from North America, there must have been a paradise of animal life, much of it very large, like the mastodon and the mammoth. Man, the hunter, has left his clues for us to follow; we have found the spearpoints with which he killed the great beasts.

The oldest spearpoints we have, up to the present state of discovery, were found in a cave in the Sandia Mountains of New Mexico in 1936. If the pack rats over the past ten thousand years had not been so eager to store things away in their own fashion, we might know a great deal more about Sandia man and his life among the Ice Age animals than we do. Unfortunately, the pack rats have got the evidence so mixed up that no one can get a clear picture of what happened back then. We can probably regard Sandia man as one of the first Americans, though where he came from or exactly when, we cannot tell on present evidence. We know that he made leaf-shaped spearpoints with which he killed camels, giant sloths, and giant bison — all of them enormous to kill by hand; and he built fires in the caves to cook his meat. That is virtually all we know about him so far.

The Sandia points were not the first ones found, though they were the oldest. In 1925 a black cowboy, George McJunkin, was out rounding up stray cattle in Dead Horse Canyon near Folsom, New Mexico, when he came upon a creek bank cut down by floodwaters where there were many large bones showing through the dirt. They probably were cow or buffalo bones, he thought. He was looking for live cows, not dead ones, and he was tired.

Still, he got off his horse to look at the bones, and his concern gave science a whole new field of knowledge. There were spearpoints glittering there in the dust among the bones. He dug them out with his pocket knife, and he took a good hard look at the way the bones were set into the ground. Then he went home and sent word to a science teacher who would go and look at his find. There have been many kinds of points found since then, some older than the ones he found. But nothing will ever be quite so exciting to the world of science as those first plain, useful, carefully made weapons found between the ribs of the big skeletons at Folsom by a tired man who took time to satisfy his curiosity.

Dinosaurs were of course much larger than the Ice Age animals, but they lived and died in a world without man. The animals that shared the great hunting grounds at the end of the last Ice Age were certainly a lot bigger than the two-legged hunters who attacked them with spears and throwing sticks and little else. Man must have felt very brave tackling a giant bison which stood nine feet at the shoulder, or a mammoth with its tusks waving fifteen feet in the air.

It is a very strange thing, but if you were to take a map of New Mexico and put a compass point down on the little Rio Grande pueblo of Bernalillo and draw a circle a hundred miles in diameter, that circle would include three things: Sandia Cave, where the first known weapons of man in North America were found; the ruined pueblo of Kuaua where, in 1541, Coronado made the first gunpowder in the New World; and Los Alamos, where the atomic bomb was made. It is a long way from a chipped stone spearpoint to an atomic bomb, but the long journey has been made in this small space.

The ice sheet did not, of course, reach New Mexico. It stopped off in a wavering line from southern New York, westward through Wisconsin, and finally wandered off the continent in Washington State. But vast herds of mastodons, mammoths, giant bison, giant sloths, camels, and giant beavers, as well as Alaska lions, saber-toothed tigers, and dire wolves (which preyed on the others), wandered down into the Great Plains and farther west by the time the ice was gone for good.

Today people go to Africa to the Serengeti Plain to see the last great animals on earth roaming wild. The Great Plains of our country once held many times the herds of the Serengeti; it must have been a hunter's paradise. Some of the animals would look familiar to us and a lot of them were quite different. Long-necked camels that look a little like the South American llama roamed in great herds, and the odd-looking ancestor of our horse was there in great numbers. One of the Ice Age's many mysteries is why, all of a sudden, these early horses all went west and north and seem to have crossed the ice bridge into Asia at almost the same time that the earliest Americans were crossing it in the other direction. Indians and horses were not to meet again for nearly ten thousand years.

There were a good many completely strange-looking animals in these early hunting grounds: bears with very long legs and short faces, rather awful-looking wild pigs, and what looked like enormous rats with short tails. Extra-large wolves and several models of lions ate very well on this collection of creatures. Giant beavers chewed down trees and must have had great fun with the watery world that came out of the melting ice. Why they were nearly all such big animals we do not know. There were plenty of small ones, too. But the big ones were so very big that there must have been a reason for it — and we do not, as yet, know what it is.

The big cats, of course, were meat eaters, which meant, now and again, a two-legged meal. The saber-toothed tiger — would

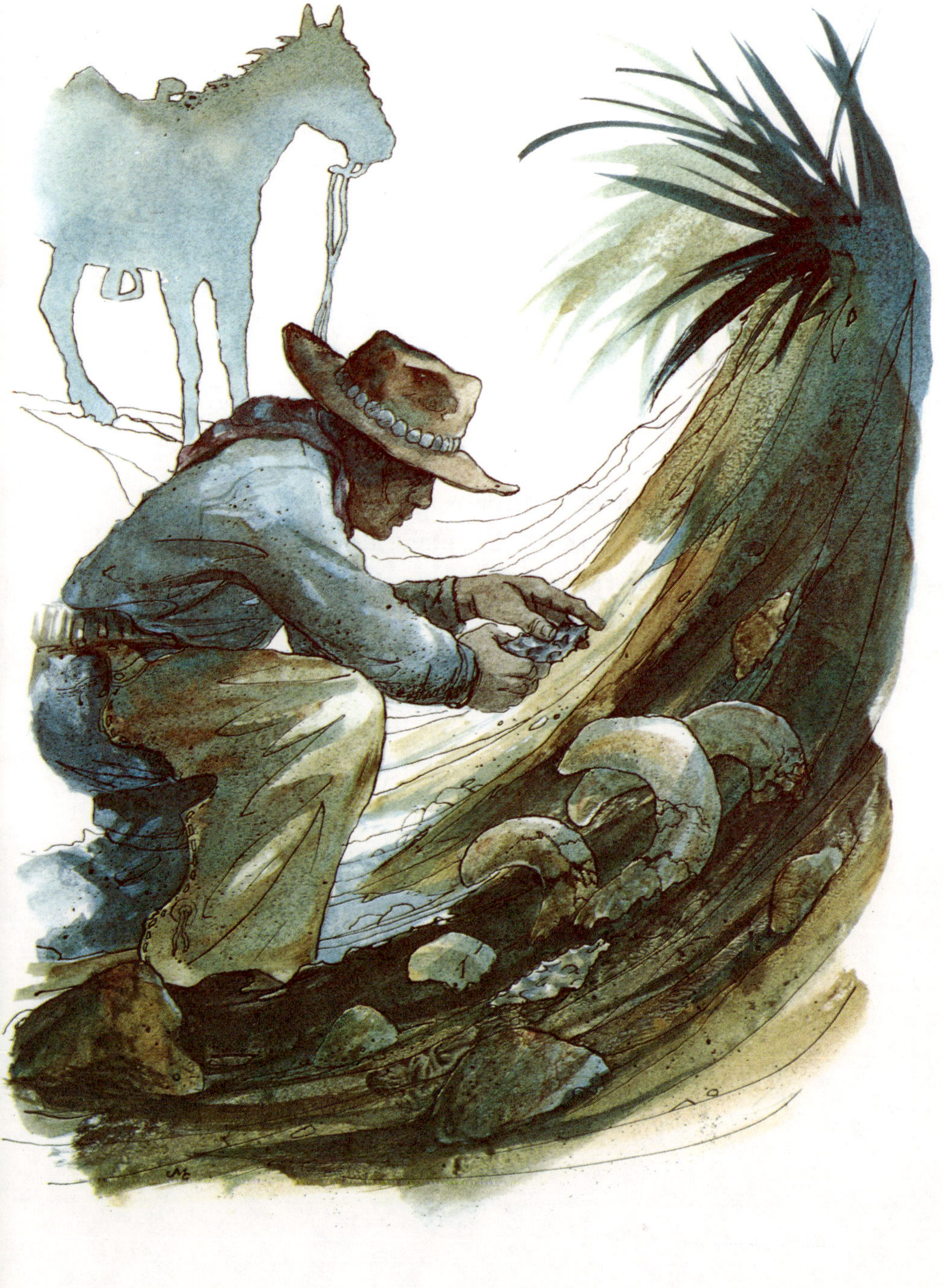

Nothing will ever be quite so exciting to the world of science as those first plain, useful, carefully made spearpoints found between the ribs of the big skeletons. *(See pages 46-47.)*

you believe it? — has the scientific name of *Smilodon* (which I like to translate as "the cat with the permanent smile"); and if anyone ever needed braces on his teeth, he did. *Smilodon* finally died out because his front teeth were so long they could not be used (your dentist calls it "overbite").

Most of the big animals were harmless vegetarians. Men were their enemies, but they were not his. Still, you would not go rushing up to a mammoth thirteen feet tall and threaten him with a three-inch spearpoint — at least you would not do it twice. So, man, who was gifted with intelligence, worked out ways of trapping big animals in pits or driving them over cliffs. Men would have to work together on a job like this; one man alone would have no chance at all. Such a killing place as a cliff or a natural pit might be the first place where men learned to work together.

Finding these places where the big hunts were held now helps us to fill in the history of this distant time. For example, the spearpoints found at Sandia Cave are different from both the Folsom points and those found at Clovis nearby. Being close together in location does not mean that these were the same people; it is thought now that these were three different peoples, living at different times in history (though all within the same general time of the late Ice Age) and that they hunted different beasts.

Folsom points were found with the bones of giant bison, Clovis points with mammoth bones, Sandia points with giant sloth, camel, and mammoth. Just recently, the bones of a mastodon have been found in the far Northwest, and the points that killed it were made of bone — the sign of still another group of ancient people, the first ones known to have killed mastodons. In all these discoveries, not one single piece of human bone has been found. All we have are the bones of the great animals and the points that killed them: points that only human hands could have made. There is much left to be found; you never need worry that all the exciting things have already happened.

It is said that the mastodon discovered America. He and his distant cousin, the mammoth, had a long hike to reach this country; both were true elephants and came from Africa. Since one could hardly expect them to swim the ocean, it is reasonable to think that the continental drift theory is right, and that they were already on the great continental raft when it finally settled here. There were several other kinds of elephants trumpeting around our prairies in the long ago. One had an enormous lower lip like a duckbill with which he scooped up food from the marshy water. Our old friend, the porcupine, came wheezing and snuffling over the land bridge from South America when he got good and ready, and the opossum dates from this time, too.

Present-day scientists think that man came to North America from Asia, across the land bridge at the Bering Strait, just before the ice broke up for the last time. (It is still possible, in years when there is a hard freeze, to make this trip across the ice.) Why did man decide to make this uncomfortable trip? Perhaps he was following the game, or, like the bear that went over the mountain, he just wanted to see what he could see. After the last Ice Age there was a long ice-free valley east of the Rockies, and perhaps the newcomers followed this road down, living on game and wearing the furs for warmth. Or perhaps they followed the seacoast, never getting out of reach of that great food factory, the sea.

There must have been several groups of people, going by several ways, but quite a few of them arrived sooner or later in the Rio Grande valley and elsewhere in the Southwest. It is fairly sure that other people came up from Mexico and that over the centuries these people blended into what we were to call the Indians. Much of this is still theory, but it is reasonable and based on good evidence. Someday we may know the answers to the questions that today's men of science are studying. They want, most of all, to find out when man came to this earth, and where.

Man has two gifts that he can leave behind him for other men to study: he can make tools, and he has the gift of speech. It is true that an animal or bird may use a branch or a stone to reach something he wants, but he does not, for example, make himself a spear and keep it for hunting. Also, many animals can communicate with each other; dolphins, for instance, have at least thirty different sounds for sending messages, sometimes a long way across the water. But no dolphin has written any how-to books for the instruction of future dolphins.

Consequently, scientists look first for weapons and for signs of messages: a carved snake on a rock — "watch out for snakes here," or a wiggly line that says "water." These are absolute proofs that man was here. On the walls of caves like those of Lascaux in France and Altamira in Spain are carefully drawn animal paintings. These are not scribbles or doodles; they are beautiful drawings. Some ancient cave paintings may be thirty thousand years old, but there is nothing "primitive" about them; they could very well be painted by a very "modern" artist. This is a type of speech as much as writing is, because you can read its story from the picture.

The men who lived in the last Ice Age, or perhaps even before the last Ice Age, were not "stupid" just because their tools and weapons were simple. There are today a number of Stone Age tribes living in remote places — the Australian outback, or the Amazon jungle, or a remote island in the Philippines — who have little to work with. They must face their dangerous world with only the simple tools of the mammoth hunter, and they have to be smart to survive. "Caveman" is a term sometimes used to poke fun at early man, as if we were much smarter and better than he. The caveman survived a very dangerous world, and he deserves our praise just for staying alive. The cave paintings prove that he did more than simply stay alive, though that was his greatest gift to us.

One of the biggest mysteries about the Ice Age animals is: *What ever happened to them?* Man survived and the animals did not. Historians call it "the time of the great dying," when forty million big animals died — young ones, old ones, practically all at once. The skeletons show this much, but we do not know why. Some of the skeletons are twisted and broken as if a tornado had killed them. What did? Was it a huge volcanic explosion? Poisonous gases? Earthquakes? Tidal waves? Meteorites?

Animals in South Africa, South Asia, India, and Malaysia survived; tigers, lions, elephants, rhinoceroses still live in those places, but the rest of the big animals died. Why? The small animals came through it, whatever it was; small reptiles, crocodiles, and turtles survived; insects prospered. Man — with only a three-inch spearpoint and a throwing stick to protect him — came through with flying colors. The plains were emptied of the herd of big animals that had made them beautiful. Young scientists still in school may be the ones to find the answers to these questions.

There are several puzzles to keep scientists awake nights besides the one about what happened to all those animals. There is, for instance, the cave full of camel bones in New Mexico. They were not the sort of camels you see today in the circus, but the long-necked llamalike camels of the Ice Age. The bones do not seem to have been in the cave that long. But there they are in one pile, thousands of them, filling the cave. We would very much like to know: (1) where they came from, (2) why nobody has found any bones like this anywhere else, and (3) why they came into the cave in the first place. Also — the million-dollar question: *How did they get into the cave?* The only way in is by way of a tunnel so low that one has to get down on hands and knees to enter it. Must we suppose that the camels came into the tunnel on their knees, following some terrible itch of curiosity, or . . .?

There are several places where one can go to study the Ice Age animals. The best, from the view of the scientists, is Alaska, where thousands of big animals are deep-frozen in the muck of the permafrost, completely preserved like the mammoths in Siberia. The problem with this is that most of the muck pits are very hard to reach, and only the most serious scientists will go to all that trouble; it is not for tourists, in other words. Much more available and very interesting are the La Brea asphalt pits in Los Angeles, California. Here, surrounded by oil deposits, is a place where liquid asphalt, which most people call "tar," has been seeping up for millions of years and formed pools on the surface. In some places the tar pools are covered with pools of water. Many animals came to what you can only call a sticky end here.

Animals have fallen into this trap all through the ages, but there must have been more animals living here at the end of the Ice Age, since most of the skeletons removed from the pits are those of Ice Age animals. Mastodons, mammoths, ancient horses, long-necked camels, and giant sloths probably began the tragedy by mistaking the asphalt pools for water, and their great weight mired them in the sticky tar. The big cats, the lions and our smiling-tiger friend, also the extra-large wolves, came hungrily to feed on the trapped game. They, too, were trapped, and the vultures hurried in to get their share and were trapped also. They all sank together into the quicksandlike pool. It was very hard luck for them, and very good luck for us, as it gives us a chance to study animals that would otherwise be ten thousand years out of our reach. The tar has preserved the bones perfectly.

The state of Wisconsin is the first in our nation to recognize the glaciers as artists, sculptors working on the lines of a bulldozer. Under a project called Ice Age National Scientific Reserve, which is part of the national parks system, the state is building a hiking trail which follows the work of the glaciers in Wisconsin. God's bulldozers have left the people of Wisconsin some beautiful gifts: fifteen thousand lakes and a lot of valuable wetlands teeming with wildlife. The glaciers have also made Wisconsin a leading agricultural state with vast acres of rich soil ground down by the ice. Wisconsin's forests are rich with hardwood trees, and its many harbors and ports on rivers and lakes are a gift of the glaciers. Since Wisconsin was the boyhood home of John Muir, the great naturalist, it is quite right that it should be the first to bring all this beauty to the notice of America.

The best place in the United States to look for glaciers is, of course, Alaska, where they abound. In the "South 48," Mount Rainier in Washington is said to have the most interesting ones, though they are not always open to the public because they continually change as the ice melts and freezes, and they are not always safe.

Chapter 5
There Are Giants in Those Woods!

The *biggest* living thing in the world is a redwood called the General Sherman Tree, which lives like the king of the forest, high in the California mountains. It has a long Latin name which simply means "giant redwood." General Sherman is 272 feet tall and 30 feet around the trunk, truly a giant.

The *tallest* living thing in the world is also a redwood tree, growing with its tall brothers in the redwood forest along the foggy coast of northern California. It, too, has a long Latin name, which means "evergreen redwood." It is 365 feet tall and still growing. In this tallest-trees-on-earth grove, there are so many other trees almost as tall, that you have to look twice to see which one is the record holder.

Very nearly the *oldest* living thing in the world is also a redwood tree; only the bristlecone pine is older. It must be admitted that the pine, which is forty-six hundred years old, shows every year of its age, while the redwood, at twenty-seven hundred years of age, is still green and beautiful.

Some people claim that redwoods live forever, as nobody has yet found one that just grew old and died. They were either killed by accident (lightning, windstorms) or cut down for lumber by their only known enemy: man.

Both redwoods, the evergreens from the coast and the giants from the mountains, were named "sequoia" after Sequoyah, a Cherokee Indian who invented an alphabet and taught his people to read and write. That was a fantastic thing to do at his time in history, and he has a fitting memorial in these fantastic trees.

Until the 1940s, botanists believed that there were only the two kinds of redwood alive today, descended back through the ages to the forests of the dinosaur age. Then in our times a Chinese scientist discovered a third kind, growing in a forgotten valley of China, a tree that all the world's scientists believed had vanished with the dinosaurs. He found a whole grove of these trees near Chungking, and scientists from all over the world came to this out-of-the-way place to study the discovery. The object of scientific curiosity was the "dawn redwood," which does not grow as tall as its two young relatives in California; but it has come down to us unchanged out of the ancient past, the only living tree that links us with the vanished world of the dinosaurs. This is the very tree that sometimes turns up as fossil leaves in coal; in fact, it was supposed to have died out millions of years ago. However, the dawn redwood is not just a fossil any more; it is alive and well in the Valley of the Water Pine and a great joy to botanists.

It would seem to be almost too much of a coincidence that the first mention in history of the great redwood trees comes from Chinese history. One Hee-Li, captain of a junk plying the China Sea, was caught in a typhoon and given a free ride across a very large ocean. Then, because a cockroach kept getting caught under the needle of his compass, he kept sailing in a direction he thought would bring him to China until the junk came to rest on a rocky coast where there were great tall red trees reaching to the sky. He carried back a good account of these trees when he did return to China — 217 B.C., by our reckoning — and it is hard to see how a good description of this strange tree got into Chinese history unless someone had really seen it.

In the time of the dawn redwoods, dinosaur times, there were several other kinds of redwoods covering a good part of North America. Many of these died out when the ice ages came, and glaciers leveled the land like giant bulldozers. Volcanoes blew up, mountains rose, seas disappeared or moved. The whole face of the earth was changed. By modern times, by which we mean a few hundred years ago, there were two million acres of redwoods left in just one location on earth, the Pacific coast of North America from Oregon to below Monterey in California. They may have been there forty million years, we are told. This sounds decidedly old to us, but they are "modern" trees beside the dawn redwood, under which dinosaurs took their afternoon naps.

The great-great-great-great-grandfather of one of the California giants might easily have been living at the end of the last Ice Age — only five generations back to the mammoth and the saber-toothed tiger! But "little" dawn redwood goes clear back to the dinosaurs!

Because both kinds of American redwood are huge, people refer to them all as "big trees," and they certainly are. But there is quite a lot of difference between the two kinds, first of all in the places where they live. The California coast, north of San Francisco, at times is one of the wettest and windiest, not to mention foggiest, places in the U.S.A. This is just exactly what the coast redwood likes. "Where the fog flows, there the redwood grows" is an old saying. These are the tall ones, tapering gracefully at the top; sometimes the branches do not begin until two hundred feet up. This means the tree is not much good for climbing. The trunk is a darkish brown, the needles dark green, and the cones very tiny for such a big tree. Coast redwoods grow both from seed and from root sprouts. Often in a redwood forest you will find a perfectly straight row of trees, standing like soldiers. If you look closely, you will see that they have sprouted from the trunk of a tree that fell perhaps centuries ago.

The giant redwood from the Sierras is a thick, heavy tree, not as tall as the coast redwood but much larger in the trunk. It can grow to forty feet in diameter. The giant redwood is also the one that lives the longest; the Grizzly Giant in Yosemite is twenty-seven hundred years old.

The redwoods are of great interest to the world not only because of their beauty or their fine lumber but because they are living history. A cross section of a big redwood will give us all the dates we know in history, recorded forever in its rings of growth. Long-ago droughts and good growing seasons and fires are recorded there, the good years and the bad ones.

The Sierra giants have a cinnamon-red bark that is nearly two feet thick and almost fireproof. Fires and other injuries may hurt the tree but they rarely kill it; the bark grows over the scar and the tree goes right on about its business as if nothing dangerous — like lightning, or flood, or a careless camper — had ever come along. These trees have a curious way of scattering their seeds, which grow in tiny cones that cannot open by themselves. First the squirrels come to the rescue; they love the seed husks, so they open the cones and scatter the seeds around the tree. If the seeds fall on the ground, well and good — they sprout. But they are quite apt to fall on the heavy cover of dry stuff that gathers on a forest floor.

Here, strangely enough, fire takes a hand. As the duff on the forest floor burns, the heat opens the remaining cones, and when they cool again, they drop their seeds. The year after a fire, there are always many little new trees. Now that forest rangers know how it works, they can keep the fire within bounds and help the seeds along. Fire, out of bounds, is still a savage enemy of the beautiful trees. Wind, too, causes the loss of many fine trees, because the root system of the redwood is not deep and it can be undermined by floodwaters.

The California Indians knew about the redwoods, and treated them with respect. They called the redwood forest "the Land of Shadows" and stayed as far away from it as they could, since it seemed to be full of grizzly bears and (for all they knew) strange gods. Treetops meeting overhead shut out the sunshine, and they liked open country better.

The first white men to see the coast redwoods were the Spaniards of the land expedition looking for Monterey Bay. When they rode into these groves of giant trees, it was like an enchanted forest; they had never dreamed that trees could grow so big. They had heard about Coronado's meeting with the giants on the Colorado River, and there were still plenty of people to say that there were giants in this western wilderness. The explorers looked wordlessly at the great cloud-sweeping tops, almost out of sight in the sky; giants, they thought, might be imaginary — but there was nothing imaginary about those trees. They camped one night under a huge redwood that towered over the oaks and pines around it. They named it the *palo alto* ("tall tree") and used it as a landmark while they explored the country. Two hundred fifty years later, in spite of having lost a twin trunk and part of its top in a lightning storm, it is still there, guarding the city that bears its name, Palo Alto.

The Sierra giants were hidden from the eyes of white men until the time of the gold rush. One of the first to see them was a forty-niner who had wounded a grizzly bear and was following it to kill it. After a while he looked up — and up . . . and up . . . and forgot the bear for looking at the trees. When he returned to camp with his story, nobody would believe him. In order to get them to come and see the giant trees, he had to tell a whopper — that he had killed the biggest grizzly in California. But even when they saw the trees, they did not quite believe it. The big trees still have that effect on people; they are so much bigger than you think they are going to be.

After a century of logging, nearly nine tenths of those two million acres of redwood are gone. The fate of the rest of them is being hotly debated and will have to be settled by the upcoming generation. Logging companies want to go on cutting the beautiful lumber, and conservationists want to set aside all the remaining forests as part of our country's parks. There is, of course, something to be said on both sides.

Interest in logging the redwoods started at the time of the gold rush, when there was a sudden demand for lumber to build ships, houses, stores, furniture, and a dozen other things. The country's lumber mills were three thousand miles away by land, and all the way around South America by ship. Many newcomers to California took a second look at the goldfields and decided they could make more money outfitting the gold diggers than in digging gold. There were those enormous trees, surely more lumber per tree than anywhere else on earth. One question they could not answer: How on earth could anyone fell a tree that size, and who had any tools for handling anything so big?

Loggers from Maine and Wisconsin and other lumber states tried one system after another and failed. In logging operations

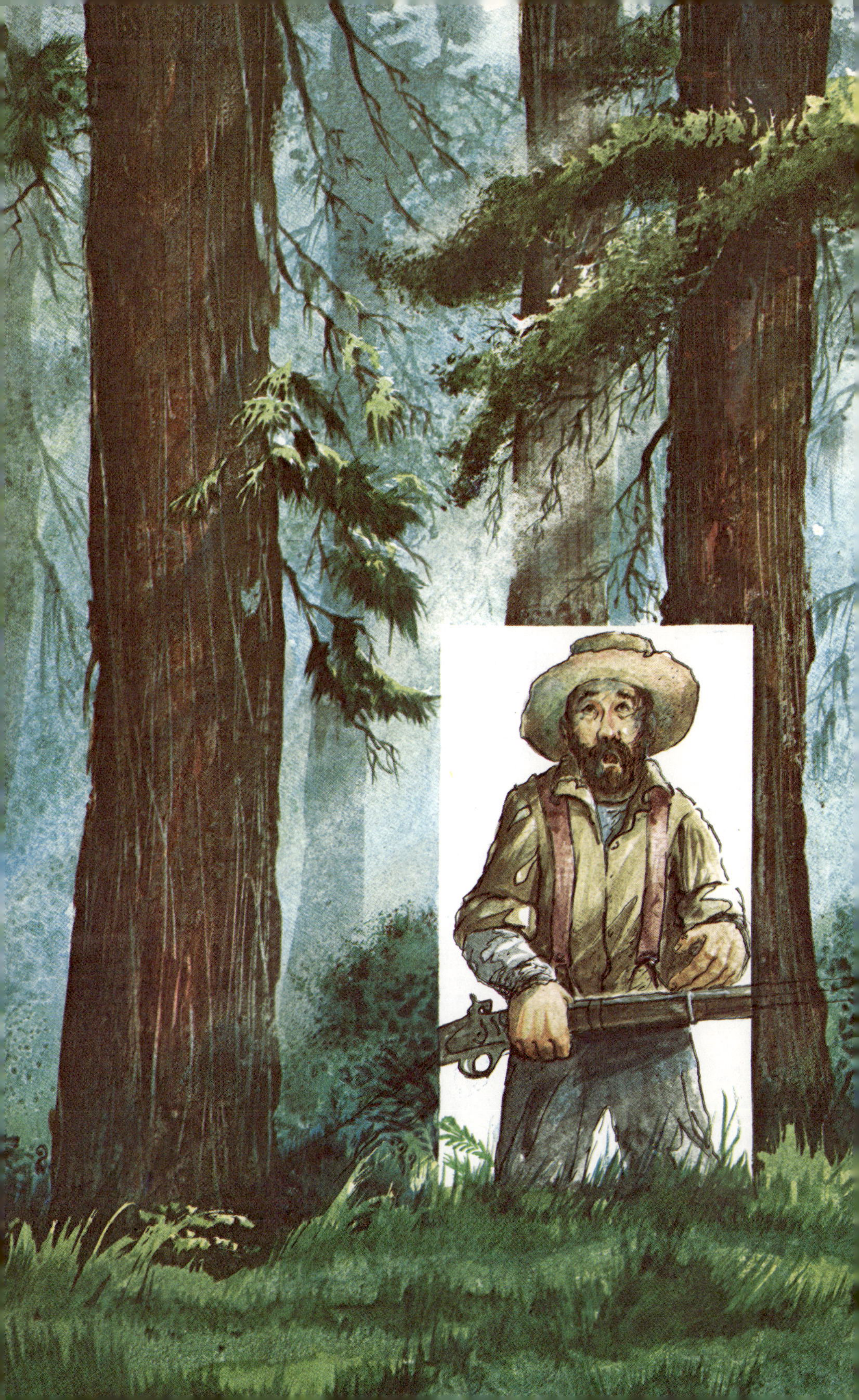

The gold rush of 1849 leads
to the discovery of the giant
sequoia by white men.

elsewhere in the country, strong teams of oxen were harnessed to pull the logs down a corduroy (a road made of small logs), until the felled timber could be rolled into the water to be floated to a mill. Getting a redwood down was bad enough, but then it had to be cut into short lengths to move, and even this was sometimes too much for the oxen. A shocking lot of beautiful trees were wasted in the years before someone finally came up with the idea of using the newly invented steam engine to power the moving of logs in the woods. The gasoline engine proved to be even better, so the donkey engine, black and smelly and as full of crazy notions as the beast for which it was named, became the logger's friend in the redwood country. People of a century ago were not as used to the smell of gasoline as we are, so they called the little engines "the skunks," because "you kin smell 'em before you kin see 'em!"

Northern California had many rivers and creeks for floating logs down to saltwater. There was a brisk trade in redwood lumber all around the world. Even shipping the lumber from the mills had its problems: an ordinary run to San Francisco took only a day or so, but sometimes the wind blew the sailing ships clear past the harbor and back again before they could make port. Even so, ships from all over the world crowded the dangerous waters around Cape Mendocino, waiting for their share of the redwood — for the wood was beautiful as well as useful.

Redwood fights disease and decay during its lifetime and, cut into lumber, it keeps these qualities. It can be used underground where ordinary lumber would soon decay, and it neither shrinks nor swells to any extent. The wood is delicately patterned and makes fine furniture and wood carvings. Unfortunately, it is also good for grape stakes. It is hard to forgive greedy lumbermen who cut down thousands of beautiful trees to chop them up into grape stakes. John Muir, the famous naturalist who tried so hard to save the redwoods, was very angry about this.

It is still a huge job to fell a big redwood, though now the loggers can call upon bigger machines, stronger cables, and even the helicopter, for help. In the early days of redwood lumbering it sometimes took days to saw through the great trunk after the falling cut was made, and both cutting and sawing were hard and dangerous work. Quite often, especially with the Sierra giants, the force of the fall would shatter the trunk, even if a bed of heavy branches had been placed to break the fall. Legend insists that one group of loggers, determined to fell the biggest tree they could find, worked at it for twenty-two days, and then the tree fell while they were home for lunch.

It finally became evident that the giant trees of the Sierras were too brittle to fell safely, and they did not make good lumber after all. Few of them are cut any more, but logging still goes on in the coastal forests. If only people had thought this through fifty years ago, we might have been spared the tragic eradication of some of the most beautiful trees (and, in some cases, forests) on earth.

The little "skunks" are still in use, and the line has grown into a passenger service which is one of the most fascinating rides in the country. The Road of the Skunks runs regularly in vacation time and occasionally at other times, from Fort Bragg on the ocean to Willits on Highway 101. It goes through the heart of the redwood country, winding up switchbacks and over trestles. Both a steam train and a diesel engine run on this line, and it is pure joy both for railroad fans and for people who have never actually seen the big woods of the logging industry.

Another redwood forest near San Francisco is in Big Basin, in the Santa Cruz mountains near Monterey Bay. At Felton, which was once known as Roaring Camp, you can get a special excursion train, the "Roaring Camp and Big Trees Narrow Gauge Railroad," which dates from the 1880s. Here you can relive history of one hundred years ago (among trees that link you with the Ice Age) as the little engine puffs its way over places called Grizzly Flat and Deer Valley. Here is the place where Daniel Boone's nephew made the first American settlement in California and picked up a gold nugget worth $32,000.

A trip of this sort brings out the fact that logging methods have changed greatly since a century ago, and that some of the lumber companies take their responsibilities very seriously. Trees now are cut after an expert tree man has gone through the woods, marking it for cutting in one of two different ways. In the first, all the older trees are marked for cutting, leaving more light and air for the growing ones which are sometimes too close together to grow fully. New trees will sprout from the stumps of those that are cut. The other method, called "clear-cutting," takes all the trees in a given area, which is immediately seeded by helicopter and cared for like a garden until the trees can make it on their own. These, too, can be weeded out when they are small, so that — two hundred years from now — they will be strong and straight forest giants like their ancestors.

The growth of young redwood trees in commercial forests like these has doubled in the years since World War II and is expected to double again by the year 2000. There are now 945,000 acres in redwood tree farms. Also, 181,000 acres of redwoods are now set aside, in more than a hundred parks and areas for public use, where more than two million trees are standing here in our world of today, telling us about the world of the past.

No one would think of going to California without seeing the redwoods. One of the handiest groves to see from San Francisco is Muir Woods National Monument, named fittingly for John Muir who was their friend. Muir Woods is like an enormous cathedral, beautifully decorated with ferns and greenery, with dogwood and rhododendron in season, or bright with colored leaves in the fall. This area, fortunately, has never been logged, and it shows us what we lost in all the wasted groves that fell to human greed.

Beautiful stands of coast redwoods are found in parks all along the California coast from Monterey up. No longer the main highway, the old coast road winds for miles among magnificent trees. They can be seen best on foot, but the drive is beautiful, too. These trees are best in spring, summer, and fall; the heavy woods are pretty wet in the winter.

The giant redwoods of the Sierras are scattered and a little harder to reach, except for those at Yosemite and Kings Canyon groves, where the world's biggest and oldest trees are. Unlike the coast, which is better in the sunshine, the Sierra giants are great fun in the snow. People who like skiing or other winter sports will not have to go far from the mountain ski resorts to see the great trees.

Why should you, who may live in Rhode Island, Florida, or South Dakota, be concerned with the redwood trees out in California? Well, first of all, because they are living history — *your* history as well as anyone else's. Also, because they are among the most beautiful things God ever made, and you cannot just stand by while greedy persons take them away from you. And, be very sure of it, the fate of the redwoods rests in the hands of your generation; you will one day have to vote on them. It will be up to you whether they remain as a beauty spot for your grandchildren — and theirs — or whether they disappear like the auk and the passenger pigeon.

Chapter 6
Those Who Have Vanished

Where were you when I laid the foundation
 of the earth?...
On what were its bases sunk,
or who laid its cornerstone,
when the morning stars sang together,
and all the sons of God shouted for joy?

— *Job 38:4, 6-7*

Nature quietly, patiently, goes to work, and over the ruins of cities the winds pile the friendly soil.... Nature waits long and lovingly for the archeologist.... She will convert fertile lands into desert wastes, cultivated valleys into... jungles, to the end that the things of man's spiritual past may be saved for the life of the future.... Nature, from age to age, has been storing under friendly soil the unwritten history of man.

— *Anonymous*

In a dry cave of southern Oregon a few years ago, someone made a discovery that one day may help us to fill in a blank page of our history. The treasure found was not gold; in fact, it was not anything that we would consider valuable — just a pile of old shoes. They are sandals, woven from grass and reeds, and rather clumsy looking; but tests have shown them to be nine thousand years old. Nine thousand years ago man passed this way, and the detectives of science are hot on his trail. As any bloodhound would know, it is a very cold trail.

What was the world doing nine thousand years ago? This was a time after the last Ice Age, after most of the mammoths and other big animals were dead; this was thousands of years before the pyramids of Egypt were built, before Moses led his people out of Egypt to the Promised Land. People would have said, just a few years ago, that this was long before man ever set foot on North America; but here is the proof that he did.

The footprints of vanished people have been found all over the West and Southwest of our country. Dr. Richard Daugherty, archeologist from Washington State University, lists one hundred ninety-three places between Texas and Alaska where archeologists have found traces of men who lived there more than six thousand years ago. It was not such a "New World" after all.

Mammoth hunters, and hunters of the great bison and the giant sloth, are known to have lived in the Southwest nearly fifteen thousand years ago. We have found the spearpoints with which they hunted, and these can now be dated quite accurately, using the new radiomagnetic system. We have found the fire pits and hearths where early man cooked his meat, and a few tools that must have been used to make the spearpoints. But fossils of man himself are few and far between. So far, the oldest ones found are three skulls unearthed in Washington State and dated at ten thousand years old. But we know little about them as yet.

These vanished peoples have been named for the places where their weapons were found: Sandia man, Clovis man, Folsom man — all in what is now New Mexico. In some places there are many layers of living conditions to be seen, from the fire pits of the Ice Age to the beer cans of last week. Man seems to be a trashy creature who refuses to pick up after himself.

One of our newest national monuments, the Jefferson National Expansion Memorial (which includes the Gateway Arch) in

St. Louis, Missouri, is within sight of an Indian mound where — eight hundred to one thousand years ago — the Indian city of Cahokia stood, very nearly as large as the white man's city that grew up around it. This is a great center of interest for archeologists, as it is the largest man-made mound north of Mexico, and the city was in its day by far the largest city within our borders. But this was a mere nine hundred years ago; the sandals in the Oregon cave are ten times as old, and they take us very far back in American history to what must certainly have been some of our earliest Americans.

It is a mistake to call these people "Indians," but we do not seem to have a better word. The first people of America did not call themselves "Indians" or "red men"; they called themselves by some name that had meaning for them — the Tall Pine People, or the River People, or the Buffalo People. They, in turn, did not know what to call the pale strangers when they came. At one time, Indians on the Oregon coast had only one word for "white man"; it meant "he who was washed up by the sea," because all the white men they had ever seen had come by shipwreck.

When the white man finally arrived in America, he took it for granted that all Indians were the same. This is like saying all Europeans are the same. The American melting pot had been working for ten thousand years when Europeans first set foot on the continent. Thousands of people, very different in appearance, language, and life-style, lived in hundreds of different places — mountains, farmlands, deserts, the seacoast — speaking hundreds of different languages. Calling them all "Indians" satisfied Columbus, but it caused endless confusion.

The Navajos have a name for themselves — Dinneh, which means "the people." Alaskan Indians call themselves Tinneh — "the people." If the names sound alike, it is probably no accident, as the Navajos probably came down through Alaska on their way south from the ice bridge at the Bering Sea, and their languages are related as, for example, Spanish and Italian are related. But the Greenland Eskimos consider themselves Innuit — "the people." The Zulus of South Africa regard themselves as "the people." So do the natives of Easter Island in the mid-Pacific. The Lapp word for "human beings" refers only to Laplanders. The Caribs, who were cannibals, surprised the Spanish (when they finally did get an interpreter and got together to talk, which is not easy if one party is a cannibal) by saying, "There is something we have been wanting to ask you. What *are* you? We alone are people!"

Present-day Indians of Arizona speak of the ancient peoples of their area as Hohokam, "those who have vanished." This at least is true; they have all vanished, probably two thousand years ago. (People on one of the Pacific islands call their ancient ones "the people of before-time," which means much the same thing: people who lived here once, under our skies, fishing our rivers and farming our lands.) Scientists call some of these early people Basket Makers, because they left beautiful baskets behind them. Probably most of these tribes live on among the present Indians of this desert land, particularly the Pimas and the Papago people, who have kept some of the ancient arts and customs from thousands of years ago. We know more about these ancient people than we do about many others which may be as old, or older. And Hohokam is as good a name as any for them.

From the evidence we have now, it is thought that at least four different groups of people crossed the ice bridge at the Bering Strait some time in the past twenty-five thousand years and spread out over the continent of North America. We know a little about them, and in the coming years will probably find out more. Some of these people crossed the coast highlands to the valley of the Yukon, which was free of ice at a time when everything else was frozen. They must have moved always south and a little east, following the river to warmer country. Some reached the valley of the Rio Grande and (like many tourists since) decided to stay there. Some went on, as far south as the tip of South America, to the bleak cold rocks of Tierra del Fuego. What pushed them on? We do not know.

Other groups, coming perhaps thousands of years later and perhaps from a different place to start with, came across the Bering Strait and down into the new country, bringing with them whatever skills they had for making tools or weapons. Someone brought in the bow and arrow during those years. Some brought the art of carving in ivory. Some of these people seem to have followed the coastline clear to Mexico. The Reindeer People came last, and they went north and east; they must have been used to cold weather.

People came north from Mexico and mixed with the people from the north and west. Kwakiutl Indians from what is now British Columbia add a note of mystery with their masks, which have great handlebar mustaches; neither Chinese nor Indian people in this area had enough hair on their faces to make such a big mustache. Does this indicate that people from the Japanese islands, people far older than the Japanese, had joined this trek to the new land? They seem to be the only people of the East who could grow enough whiskers to make such a great mustache. The Kwakiutl masks, and the totem-pole faces, stare at us out of the past, and keep their secrets in spite of our searching.

Coming years and new discoveries may clear up some of these mysteries. At least we can now make some educated guesses about the people who made grass and reed sandals and beautiful baskets, thousands of years ago and then vanished: the Hohokam.

Careful research tells us that there were at least two kinds of Hohokam people in the Arizona country: the River Hohokams, and the Desert Hohokams. The River People farmed, counting on the flooding of the Gila River in the same way that the Egyptians used the Nile. But the Gila was not "old faithful" like the Nile, rising every year right on time; sometimes the river failed them, and the crops were lost. So they set up an irrigation system in the valleys of the Gila and Salt Rivers. Parts of this have been dug out of the sand in the past few years, and it looks remarkably like a modern irrigation system. The Hohokams must have been the first people of the New World to build a system of canals and water gates for farming. We do not know exactly how long ago they built it, or what engineering genius among them first figured out how to build gates out of reeds and branches — the same way you make baskets — to control the flow of water. In any case, he ranks with Robert Fulton and Thomas Edison.

At some point, very long ago, someone brought the Hohokams the gift of corn. We think it came up from Mexico, and it was in a very small and early form, hardly more than a grass with heavy heads like wheat. Wherever it came from, it made a great difference to the lives of these early Americans as it does to ours. Before the coming of corn, people had gathered wild fruit and vegetables and many kinds of seeds. But corn was to become the heart of their farming as it is of ours as wheat is in Europe, and rice in the Orient. Corn had to have care, and it stayed in one place. A wandering people had to settle down if they wanted to raise corn, so they began building houses rather than just camping out in a cave or making a shelter out of brush. The new houses were dug into the earth and roofed with branches and mud. Like the Dakota "soddies" of pioneer days, they were not very pretty, but they kept out the cold and the heat.

Corn and man seem to be made for each other; neither one can get along without the other. Corn is called "the civilizer" and "the grain that built a hemisphere." Our whole Western half of the world has a debt to corn, which is still America's best food crop, and the best little chemical factory for trapping the sun's energy into a form we can use for food. We have also a debt to those people, those very early Americans, who first learned how to use it.

The Hohokam ground the dried corn kernels in the hollow of a big rock, using a small rounded rock to grind it. This is not the kind of a kitchen appliance you could easily carry around. It worked fine if you stayed put, but it was not much help if the tribe was on the move. Since women supposedly constitute the talkative half of the human race, they are probably the ones who thought up the idea of living in neighborhoods where there were other families to talk to, even if all the men were away hunting. This way, the women could talk while they ground the corn, or they could sing together. Little pueblos (villages) grew up around corn.

If you have a crop in, the weather is something to worry about. You could plant your corn, but if the gods did not send rain, it would not grow. So people prayed together, in songs and dances in honor of the rain god and the sun god, to help the

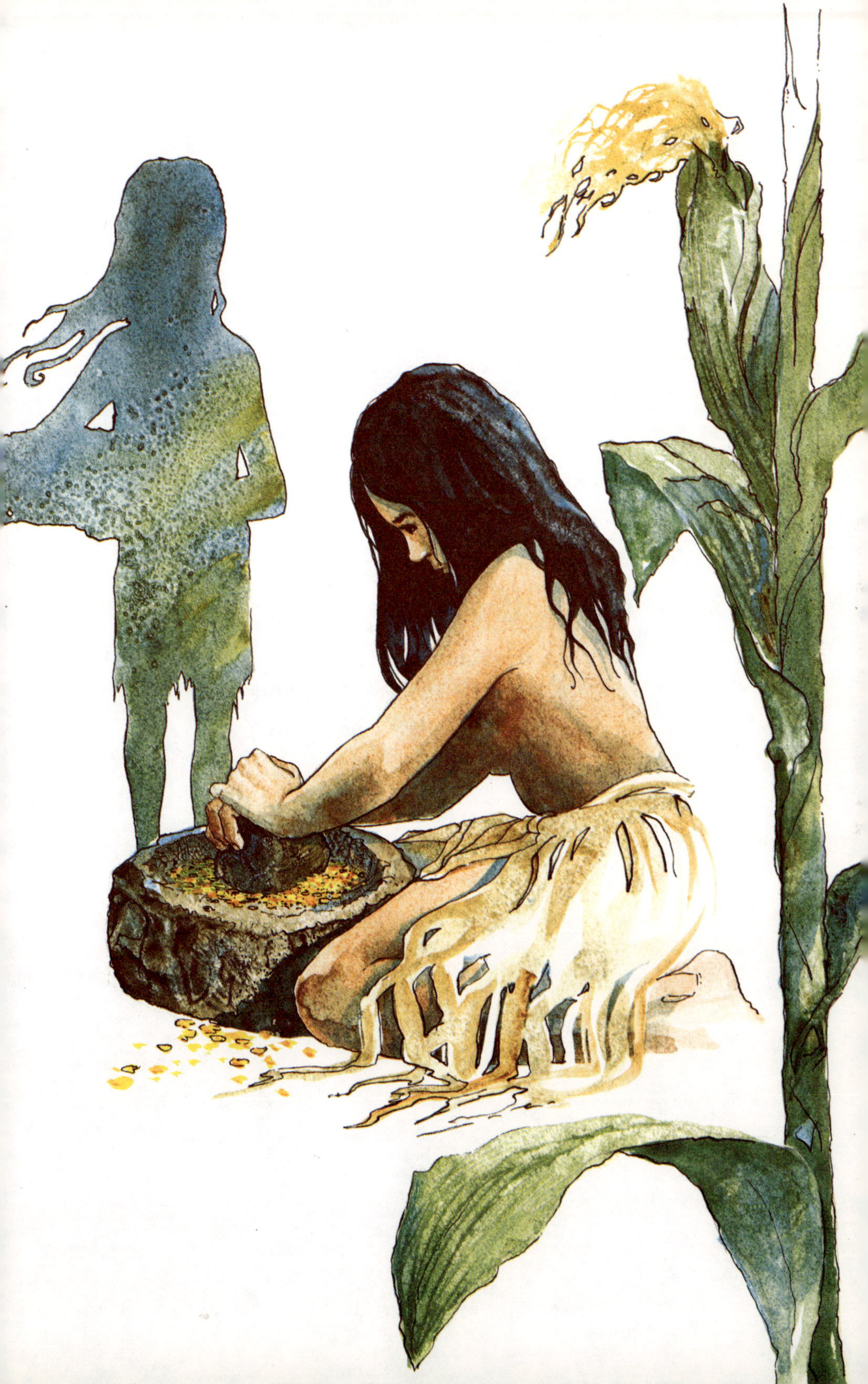

Hohokam Indians, early settlers of the Southwest, grind corn, called "the civilizer" and "the grain that built a hemisphere."

weather along. Many stories, songs, and dances grew out of the raising of corn — corn, which wore plumes like a warrior when the harvest was ripe. Indians of today still perform these ancient dances, asking the gods for rain — the right kind of rain at the right time, which is very important. Many of the white man's dances are just for fun, but Indian dances are very serious. These are the words to a Basket Dance from the pueblo of Cochiti, in New Mexico:

> Let the thunder be heard, O ye ancients!
> Let the sky be covered with white blossom clouds,
> That the earth, O ye ancients,
> Be covered with many-colored flowers.
> That the seeds may come up,
> That the stalks grow strong,
> That the people have corn,
> That happily they eat.
> Let the people have corn
> To complete the road of life.

That sounds very much like the Christian prayer, ". . . Give us this day our daily bread. . . ." If your daily bread were corn bread or tortillas, it would be just right.

By the time the Spanish came to the Southwest in the sixteenth century, the Indians had worked with corn for a long time, and it had changed a good deal from those first tiny ears in the time of the Hohokam. The Spanish found flint and flour, as well as dent, sweet, and pop corn, in six colors, colors that were sacred to the Indian. Europeans were strangers to this plant, but they caught on fast, from the Pilgrims of New England who were taught to plant a fish with the corn to make their crops grow (and *that* must have sounded like a wild tale when the Indians first told them!) down through the centuries to now, when corn is grown from the tall stalks of Iowa to the rich little dwarf plant that will help to stamp out hunger in the poor places of the world.

Snaketown, Arizona, is the best example of the early Hohokam culture that we have. It is only in the past few years that this place was recognized for what it is — a window on a lost world, a civilization that was here in our own country before the Cliff Dwellers or the Mound Builders. These people must have been very good farmers to have lived so long in the desert. Hundreds of miles of old canals, part of their irrigation system, have been dug up, along with the remains of nearly five thousand houses. This was not just a little village and a few farms; it must, at one time, have been a sizable group of people.

These were a basket-making people; even the floodgates of the canals were woven of grasses and reeds. Baskets were made by many of these early peoples, long before anyone thought of the pottery which is now so much a part of the Southwest. Baskets were light and easy to carry, while pottery — like the stone corn grinders — was heavy. It is likely that the very early people made baskets in the years before corn, when they had to move around to gather roots and seeds for food. Perhaps pottery was discovered when some smart woman decided to plaster her basket with clay to make it waterproof. Some of the very early pottery had marks on it as if it had been wrapped with a grass rope. Pottery seems to have caught on wherever there was the right kind of clay to make it. The first pottery may have come from either South America or Japan, traded from tribe to tribe (originating with those who lived on the seacoast). Wherever it came from, it found a good home in the Indian Southwest, and some of the world's finest pottery now comes from there.

Each of the scattered tribes worked out its own designs to use on pottery and baskets, and today these designs help us to tell where these ancient household wares came from; sometimes the pottery is thousands of miles from where it was made to where it was found in modern times. Regular trade routes from tribe to tribe moved all kinds of goods across the country for years before the white man came. An Indian mound in the Mississippi valley had copper from the Great Lakes region, obsidian rock from the Rocky Mountains, mica sheets from the Southern Appalachians, shells from the Gulf Coast, fossil shark teeth, grizzly bear teeth, red jasper stone, fresh-water pearls, and pottery, all from elsewhere. Today, if you were to pick up a piece of black-on-black pottery in Sweden or Singapore, you would know that it was from San Ildefonso pueblo in New Mexico and made by the world-famous artist, María Martínez. From the very beginning of both basketry and pottery, the woman who made it put her signature on it so strongly in its style and finish that we can identify it even today.

All the early people seem to have had animal legends which they used to teach tribal history, or good behavior, to the children. Coyote was a troublemaker, fox was clever (we say "foxy"), black bear had a bad temper, and so on. Animal and bird designs were used on the dishes and baskets and on some of the clothing. Living must have been very hard for those early people, and they could not have had much free time, yet they took time to make all their useful things beautiful.

The people of Snaketown worked out an art that no other tribe seems ever to have thought of: they discovered the process of *etching* which, with a few changes, is still used in modern art. Using tar or pitch to draw their design on a large shell, they would etch it with acid from cactus. We use different acids today, but the process is the same: the acid eats away all but the design which is protected by the tar, and when the tar is washed away there is a design on the shell, raised a little from the background. Modern scientists were quite surprised to find that the Hohokam had been doing this kind of art for a couple of thousand years. We were quite a long time in discovering the process for ourselves. The Hohokam used it for jewelry; piece by piece it is coming to light from the sands of Snaketown.

In time, the Hohokam moved away from Snaketown. There was a terrible drought in the Southwest in the thirteenth century, and bad floods a few years later. Many of the old inhabitants moved away at this time, and the Snaketown inhabitants probably went at this time too. From evidence left behind — pottery and buildings destroyed, "killed" (which meant they were leaving for good) — it looks as if they all went at once. They found better places for farming, and over the next two centuries blended with other tribes from the east and the south. In the fourteenth century this new people built Casa Grande (Spanish for "Great House") which is still with us, a majestic ruin in the desert south of Phoenix.

One of the reasons we have for thinking that some of these Hohokam may have come from the south, from Mexico, is that they had a big ball court, much like the ones built by the Mayas of Mexico. The game played was rather like volleyball, except that neither hands nor feet could be used on the ball; it had to be bounced off the hip. It was the sort of game you had better not lose, because the winners (at least among the Mayas) ate the losers at the victory banquet. Not really a good place to turn out for volleyball.

There are many unsolved puzzles at Casa Grande. One is a carving on stone, a petroglyph of a maze, exactly like the one at a very ancient ruin in Crete. How did anyone from Crete ever find the Arizona desert?

A man by the name of William Coxon made a hobby of studying Indian petroglyphs and spent most of his life working on it. He found some very interesting signs around Casa Grande. People who do not know much about it will tell you that these petroglyphs are just Indian doodling, like you might find on a telephone pad. Some Indian with nothing much to do just sat there (in the blazing sun) and doodled signs on the rock and they do not mean anything at all, according to this. It might be possible if the Indian had a crayon or a felt pen; but petroglyphs have to be pounded or chipped into the stone, and making just one figure would take all day. So Mr. Coxon assures us that they are not "doodles": they are messages — and they can be read if you will take the time to study them.

Most of these figures are taken from Indian sign language, which is done mostly with the hands. If an Indian were trying to tell you, "I saw it," he would point to his own eyes and then indicate himself. To get the message "See!" on a rock, he would carve two dots for eyes. The message, to any Indian passing by, would be, "Look! There is something here that you should notice!" The Indian never wastes words like the white man, who always uses more than he needs. So all the little marks and *symbols*, which is another word for "signs," were messages for other people. A symbol might say, "There is good drinking water up to the left behind the big rock," or, "Good place to get elk ahead." Some symbols were like our highway signs — an arrow with a curved shaft, or crossed lines — which tell us: "Turn left — winding road (or crossroad)." They were very simple road maps, in a time when there were no roads, only game trails.

Perhaps the most interesting thing about the petroglyphs in this Hohokam country is the fact that William Coxon, in traveling around the world, has found exactly the same symbols on rocks in the Gulf of Mexico, the Canary Islands, and along the rivers of Ireland, Australia, and South Africa! That doodling Indian really did get around, and he must have had a lot of free time. Mr. Coxon concludes: "The Scriptures have been challenged so many times by those who thought they knew better, yet the holy word has endured while those who doubted them have been forgotten. There is a passage which reads, 'And the whole earth was of one language and of one speech.' (Genesis 2) The petroglyphs testify that at least the writing was understood."

Chapter 7
Land Beyond the Sunset

Coyote has been at it again. Not the white man's coyote, which sometimes steals chickens or lambs and makes such scary noises under the moon, but the mythical coyote of the Indian legends: Ol' Man Coyote, mischief-maker, who stirs up trouble in the world, who deliberately took two bites out of the first day, so that — no matter how you added them up — you could never make the days come out even to be a year.

Today our calendar has 365 days, 5 hours, 48 minutes, and 46 seconds, divided into twelve months, with an extra day slipped in every four years for leap year. We use this system, not because it is accurate, but because nobody has come up with a better one. No one wants to change to thirteen months of twenty-eight days each, and even that is not exact. Eight hundred years before Christ, people discovered that they could not settle it with twelve months of thirty days, either. Whatever system they dreamed up just turned out to be one of those pesky arithmetic problems that have a remainder. It got so that rulers of kingdoms looked on the calendar as their biggest headache. A ruler was supposed to know more than his subjects did, and it was embarrassing to have his wise men forever pointing out to him that he could not even balance the calendar.

Julius Caesar, who is supposed to have invented leap year, established a new calendar in 45 B.C. and enforced it wherever the Roman legions ruled. Ireland had never heard of Julius Caesar, so they had a calendar worked out by their own wise men. When

Ireland was converted to Christianity, they simply added the Christian feasts to this calendar. Hundreds of years later, when all the bishops of the Western world went to Rome for a meeting, there was a great hassle between the Irish bishops and those from Europe over the date of Easter, which differed on their calendars.

At one point in history, countries following two different calendars were running eleven days apart! You can imagine what that did to trade, for one thing. Even Kublai Khan, far away in Cathay, was struggling to work out a calendar. The Mayas, who lived in Mexico over two thousand years ago, came closer than anyone has, since then, to an accurate calendar. It has been a problem as far back as history goes, and it still is.

Thinking about our ancestors — and their attempts to find a time system they could agree on — should give us more patience with the mathematical stew we are in at the present time: trying to convert to the metric system so that we will have a common set of measurements with the rest of the world. Possibly Ol' Man Coyote took a few bites out of our measurement system, too, just to stir up trouble.

If someone asked you how you measure time, you would say, "That's easy — with clocks and calendars!" You would be right, but we ought to remember that man did not come equipped with these things. He had to invent them, and it took him thousands of years of hard work to get as far as he has.

There were, of course, many ways of telling time in the years before clocks and watches started flowing out of Switzerland in such quantities. Living out in the country fifty years ago, your mother would say to you, "When the mill whistle blows, that's suppertime!" Or, "When that big tree shadow starts up the wall, you come home running!" Back in the Middle Ages, when people were very religious, a mother would say, "Now, be careful, daughter, and remember that your father wants his egg boiled just one Act of Hope." In Ireland they will tell you, "Oh, it's just a couple of Rosaries down the road!" Someone is sure to have taught you that when you can stand on your shadow it is noon. French-Canadians in the fur trade used to count the length of a canoe portage by the number of pipes they smoked in crossing it; the longest was a nine-pipe portage near Lake Superior. And here is a good question for you concerning the nine-pipe portage: Were they measuring time or distance? There are places where it is pretty hard to tell.

One of the oldest, surest clocks in the universe is the sky clock, the stars. Polynesians sailed across thousands of miles of open ocean to Pacific islands they had never seen, with no guide but the stars and a pilot who could read them. Even today, in our wonderful world of gadgets, the sky is the last authority on time and directions. It has only one fault — clouds. Sailors pray for a cloudless sky so they can get their bearings, and they have a real affection for the North Star, which never changes.

Calendars came long before clocks. A calendar marks the things that are important to the person who makes it. No doubt you take your new calendar each year and mark in dates connected with family members, relatives, and friends: birthdays, graduations, weddings, family vacation, first and last days of school, the date of spring vacation, Thanksgiving and Christmas get-togethers, and so on. Quite reasonably, then, this record of the Indian year marks the things that are important to a tribe who lived perhaps two hundred years ago.

The year began in October, which they called "back to back" because it was the place where the hot and cold seasons parted:

- Time of the Thin Winds (November).
- Great Winds (December).
- Crusted Snow (January).
- Baby Eagle (February).
- Month of the Blue Wind (March).
- Month of the Little Leaves (April).
- Month of the Yellow Wind (May).
- When Few Seeds Ripen (June).
- Great Seed-Ripening (July).
- Little Ripening (August).
- Harvest: Ceremony of All Blessings in Thanksgiving (September).

This is an Indian calendar from a different part of the country, from a people who must have been full-time farmers:

- Month When the Little Lizard's Tail Freezes Off (January).
- Plant Root, "Daughter of Spring" (February).
- Plants Above the Ground (March).
- Sticky Ground: Wheat-Planting Time (April).
- Soft Ground: Corn-Planting Time (May).
- Corn-Tassel Time (June).
- Corn-Ear Time (July).
- Beard of the Corn (August).
- Corn in the Milk (September).
- Corn Fully Matured (October).
- Fall of the Year (November).
- Middle of Winter (December).

Almost as far back in history as we find man himself, we also find evidence that he was trying to measure time and distance. Time came first, because his idea of distance was limited by how far he could walk, and he did not know enough about the rest of the world to be curious about it until he discovered trade. This probably came about by accident from hunters meeting and bartering in sign language.

But long before this, man would have noticed the seasons: the hunting time, when everybody had enough to eat, and the frozen cold time when the old people and the babies died. They would see every year the time of young animals, the salmon runs, the season of fruits and berries when it was always hot. Sooner or later, these things would be related to the sun, that great, silent, golden monarch in the sky. Someone would notice that the sun seemed to travel in the sky, to go away and come back again regularly. They marked the time when the night was so long they thought it would never end, and another time when there was a glorious long day and a short night. We know these as the summer and winter solstices, in June and December, dividing the year in half. Thousands of years ago, with no one to explain it to them, people worked out the four landmarks of the year: the solstices on which they celebrated the midsummer festival and the midwinter festival, and the two days just halfway between them when day and night are equal, the spring and fall equinoxes. If you ever get to worrying about how many legs has an equinox, just remember that *nox* is the Latin word for "night," and *equi* is the same word as our word "equal." In other words, day and night are the same length.

It is not hard to understand how pagan peoples of thousands of years ago, who did not share with the Jews the revelation of the true God, would have worshiped the sun. It was the source of their light, warmth, and growth, and it was very beautiful. It was the greatest natural power in their world, with the moon coming along second.

In building a temple to the sun-god, these various peoples were not only building a church where they could worship, they were also setting up a scientific device — a sun-clock — for keeping track of the sun's course across the sky. This knowledge seemed a sort of magic to ordinary people, secrets to be known only by their wise men. This information was very important because knowing what to expect might mean the difference between starvation and survival. They very cleverly worked out ways of trapping the sun into telling them what they needed to know. Stones placed at a certain angle would catch the sunrise glow on the day of the spring equinox. Stones placed in another fashion would catch the first gleam of the fall equinox. It would take a long time to work this out, and some of the people carried their worship of the sun-god to the point of making human sacrifices when there was a drought, for example. Their religion was a great confusion between science and fables by the time they stepped into history.

It was probably fishermen who first connected the tides with the phases of the moon. They saw that the moon went through the same changes every twenty-eight days, and that twice a year there were very high tides and very low ones. So the lunar (moon) clock became the guide for those who lived by the sea.

Most of us have heard of Stonehenge in England and perhaps have seen pictures of it, with its tall black stones standing in

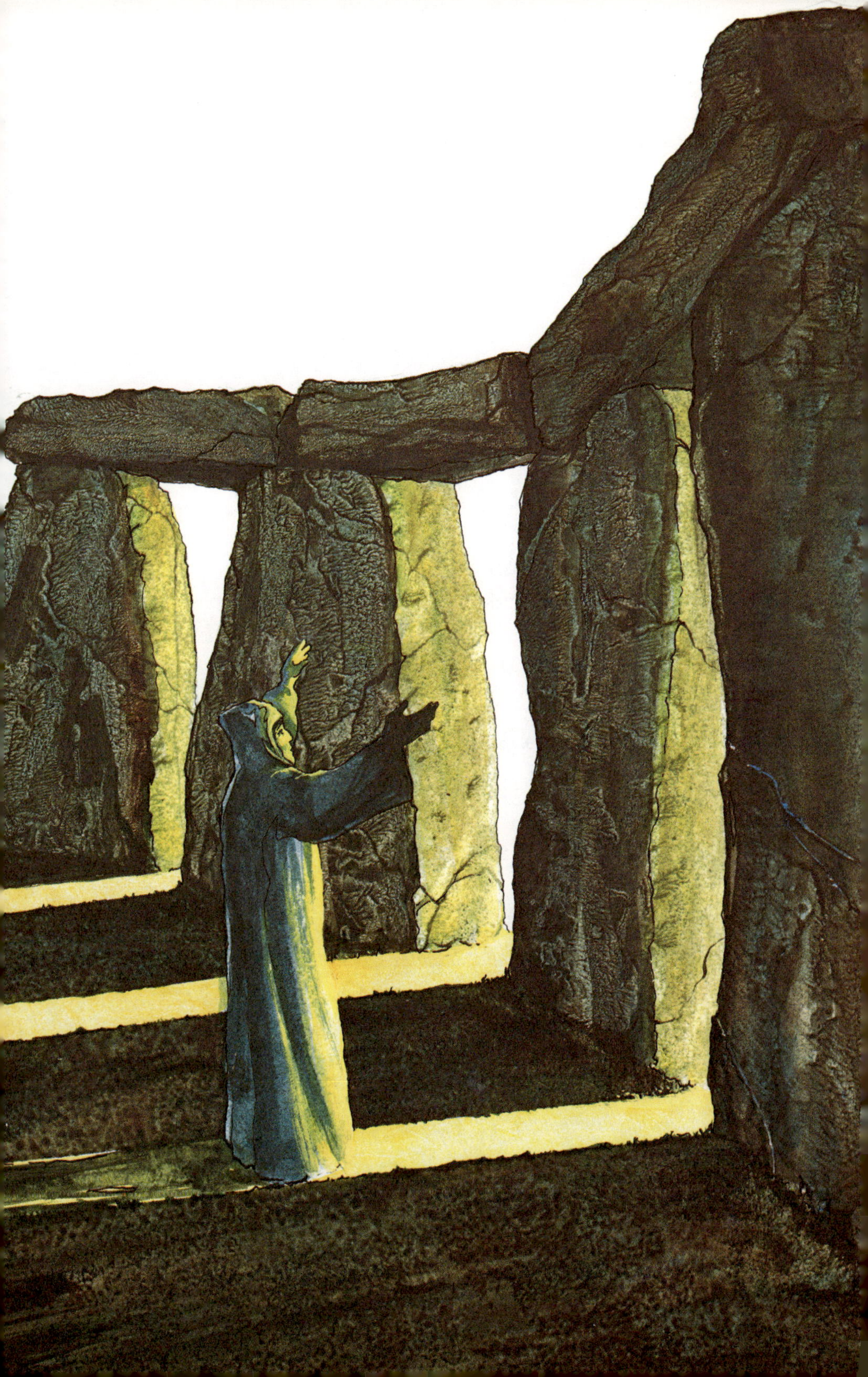

Stonehenge in England: Is
it an astronomical device, or
a temple to the gods? The first
Western Hemisphere inhabitants
built temples (similar in structure)
to various deities, including the sun-god.

a circle. This was most probably a solar (sun) clock for people who lived there four thousand years ago. Few of us realize that there are buildings in our own country made for exactly the same purpose — to keep track of the sun's journey across the sky. The ruins of these buildings are not as old as Stonehenge, but they are a lot older than any other old buildings we have, and they tell us a story that few people ever heard before.

To understand these buildings, we have to go back in history nearly four thousand years, to the city of Tyre on the coast of Palestine. These people were called Canaanites in the Bible, but history knows them as Phoenicians, the people who gave the alphabet to the world.

More than three thousand years ago, Tyre was one of the greatest cities in the world, and the center of trade for the Mediterranean. Tyre was first to build a fleet of fast, sturdy galleys rowed by slaves. The ships were captained by a tough, curious people who were not afraid of anything. They moved out of the Mediterranean to the coast of Africa and built cities on the Spanish coast and on the North Atlantic coast of Africa. One city was called Tarshish. It was a trading point for the strange things they brought home to Tyre. Outgoing from Tyre, they carried cedars of Lebanon for Egypt, which had no wood, and also a purple dye for the cloth which was made from shellfish found in their waters. Kings and important people all around the known world dressed up in "Tyrian purple," and after the people of Tyre had discovered how to make glass dishes, every banquet table of all the nearby kingdoms used Tyrian glass. Going home to Tyre from Tarshish, they brought back sandalwood and precious stones, ebony and elephant tusks, "ivory, apes, and peacocks" (as it says in Scripture), and many curious things out of Africa. This was the Bronze Age, and to make bronze — for tools, weapons, or jewelry — you had to have tin. The only tin came from a foggy island called Britain, and nobody but the Phoenicians knew where to find it.

The sailors who made these daring journeys into the unknown had one thing in common (otherwise they departed this life in a hurry): they knew the paths of the seas, they kept all kinds of charts in their heads, but they never wrote down anything that would give an enemy a chance to dip into their trade. More than one Phoenician ship captain sank his ship rather than let his cargo and maps fall into the hands of an attacking galley.

Jonah — who had trouble with the whale, remember? — was on a "ship of Tarshish" when it happened. They were the finest and biggest merchant ships of their time; but the men of Tyre left us very little evidence of how they managed those terrifying journeys over the dark seas. We cannot imagine, for example, how they managed to set up a trade route with what, two thousand years later, would be known as New England. Yet there is very strong evidence that they did.

After the Pilgrims came to our northeast coast, many more English immigrants came and settled in what is now Massachusetts, Rhode Island, New Hampshire, and other areas nearby. Most of these people were farmers and they built farms. They were mildly surprised to find so many stone buildings lying about in ruins. Some were partly underground, and in the days before refrigerators, people stored their winter fruit and vegetables in just such pits. So the thrifty New Englanders stored their apples and turnips in the underground caves and thanked heaven that the Indians had known how to build root cellars.

Only recently, when Dr. Barry Fell from New Zealand came to see the "root cellars," did the secrets come out. They were not root cellars and the Indians did not build them. In a place called "Mystery Hill" at North Salem, New Hampshire, one of the "root cellars" turned out to be part of a scientific observatory which had been used as a sun calendar two thousand years ago! Dr. Fell was able to translate some of the "root scratches" on the stones, which told him that it was a building in honor of the god Bel (in the Bible it is spelled "Baal" and he was the god of the Canaanites — the Phoenicians).

It all adds up to a New England settlement of people from Tyre and Tarshish who set up a trade route across the Atlantic before the birth of Christ. The men of the new country were in the fur-trapping business, and our country must have been a hunter's paradise in those days. The bold sailors from Tyre and

Tarshish must have done very well in the fur trade. In return, they brought to the edge of the world cargoes of weapons and dishes and jewelry made of bronze. These things have been found in America, and they had to come from Celtic Spain because nobody else could get his hands on the tin that was mined in those foggy islands north of Spain.

It was quite natural that once they had crossed the ocean and founded new colonies in America — which they called Iargalon, "Land Beyond the Sunset" — they would build temples like the ones in their own land in honor of the god Bel, many of which were observation posts for studying the skies and the seasons.

Dr. Fell has translated many inscriptions which are cut into rocks in different parts of our country. These are in several languages, and there is evidence that not only the men of Tyre and Tarshish came here, but also the Egyptians and the Libyans from Africa, and the Celts from Western Europe. Some American Indian languages contain words from Phoenician, Libyan, Chaldean, Moabite, and other ancient nations we hear of only in the Bible. There are two messages carved into rocks on the Atlantic coast that come to us out of the darkness of countless centuries; at Mount Hope Bay near Bristol, Rhode Island, is a "Kilroy was here" that makes you think. It says, "This Stone Proclaims Voyagers from Tarshish." On an island ten miles off the coast of Maine, near Monhegan Island, is a simple direction: "Ships from Phoenicia Cargo Platform."

Another puzzle is a flat stone on a hillside twenty miles from Albuquerque, New Mexico, with this message carved into it in characters that are a mixture of Phoenician, Greek, and Moabite: "I am Yahweh thy God who brought thee out of the land of Egypt, out of the house of bondage. Thou shalt not make unto thee a graven image. Thou shalt not take the name of Yahweh in vain. Remember the day of the Sabbath to sanctify it. Honor thy father and mother that thy days may be long on the soil which Yahweh thy God giveth thee. Thou shalt not kill. Thou shalt not commit adultery. Thou shalt not steal. Thou shalt not testify falsely against thy neighbor. Thou shalt not covet thy neighbor's wife."

Does it sound familiar? It should. But how do you suppose it got on a rock in New Mexico?

Though the Phoenicians seem to have gone a long way without written charts or maps, our world today is more complicated. In the business world, time *is* money, and things must operate on schedule. We need to know exactly where everything is and how to bring people together at times and places for trade and many other reasons. In other words, we need *accurate* maps and charts, and a time that everyone agrees on. When World War II started, we all discovered at once that the world was not properly mapped. Thousands of lives were lost simply because military leaders did not have a correct picture of any country, not even of their own.

In the years since the war, all the countries of the world have been trying to get under way what would be the biggest international project so far — a complete, accurate map of the world. The National Geographic Society has made some of the best maps we have, but there is still much more to do.

From the time of Julius Caesar, maps have been a source of trouble. Caesar kept all the complete maps locked up in his own strongbox, lest some enemy lay hands on them. Maps were as much military matériel as a shield or a spear; they could tell an invading general which was the easiest point to attack, where to find water, and many other vital facts. During the years of discovery, from the fifteenth to the eighteenth centuries, maps were the key to power and fortune and had to be kept from other countries at any cost. Spanish ship charts were always weighted with pieces of lead, so that if the ship were taken, the charts could be tossed overboard and would sink by themselves. Maps and charts were the first booty claimed by a pirate on capturing a ship, and there was a huge black market in phony charts and maps.

We hope that we have got past this point, to where we can view a map as a means of understanding our neighbors rather than a tool for defeating them. But we still have the job to do, to find a method we can agree on and get it all down on paper. All countries recognize the need of a world map project, but we will have to agree on methods first. For one thing, there are no less than eighty ways of indicating "mountains" on a map at the present time. Seventy-nine countries must give in on that one. We will have to have a standard system of measures, which we do have in the metric system (provided everyone agrees to adopt it). These are the big problems; there are also many small ones.

We have done better in the matter of regulating time, though that was a rough fight while it lasted. We have now an international agreement to have one prime meridian, the one passing through the Greenwich observatory in England; from this, all longitude is calculated and all time is taken. The civil day begins at midnight and lasts twenty-four hours. When Big Ben strikes midnight in London, a new day is beginning. There are, of course, different time zones, of which the United States uses four. We take all this for granted now, but all these details had to be debated. Not everyone wanted the day to start at midnight. Some countries had a tendency to feel that *their* country should set the time. Easter Island, a lonesome rock in the vast Pacific, two thousand miles from land in any direction except down, calls itself "The Island at the Center of the World." A lot of other countries, including ours, feel that they are the center of the world.

So our country, as we all know, is in the process of converting to the metric system of measurement. People who do not know much about it are apt to get angry at the confusion and say, "What was good enough for my grandfather is good enough for me!" But it is not that simple. (Your grandfather, for one thing, was not planning to fly to the moon.) We are the last big country in the world to hold out on adopting the metric system; the others are Brunei, Burma, Liberia, and Yemen. It does not matter a great deal if they do not convert, but it makes a whole lot of difference whether we do. And this is not simply a matter of mapping the world, though that is very important.

The system of measures that we have been using resembles nothing so much as a trunk full of odds and ends from the attic. Start with the foot measure: it was Charlemagne's foot, we are told, long ago measured and set up as the standard foot. A sixteenth-century German, who felt that there should be some note of the fact that not all feet are the same size, suggested this way of solving the problem: "Stand at the door of a church on Sunday, bid sixteen men to stop, tall ones and short ones as they happen to pass out as the service is finished, then make them put their left feet one behind the other and the length obtained shall be a right and lawful rod, and the 16th (of it) shall be a right and lawful foot."

Then we have the inch: the length of the knuckle on King Edgar's thumb. You may never have heard of King Edgar, but he left us with the puzzle of fitting twelve of his thumb knuckles into Charlemagne's foot to make an ordinary twelve-inch ruler. A yard, as ruled on by King Henry I, was the distance between the end of his nose and his fingertips.

The meter was set up mathematically as one-ten-millionth of the length of the earth's meridian between the equator and the North Pole. The final measurement turned out to be a little over thirty-nine inches, near enough to a yard to be reasonable to us. If King Henry's arms — or his nose — had been a little longer, we might have hit it exactly right.

The pyramids were built using cubit measure (a cubit was the distance between the elbow and the fingertips). There were at least two kinds of cubits, a big royal one and a small everyday one, much in the way that the United States has three kinds of miles and six kinds of tons. Noah built the ark to cubit measure, as you can read in the Bible. Thousands of years later, Henry Ford built the Model T using measurements to a sixty-fourth of an inch. By the time he got around to making the Model A, he was using a "decimal inch" divided into hundredths. Nowadays, most cars are built according to metric system specifications.

World efforts to work out a system of common measurement are much the same as trying to work out a common language. The only people who seem ever to have done so were the Plains Indians of our country, who talked with each other, and with the white men from different countries, with the sign language. The more we see of the efforts of other people to find a common language, the greater mystery it is how the Indians ever worked it out.

It is easy to see that we cannot communicate unless we have words that both understand. If you speak in Dutch and I answer you in Japanese, we are not apt to agree on much. What is the language spoken by the most people on earth? As a matter of fact, it is Chinese; one fourth of the world's people speak it. Now, if the other three fourths of the world would learn Chinese, we would have the problem solved; it is said that it takes a person of average intelligence forty years to learn it, so it would take a while. English and German are increasingly becoming the business languages of the Western world, except for that enormous chunk of the Western Hemisphere that speaks either Spanish or Portuguese. It is, as you can see, quite a large problem. And if we cannot even agree on a system of measurements so that we can map the world, how can we ever solve it?

Chapter 8
The Land of Sometime

This is the land of *poco tiempo;* the land of "after a while," or perhaps, "sometime."

—*The Author*

Walk on a rainbow trail, walk on a trail of song;
And all around you will be beautiful.
There is a way out of every dark mist,
If you walk on a rainbow trail.

—*From a Navajo song*

The Grand Canyon is in northwestern Arizona, set like a jewel in a wealth of parks and scenic wonderlands reaching out into New Mexico, Colorado, and Nevada. It is not as big as the "Grand Canyon" on Mars, which is five times deeper and four times as wide, but it is big enough: a mile deep, some 4 to 18 miles wide, and over 200 miles long.

In 1858, one of the first Americans to see it wrote glumly in his notes: "It seems intended by nature that the Colorado River [which runs through the Grand Canyon], along the greater part of its lonely and majestic way, shall be forever unvisited and undisturbed. It appears to be altogether valueless. Ours has been the first, and doubtless will be the last, party of whites to visit this profitless locality."

Millions of tourists have proved him to be absolutely wrong. It has now reached the point where you must make a reservation in advance if you want to do anything with the river but look at it, such as hiking, riding horseback over the hundreds of trails, or running the rapids in a rubber boat.

The Grand Canyon country and its surrounding cliffs and deserts are not even yet densely populated. Old-timers say that in the early days (by which they mean *our* early days, a hundred years ago, not the river's, which were millions of years ago) it used to be so lonesome that the rabbits spoke politely to the rattlesnakes when they met, and so hot that when a dog chased a rabbit they both walked. The automobile has changed all that, though the people who come in covered with dust from every state in the Union are tourists, not settlers. They come to see, take pictures, and go away again. Only the Indians — the Navajo, Hopi, Hualapai, Havasupai — call this wild and beautiful country "home." It takes a certain kind of people to live in such an enormous land and not be crushed by it. Indians have always known how to live at peace with their land.

More than three million visitors a year pour through the park gates, driving or on foot, coming from or going to a dozen beauty spots nearby — or, as "nearby" as anything is in this huge country. To the north are fantastic Bryce Canyon with its goblin-shaped rocks, and Zion, "heavenly city of God, not made with hands," named by the early Mormon pioneers. To the south are the Painted Desert and the Petrified Forest National Park; eastward, across the Navajo-Hopi country, are Canyon de Chelly (pronounced CAN-yon d'SHAY) National Monument and Pueblo Bonito. Glen Canyon Dam has a backwater lake with enough water to cover Pennsylvania a foot deep, creating a huge recreation area.

Surrounding the Grand Canyon National Park, which runs along both banks of the Colorado, are more national and state parks and monuments than you could ever hope to visit: Arches, Canyonlands, Capitol Reef, Dinosaur, and Rainbow Bridge in

Utah; Saguaro, Organ Pipe Cactus, Monument Valley, and Inscription House Ruins in Arizona; Mesa Verde, Cripple Creek, Ute Mountain, and Rocky Mountain in Colorado; Chaco Canyon, Bandelier, Gran Quivira, White Sands, and Carlsbad Caverns in New Mexico, for starters. Through all this fabulous country you can see the people who call it home — the modern Indians who are not at all the "vanishing Americans" of fifty years ago, but up-and-coming people who are working out their own future. Behind them, in the shadows, under the great mesas ("mesa" being Spanish for "table") where the cliff dwellings silently wait out the centuries, are the Anasazi, a Navajo word meaning "the ancients — the old ones — those who were here before us." Their spirit remains in the country they once lived in and loved. We need what they have to teach us, for they were people of peace, who lived under democracy long before it became our way of government.

Much of the Grand Canyon country is Navajo now, but the Navajos have not been in this area long. The Anasazi lived here, perhaps two thousand years ago, in a world without white men; the Navajos came on the scene as wandering people from the north, just in time to be at war with the white man who wanted this land. The Navajos were bold and warlike, even when fighting on foot. At the time of the Pueblo Indian rebellion against the Spanish, the Navajos, Apaches, and Comanches stole all the horses they could get and went into the business of raising horses. The Pueblo tribes never did quite catch on to the idea of horses, but their more warlike neighbors did.

After the gift of fire, which was lost in the past, the horses were the nicest thing that had ever happened to the Indians. There was no more trudging along on foot after the tricky buffalo or the savage grizzly. A whole new style of fighting emerged. Perhaps the happiest of all were the women, who had been carrying the baggage since time began; now at least the heavy tepee poles and covering hides could be carried on the backs of these wonderful animals. The mounted tribes took to raiding the pueblos for food and slaves; it was much more exciting than simply trading for what they wanted. Some medicine man hit the jackpot with an idea that caught on right away: for a price, he would personally guarantee that a little boy got special magic, and lessons, which would make him an expert horse thief when he grew up. The time of the beautiful Appaloosa, the horse thief's dream, was still in the future in those early years, but horses of any kind were wonderful.

In the middle of the last century, the American army was sent to subdue the Indians (not the whole army, naturally, but a lot more soldiers than there were Indians). Thousands of dead soldiers later, the army agreed that the Indians were not, after all, a bunch of ignorant savages who could be easily conquered and pushed around (for their own good, of course). The problem was just not as simple as some of the rocking-chair thinkers on the civilized East Coast seemed to think; what was needed, they insisted, was to take a hard line with these scalping savages. A few good hangings would do a great deal of good, they said; a dead Indian gave no one any more trouble. The army would no doubt frighten them into submission.

There is a very old recipe for squirrel pie which begins, "First, catch your squirrel." The army had first to catch the Indians before they could punish them for attacking wagon trains. Today we can see a lot of things more clearly than our great-grandparents could. There was so much killing on both sides that it was hard for people to think clearly about the problem. Land-hungry Europeans and Americans wanted all the Indians removed from their path — killed, if need be — so that they might take over the lands that the Indians loved and would never leave of their own accord. Some very terrible things were done to the Indians in the process of trying to get their land away from them, and thousands of people of both races died horribly because of greed.

The Navajos and Apaches did not consider themselves friends of the Pueblo Indians, but they banded together against the white man and they almost drove him back where he came from. In later years, when the Indians were crowded into rocky corners that nobody else wanted, heaven played a sly joke on the white man: most of the worthless land that had been given to the

Indians turned out to be full of oil, or gold, or — as of now — uranium.

Today the Navajos are interesting to us for a great many reasons. They are the only people in the Americas who live with their herds out on the lonely hillsides. Against the background of the burned hills, they look as if they had just stepped out of the Old Testament. The Navajos live by single families, scattered over this desert country. Though many of the young people work in the city of Shiprock, New Mexico, making transistors no bigger than a dime for the most modern of electronic equipment, they live in a style reminiscent of long ago. Navajo women, who are used to memorizing very complicated rug patterns for their weaving, find that making the transistors is very simple.

The Anasazi did not live with their sheep as the Navajos do; the Anasazi lived in the Southwest long before the Spanish brought in sheep. They lived, these people of so many centuries ago, in apartment houses; they may have been the first people in the world to live this way. Certainly they were the first to build a big apartment house in our country; it was called Pueblo Bonito (Spanish for "Beautiful Town") and was located in Chaco Canyon, New Mexico, twelve hundred years ago. It had at one time six hundred fifty rooms, which was a world's record for apartment houses until some New Yorker built a bigger one in his city in 1884.

Pueblo Bonito is probably older than the cliff dwellings, but both of these called for apartment-house living, which makes them different from almost all the other early homes of ancient people. The cliff dwellings, real "high-rise" apartments, made it an adventure simply getting into and out of the house, and they were safe from even the boldest enemies. Pueblo Bonito must have been built in a time of peace, when the Anasazi could safely plant their fields and live beside them while the corn ripened. Corn was new, then, to the Southwest peoples, and "corn, the civilizer" left its mark on the great apartment house, for it has all the marks of a highly civilized place.

Chaco Wash would have been running full of water then, keeping the Indians' gardens green and giving them a supply of good drinking water. Scientists who can read evidence say that the building of Pueblo Bonito, which took many years, took place in the fall of the year, after the harvests were in and the planting done. The trees, they can tell, grew where there was much water, were felled green, and carried to the building site to dry. (The Navajos say it was Mockingbird Canyon where they cut the trees; there are no trees now in Mockingbird Canyon.) Men brought the trees and, when they were ready, placed them for beams and roof supports. The women laid the mud walls and plastered over them; this was women's work. The prints of beautifully shaped hands, women's hands, can still be seen here and there in the twelve-hundred-year-old plaster.

At what point Chaco Wash started to dry up we do not know for certain, but about eight hundred years ago there was a bad drought, as the tree rings will tell you. Then there was a destructive flood when the river overran its banks for a hundred miles. When the harvests had failed too many times, and too many old people and children had died from hunger, those remaining of the Pueblo Bonito people moved away from Chaco Canyon to search for another river.

The river must have filled up again, because another people came, a long time afterward, and settled in the shell of the big apartment house. They rebuilt it, using mud and stones in a different way from the first builders, repairing the broken walls and using the broken pieces between sandstone blocks. The old beams, cut by the early Anasazi, had been cut with stone axes and were rounded at the ends as if beavers had cut them. The new people had better tools; you can tell it in the cutting marks. They built some of the mysterious "keyhole doors," what for, we cannot discover. They made built-in shelves and hanging poles to store household things (probably, even that long ago, women were fussing about never having enough cupboards); they also laid stone fireplaces in the middle of the rooms for cooking and warmth. One thing they did not build was doors on the ground level; their world was not so peaceful any more. So the only way into the apartment house was up a single ladder, which was pulled up and put away when the last citizen was home for the night.

And then, one day, tragedy came to this second people and they, too, moved away from this pleasant valley, seeking a safer place to live. By this time there were tribes that had come down from the north, raiding the pueblos, and peace was only a memory. Pueblo Bonito was left to the desert winds, which whip the sand up the canyon by day and down the canyon by night, sanding the walls of the great house which stands in the desert like a ruined castle, still beautiful in age as it was in youth, twelve hundred years ago. These things were told us by the stones and the roof beams, for these are records we can trust.

The peaceful people of the river valleys must have discovered by this time that they were no longer safe living on the valley floor. Some genius among them discovered cliff caves, and the cliff dwellings came to be. At Puye, or "Place of the Cottontail Rabbits," are some of the earliest of these, along with a ruined apartment house like Pueblo Bonito. It is just as if, a thousand years from now, some archeologist would try to puzzle out why some of the electronic-age people had solid roofs over their houses, while some had glass — which surely must be an early form of sun-heat?

This interesting place is now in the Bandelier National Monument, named for a Swiss naturalist who was the first white man to explore and love this country. Here, on a pleasant little river known as El Rito de los Frijoles ("Little River of the Beans"), are the ruins of an apartment house once called Tyuonyi and a group of cliff dwellings that have been dug out of the soft stone. Later, the people would learn to build walls and rooms in the natural caves they found, but here they simply burrowed in like an owl or a prairie dog and made themselves a snug home that could be easily defended.

Cliff dwellings are scattered all over this country of the brown deserts and red sandstone cliffs. Americans did not discover these "silent cities of stone" until about a hundred years ago. Two cowboys out chasing strays came out on a ravine and saw, across from them, what looked like great castles in caves under the mesa top. They climbed down the ravine, half afraid that the castles would disappear as they came closer, and finally made

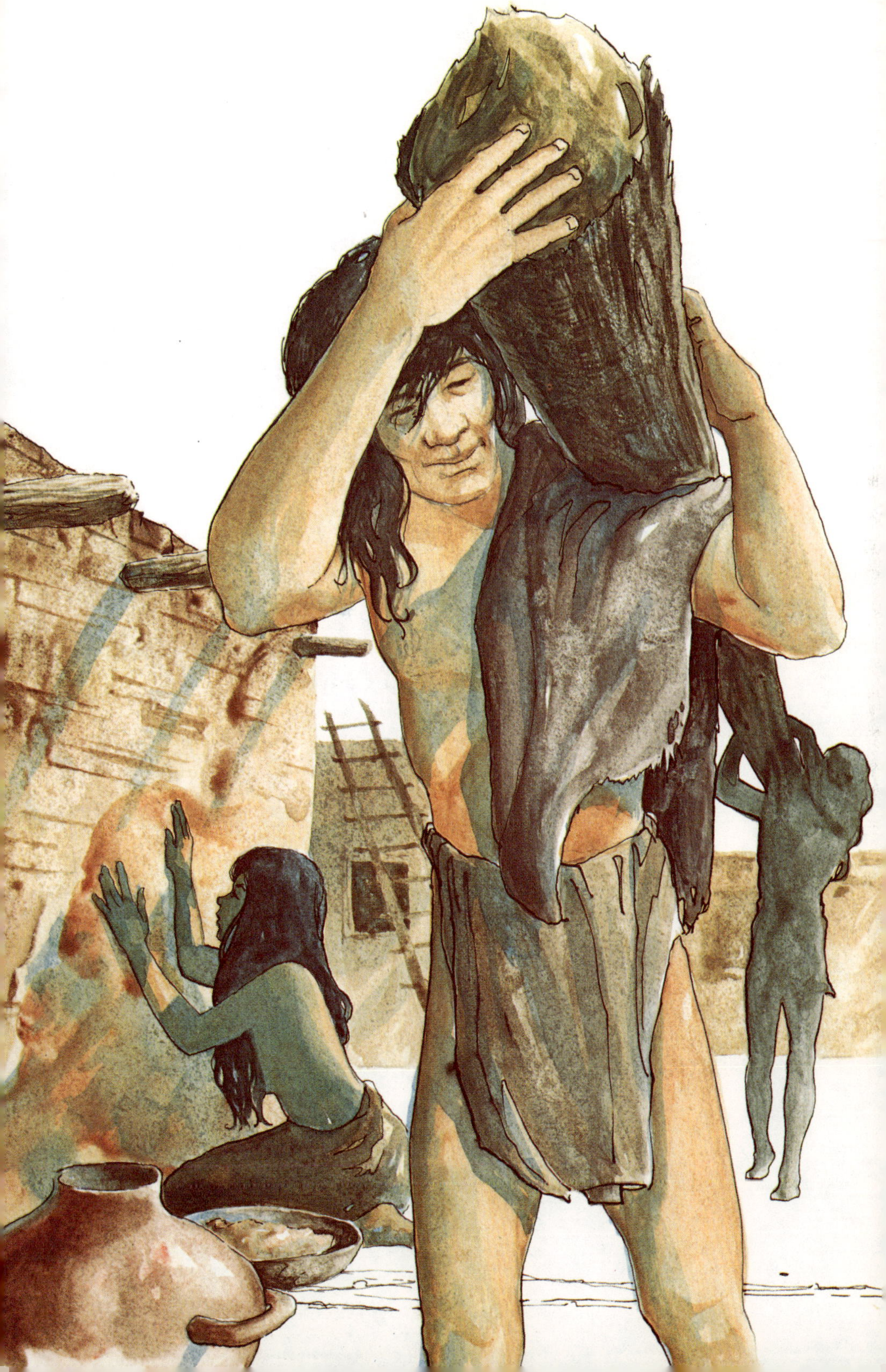

The ancient Anasazi of the Southwest build Pueblo Bonito, using timber which once grew in Mockingbird Canyon.

their way up the slippery path to the caves. Here they found baskets and pottery and other signs of human life from some time, long ago. They noticed how carefully the apartment houses were built, and how well they were protected from wind and rain and dust, and of course from enemies. Some very intelligent people must have lived here, they decided.

One of the cowboys, Richard Wetherill, went home and got his brothers to help explore this silent city from out of the distant past. The site is now a national park, Mesa Verde (meaning "Green Table," in Spanish). It is in Colorado, not far from the "Four Corners" area where Utah, Colorado, Arizona, and New Mexico meet. It is still one of the most beautiful Cliff Dweller sites in the country, and one of the easiest to reach.

This is one of the problems of seeing the cliff dwellings: so many of them are far away and hard to reach. (One tourist was heard to remark that she felt it was very thoughtless of the Indians to build their homes so far from the railroad!) Canyonlands National Park can be reached only by jeep, and it is an all-day trip on horseback to the ruins at Keet Seel. Canyon de Chelly National Monument is a half-day trip. This is *big* country. But tours — by bus, by jeep, by boat, by plane — are available, and certainly the scenery is unique in all the world.

Most of the cliff dwellings show the same features, but some are different because of their location. Balcony House is on a sheer cliff where little Indians at play might roll off and fall a half mile before reaching land; so a sturdy balcony was built to protect them. All the cliff apartments have the simplest of ladders, a set of toeholds in the cliff. This was the sort of apartment where you did not need a door key — just good strong toes and a head for heights. You also needed to be well balanced, since everything for your apartment had to come up that ladder on your head. Towers of the cliff dwelling are usually square, but some are round, and all are beautifully made. In all of them are *kivas*, ceremonial structures used (among other things) as religious meeting places for the men of the tribe, for the Anasazi were a very religious people.

Some of the most beautiful artifacts have been found at White House Ruins, Canyon de Chelly National Monument. This fantastic canyon was the last hideout of the Navajos when they were trying to avoid going to the reservation. It is not the sort of place where any white man, even with quite a large army at his back, would choose to go hunting for Indians. Kit Carson, who had always known the Southwest better than any other white man, finally defeated the Navajos there, by killing all their livestock and burning their homes and orchards. Canyon de Chelly will always be a sign of betrayal to the Navajo, for Kit Carson had been their friend. But to us of a later day, it is simply a place with marvelous scenery, and memories that go back before time.

In the Grand Canyon itself, high up on the banks, are caves used by hunters four thousand years ago. Small figures made out of willow branches represent animals that they hoped to kill; putting them there in the cave, which was kept for this use, was like saying a prayer for good hunting.

Along the north rim of the Grand Canyon, three thousand feet below the rim, is a place called Indian Gardens. Here, many years ago, a tribe of Indians who are called Havasupai, or "People of the Blue-Green Water," used to live while they hunted on the north rim. The place had a good spring, as well as shade trees, and they planted some of their crops there because their own home — on the south rim — was not very big. When the land in this area was being surveyed for the park, the Indians did not want to let go of this small and pleasant place. President Theodore Roosevelt asked them personally to give up their gardens so that all Americans could enjoy this beautiful place. Now, the People of the Blue-Green Water live on the smallest Indian reservation in the country, the Havasupai, on Havasu Creek.

One of Hollywood's better efforts at movie-making was called *Lost Horizon*, and it concerned a lovely lost kingdom hidden among the great mountains of Tibet. The kingdom was called Shangri-la, and the word passed into our language to mean a beautiful, faraway place that man is forever seeking — like the fountain of youth, or the Isles of the Blest (also known as the Fortunate Isles). An American Shangri-la, little known, hard to reach, and absolutely beautiful, is Havasupai Reservation, which rests between the great red cliffs just off the south rim of the

Grand Canyon. Three of the world's most beautiful waterfalls are in this hidden canyon, and they give the name to the people who live there: People of the Blue-Green Water. The pools are like fine jade under the falls, which are made by Havasu Creek. The creek furnishes the Indians with fine drinking water and water for their fields, and then, twenty miles away through twisting canyons, pours into the Colorado. In this tiny corner of a huge land, three hundred fifty Havasupai Indians live.

As a matter of fact, it is an extremely inconvenient place to live, despite all its beauty. Indians have always known how to make peace with their land, and they do so with dignity even though most of the land given to their people has been taken back by the government, and the present reservation is so tiny that they cannot even raise feed for their horses. The horses are their link to the outside world, for every bit of merchandise and most of their food must come down by horseback from the canyon rim, eight twisting miles away. Surrounded by the great burned cliffs of red sandstone, the velvety green of cornfields and other garden vegetables look like a painting of a lost green paradise. They raise whatever they can, but there simply is not room for much variety. Their diet has no milk, no eggs — or very few; eggs and milk were not designed to be carried around on horseback.

Now that tourists have discovered this beautiful place, more and more visitors come down the switchback trail, either hiking or on rented horses. In the past few years freight has been dropped by helicopters, which is convenient, but expensive.

Stamp collectors are alert to letters with the Supai postmark; this is the last U.S. post office which still gets its mail by packtrain. Havasupai postal carriers make three round trips a week. The post office is the center of town, as it used to be in all of the old West. Huge trees shade the only street, and there are no cars or trucks to stir the dust.

In spite of its travel problems, fifteen thousand visitors a year have found their way to the little Shangri-la hidden among the red cliffs. All must come down the same switchback trail from Hualapai Hilltop, where of old the Pinetree People lived. The town of Peach Springs on Highway 66 is the departure point for the trip to Supai, and arrangements must be made ahead of time for anyone who wishes to stay overnight.

The Havasupai people must have been around for a very long time, or someone else found this beautiful place long ago, for there is a rock carving of a man attacking a mammoth that really dates the artist. Over the years the Havasupai Indians have built up a reputation for several things: for one thing, their baskets have been eagerly sought after for years without number, and also — a thing which other Indian tribes have known about for centuries — nobody can tan a deer hide the way the Havasupai people can. Tribes far out on the plains arrange to trade for their deerskins. The Havasupai are also fine horsemen, as they prove every year at the annual peach festival. They invite the Navajo, Hualapai, Hopi, and Mojave Indians to compete in the rodeo.

The local school has about forty children in grades one to four. After that, they must go away to boarding school to finish. Even so, it is a wonderful place for children, where they learn to ride and swim as soon as they can toddle, and have those lovely blue-green pools to play in when the summer comes. Saturday night movies are in English, but you can always make up the dialogue as you go along, and it probably makes as much sense as some of the white man's talk anyway.

Like most old places in the Southwest, Supai has its outlaw legends. Butch Cassidy and the Sundance Kid roamed farther east, but one black-hatted gunman named Lee once stayed for three years with the Havasupai. He has left his name to Lee Canyon, where the Topocoba Trail from his hideout down to Supai makes twenty-nine switchbacks in the first thousand feet; whatever the late Mr. Lee had done wrong, he must have had good nerves.

This whole Grand Canyon country is filled with puzzles that the scientists of the future must unravel. If we do not know the past, we cannot provide for the future. And this country, as well as exposing much of the earth's history in its rocks, also tells us a great deal about the people who have lived here in the past four thousand years. Scientists think that one extra inch of rain a year would have saved Pueblo Bonito; on such things the movements of people depend. Frijoles Canyon, where once the Little River of the Beans flowed sparkling past, watering the squash, beans, and corn of a contented farming people, was in the beginning the "Garden of Eden" to the Indians who lived there, as their legends tell us. The mummy of a young girl was found near here; she was wrapped in skins and bound in yucca-fiber woven cloth. She is perhaps ten thousand years old, and not even the Egyptians were weaving cloth that long ago.

In and around the Navajo country, though much older than the Navajos, are the petroglyphs carved on the rocks long ago by the Anasazi. Some are quite plainly pictures of Europeans — men on horseback, wearing hats — and these date to the sixteenth century, but many are much older. Newspaper Rock at Indian Creek State Park in southern Utah is covered with what must have been headline news two hundred years before Columbus. There are thousands of other petroglyphs, also some pictographs, which are paintings on rock; on the whole, these do not last as long as the petroglyphs, which are carved into the stone.

A man named La Van Martineau has spent much of his life decoding Indian petroglyphs, which is an art something like that of the cryptographers who work on messages in wartime. The Indians were not trying to hide their messages, as a war signalman would, but you have to read them in much the same way. Most of the Indians' choice of signs can be worked out with reasoning (and practice) and they do make sense. Like that very old joke about . . .

Wood

John

Massachusetts

. . . which you are supposed to read as "John Underwood, Andover, Massachusetts"; the position of the signs is just as important as the marks themselves.

Mr. Martineau explains in his fascinating book that many

carved symbols come from the hand sign language; for example, you are telling someone he must look for something which is hidden out of sight, and you double up your right fist and then hold the left hand curved over it, hiding it. If you want to put this on a rock, you carve a dot, and "hide" it with a curved line over it. The sign for "I wish to trade" is to hold out the arms, crossed. To indicate the same message on a rock, you would carve an X. This all sounds very reasonable when Mr. Martineau explains it, but he has worked very hard at this study and has discovered some very interesting Indian "news" around the country, particularly in the Southwest.

We have a good account in Spanish of the first crossing of the Colorado River by white men, two Franciscan friars who were trying to find a road from Santa Fe to California. We did not know, until Mr. Martineau came along, that there was another account of the same thing, carved on the rocks by the Indians who were there. The friars wanted the Indians to guide them to a crossing of the mighty river, and the Indians said they could not walk that far because their moccasins were worn out. The Spanish gave them leather and they made new moccasins. They came to a point on the journey where the Spanish did not believe that the path could possibly be where the Indians said it was, and they wondered if they could trust the Indians. Then they went the way the Spanish wanted to go, and it was the wrong way, and they had to come back. It is all there, in the little carvings on the rocks. Since 1776.

Tourists have been very hard on the Grand Canyon, not just the inconsiderate ones who carve their names on rocks and trees and otherwise spoil the beauty.

Perhaps as time goes on, someone will have discovered a way to cope with the vandalism and with the mountains of litter that are cluttering the riverbanks and messing up the most beautiful park we have. It is the responsibility of every American to protect this and our other parks from the worst enemy he or she has — carelessness.

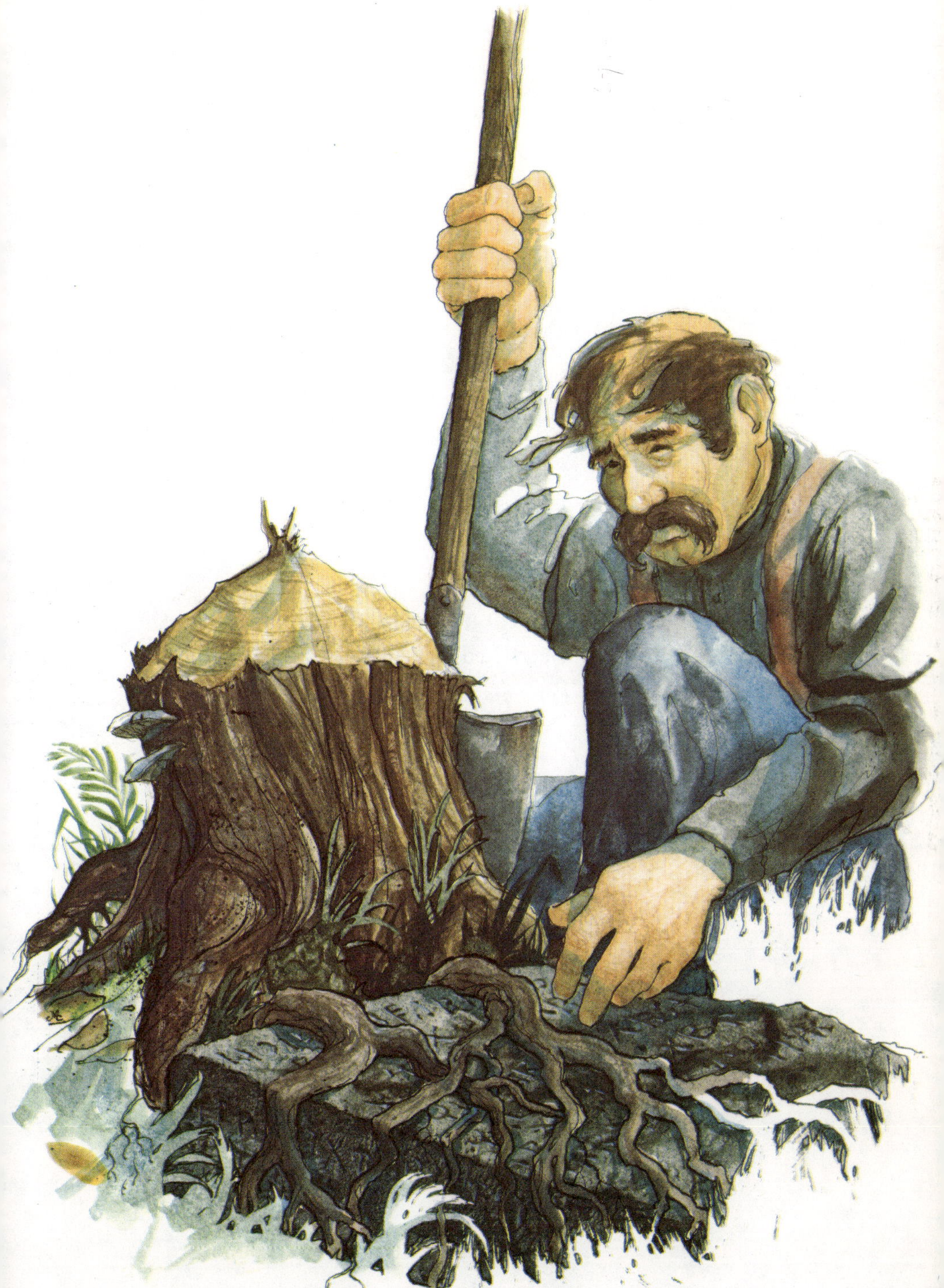

**The Kensington Rune Stone
is unearthed in Minnesota.**
(See pages 118-120.)

Chapter 9
Frostie Seas With Myghty Yslands of Yce

The English and the French just numbered their kings: Henry I, Henry II, Louis XI, Louis XIII. This was rather a tiresome way to do it. Philip the Fair and Philip the Fat came about because there were just too many Philips. Alexander the Great certainly earned his title, but few men in history are big enough to be called "the Great." Eric the Red and John the Short are quite ordinary descriptions, not reserved to kings. Ethelred the Un-ready, Ivan the Terrible, and Egbert the Foul all must have got on somebody's nerves. Harold the Fair-haired was everybody's darling until he began taxing his people so heavily that his angry subjects rather rudely renamed him Harold the Lousy. But the prince of these colorful monarchs was King Magnus Barefeet, a title which translates freely as "Great Big Bare Feet," surely an interesting sort of royalty. If this were a once-upon-a-time sort of story, it would have to begin: "In the reign of King Magnus Barefeet, when Sweyn Forkbeard, the son of Harold Bluetooth, was 'viking' along the coast of Ruritania, two Icelanders, Ari Marston and Ulf the Squinter, on a voyage to Greenland, sighted land to the west. As they were in a hurry to make port they did not stop to name the islands Ariland or Ulfland, Squinteria or even, possibly, New Barefeet. Later voyagers named the land for Amerigo Vespucci, who did not really have much to do with discovering it."

The trouble was islands. Mapmakers in medieval times were very generous with land. Anywhere that a map tended to look a little bare, they tossed in a few islands, like raisins in a cake. Unfortunately, once the island was drawn in and named, it was almost impossible to convince anybody that it was not there, had never been there, and could not be found there. The names and stories of these islands remained to plague explorers for centuries.

The Greeks began it with their stories of the Elysian Fields, "The Happy Isles," where dead heroes could rejoice forever. But the new nations of Western Europe soon caught up with, and passed, the wildest Greek fancies.

To begin with, there was Hy Breasil: the Isle of the Bright Gleam. The Irish dreamed this one up, though the Portuguese were right behind them with their tale of the seven bishops who fled Portugal with their people during the Moorish invasion of the seventh century, and settled in seven cities on the Isle of the Blest. (Watch those seven cities; they really got around.) Mapmakers were still drawing in the island of Hy Breasil even after its name was given to Portugal's huge colony, Brazil.

Next in popularity was St. Brendan's Isle. There really was a sailor-monk named Brendan who was very holy, and who ought to be a great comfort to librarians. He is said to have borrowed a book from another monastery — this was in the days when books were lettered by hand and might take up to ten years to make, so they were very precious. He kept the book too long, and in those days you could not just pay a five-cent fine for every day overdue: you got a whopping penance. Brendan was told to find himself an island and live there "far from all earthly comforts" for seven years. It is recorded that he set out with seventeen companions in a skin boat to find an island in the Atlantic where they could pray in peace.

He came back with a fund of astonishing stories, as the Irish are apt to do, stories that are still related around the peat fires as though they happened yesterday. One that you might call a whale of a tale told how he and his tired companions beached their boat on a small island and set about building a fire to cook a warm supper, whereupon the island rudely flipped its tail and dove off into the deep. He said they had found the Green Isles of the Floods, the place where the talking beasts swam out to meet them (seals, perhaps?) and the fragrant breezes blew from the lovely isles where everything was green but fruit was ripe for the picking. One could expect no less from the people who practically invented poetry and folk music.

A less happy landfall was the Isle of Demons, where hideous little devils ran about, working at a great black forge that people might think was a volcano at first sight. Next to this was a bare rock where Judas Iscariot was doomed to sit forever staring at the sea, with the Isle of Fleas on one side of him and the Isle of Mice on the other. People tried for centuries to find St. Brendan's Isle, but, if anyone ever did, he did not come back to say so.

Somewhere in the farthest seas was the island with the Fountain of Youth on it, where the old would grow young again just by washing in the fountain. Not only the women were interested in this. Returning sailors had heard rumors, and some claimed to have sighted the island — but nobody actually set foot on it.

Someone wrote about "frostie seas with myghty yslands of yce." Iceland and Greenland were strictly in this class, though both of them — unlike the mythical ones — were really there. And both of them, cold though they were, held out new hope for the Norsemen who settled them. They were to prove very important to the future America.

Oddly enough, as Norway was nearest, Norwegians were not the first white men to settle the two chilly islands. Irish monks and fishermen had been there off and on since the sixth century, which takes it back to St. Brendan. Brendan, like everyone since, must have been following the island-hopping route across the North Atlantic: Ireland to Bristol to the Outer Islands to Iceland to Greenland to America — possibly Nova Scotia. (Some people, remembering the flowers and the birds, think it was Florida, and claim they can prove it by an Irish bell and ironwork dug up there.) Wherever it was, he named it "Greater Ireland," and sailed home to tell them all about it. The year was 535 A.D.

There must have been something in the atmosphere of the sixth century; the Irish were not the only island-hoppers at work. On the other side of the unexplored new continent, on another ocean even bigger than the Atlantic, a Chinese junk with five Buddhist monks was doing the same thing headed east. Led by a scholar-monk named Hsu Fu, they crossed the mighty Pacific by the same trick of island-hopping from Japan to the Ryukyus to the Aleutians and down the long coast to Central America. Chinese history accepts Hsu Fu's carefully written journal, and in Central American carvings there are stone elephants — which never lived there, even in ancient times — and Oriental faces. Hsu Fu stayed in "Fu Sang" for forty years, then returned with many gifts for the Chinese emperor; it was a fabulously rich country, he said, where people could live forever. He had named it "Greater China." He returned to China in the year 539 A.D. (our time).

All this was four hundred years in the past when a Norwegian Viking ship, off course in a storm, found Iceland. In 930 A.D., Norway was getting crowded for farmland, and most of the trees had been cut. A great many of the subjects of Harold the Lousy were anxious to get away from him, and settlers flocked to Iceland as fast as ships could be found to take them. In Norway all lumber was heavily taxed by the king; in Iceland it was free for the taking. Some smart citizen tapped the hot springs with which volcanic Iceland is filled, and set up sauna baths which were greatly appreciated. They set about making a government that would be free of the heavy hand of Harold and set up the first parliament in Western Europe. The Norse were delighted with Iceland, and their fierce loyalty to this cold little country is still operating, as is their democratic government.

People who settled on Iceland tended to stay there, partly because they considered themselves a separate country (much as the thirteen states of America were one day to think of themselves as separate from England) but mostly because of the terrible trouble of getting there. From Norway to Iceland could take as little as four days' sailing (a Norse longship averaged about one hundred fifty miles in a twenty-four-hour day — if the weather was good). If the winds were against you, it might take the better part of a year — if indeed you lived to get there at all. The Icelanders very early had a great loyalty to their country, and, like Ireland, had many poets and singers to preserve their history.

Europe in the tenth century was a very rough place. There was violence and fighting everywhere. A hot-tempered character named Eric the Red was part of the reason that there is a Norse strain in our history. Eric was already exiled from Norway for murder, and living in Iceland, when he got into another fight and killed two men, and was exiled from Iceland also. With no place to go, he took a longship and crew and sailed westward. Blown off course by a great storm, he made a landfall on an island, much bigger than Iceland as far as he could tell. He named it "Greenland" in the hope that people would think it was green and fruitful, and when he had finished his three-year sentence of exile, he returned to Iceland and gathered up a great number of settlers and hurried back to his new island.

Unfortunately, the only thing green was the settlers. The growing season was short and the winters long and cold. Eric had found the most sheltered place on the island and was rich enough to build a good house and barn so that his family and animals were safe and comfortable. Not all the colonists could do this.

Eric's son, Leif the Lucky, was born on the Greenland farm and grew up there; he considered himself a Greenlander as distinct from either an Icelander or a Norwegian. When Leif was a young man, he sailed his ship to Norway on a trading trip, taking his mother with him. They were both converted to Christianity in Norway, and when they returned to Greenland his mother planned to build a church there. Eric was not interested in churches, but if she wanted to use her private fortune that way, he made no protest.

Leif saw no reason to go to Norway for their lumber, pay the king for letting them cut it, then ferry it on the long trip home to Greenland. There was a story, not too reliable, about a boat full of Icelanders blown off course for Greenland, who had seen islands far to the west. There were trees on two of the islands, the story said. In 987 A.D. Leif gathered a crew and went to find out. Leif came home a year later, with a cargo of good lumber and a lot of fantastic stories which made the shivering Greenlanders sure that he had found the Green Isles of the Floods that the Irish were always praising.

Now that Leif's adventures in this unheard-of land have been told and sung for a thousand years, it is impossible to sort out exactly what happened to this boatload of adventurers. Leif told them that he and his crew had wintered in the new land, in a good warm house: you never saw such trees, you could cut them for years and years and never run out of trees. (Leif was wrong about this.) Everything there was a little bigger and better than it was anywhere else — plenty of fat deer, huge salmon, and even grapes. Norway could not grow grapes: it was much too cold. Because of the grapes they had named it "Vinland the Good."

People talked longingly of living where sheep and cows would not have to be kept in the barn all winter, a place where there were endless trees for building material and firewood. It sounded like the "Promised Land." Yet Leif made no plans to go back, and we do not know why.

After a few years, Leif's younger brother took a ship to look for the forested land his brother had talked about. He wanted to set up a lumber company. They could not find Leif's camp, where there was a solid house built against the winter, but they set about building a camp on one of the beaches. They got into a fight with the Indians and Leif's brother was killed. They buried him on a great headland overlooking the stormy sea and hurried back to Greenland.

The following summer, Leif's next youngest brother took his ship westward. When the crew discovered that he planned to bring his brother's body back to Greenland, they mutinied, as they were very superstitious about the dead. Finally the ship was caught in a bad storm and most of its crew were lost at sea.

Gudrid, the widow of Leif's brother, married again, to an Icelander named Thorfinn Karlsefni, and it was he who led a group of one hundred sixty people westward to start a colony in Vinland the Good.

They planned to go to Leif's camp and build there around the house he had left. Leif and Karlsefni were old friends and shipmates, yet Leif did not give him sailing directions to find his camp. Why? Was it jealousy between Icelanders and Greenlanders? We only know that Karlsefni's party hunted in vain for Leif's landfall and never found it. They settled and built a colony in what is now Newfoundland. They had brought cattle, sheep, and hogs, and they lived well for the three years they stayed. The son of Karlsefni and Gudrid, born the first winter, was the first, last, and only born citizen of Vinland the Good. At the end of three years, for fear of the Indians, they went back home.

Not until 1960 was it known for sure where this colony had lived. Leif's camp has never been found. But at L'Anse Aux Meadows, Newfoundland, archeologists turned up the remains of a white man's settlement. They found a blacksmith shop, an anvil, charred wood that can be carbon-14 dated to the right time in history, a spindle whorl, which proves there were sheep to grow wool and women to spin it, and a great steam bath. A pile of rocks against the skyline was probably their sun-clock. It had to be the settlement of Karlsefni and his people.

Church records show that in 1055 a bishop was appointed for Iceland, and another for Greenland and Vinland. This is solid evidence that there was a colony of Christians in each place at that time. The crusade was preached in Iceland in 1271, so these countries were still in the mainstream of religion as they were of commerce; exports of walrus ivory, eiderdown, and — most especially — of the rare white gyrfalcons which every king in Europe wanted for his hunting, were shipped for three hundred fifty years to Bristol, Flanders, and Cologne. The curtain was falling on the Northern scene when, in a letter to one Matthew Knudson, to whom he was offering the bishopric of Greenland, the pope wrote sadly that "navigation is very rare; landing can take place only in August, after the ice is melted."

For well over a hundred years at this time — during the 1300s and 1400s — the seas to the north of Europe were so stormy that no supply ships could get to Norway, let alone Iceland and Greenland. In 1347 a trading ship bound for Vinland was driven by heavy seas to Iceland and could not get away. A few years later, a captain wrote in his log that "now there comes so much ice that no one who values his life dares to follow the old routes."

During these terrible years, even the big colony in Greenland gave up. With neither wood nor metal on the island to build ships, they had no way of getting off the island. The seas got colder and stormier, and people died from the cold and from sickness. Finally, all that were left of them went north and joined the Eskimos, who seemed to be the only people who knew how to live in such country. The white men disappeared without a trace. During the fifteenth century, pirate ships darted into the Greenland harbors in August, hoping to take slaves, but not a living person was to be seen. According to the *Icelandic Chronicle*, more than two hundred little villages had been in Greenland before the bad years came.

Little Iceland seems to have fared better, perhaps because of better natural resources and also, it seems, because of a better government. Icelandic gyrfalcons were still shipped (whenever a ship would dare those terrible seas) along with hides, mutton, and walrus ivory. Sturdy Icelandic ponies, descended from Viking horses, thrived on the island. Inventive individuals thought of ways to use the host springs to make life more pleasant; for a singing people, it was a fine place to live, even if you did have to move out once in a while to let a volcano blow up.

There is a strange little footnote to the story of the Greenland colony that was found in, of all places, Minnesota. It is a flat stone, about the size of a tombstone, and there are strange marks all over one side and one edge. It is called the Kensington Rune Stone, and a replica of it is in the Smithsonian Museum in Washington, D.C. (The original stone is held by the Chamber of Commerce in Alexandria, Minnesota.)

The stone was found in 1898 at Kensington, Minnesota, by a Swedish farmer named Olof Ohman. Minnesota is a land formed by glaciers, which means that every farmer must spend time digging rocks out of his fields. Mr. Ohman had cut down a tree and discovered that its roots were wrapped around the stone. The tree was later examined and noted to be at least seventy years old. This became very important later, since seventy years before Mr. Ohman dug up the tree, Minnesota was the heart of the Indian country and no place for anyone to sit around carving messages on stones. Scholars have been arguing over the Kensington Rune Stone for nearly a century now.

The argument came about because someone pointed out to Mr. Ohman that the scratches on the stone looked like some kind of ancient writing. Since it seemed likely to be Scandinavian runes — which were common in Norway and Sweden in the Middle Ages but almost forgotten by the world of 1898 — they called in the experts. As will happen sometimes, the experts did not agree. One of them thought the stone was genuine, a relic of far-off times and people. The other one insisted that Mr. Ohman was trying to pass off a fake on the public.

If Mr. Ohman had worked up a hoax, he did not get anything out of it but a headache. No one has ever been able to suggest any good reason why a respectable, hardworking Swedish farmer should try a stunt that was worthy of P.T. Barnum.

The translation of the writing on the stone is given in lines (with words supplied where they are understood — as part of a verb, for example):

ON THE FLAT SURFACE
Lines 1. (We are) 8 Goths and 22 Norwegians on
2. (an) exploration-journey from
3. Vinland through the West. We
4. had camp by (a lake with 2) skerries one
5. days-journey North from this shore.
6. We were (out) and fished one day. After
7. we came home (we) found 10 (of our) men red
8. with blood and dead. AV(e) M(aria)
9. save us from evil.

ON THE EDGE
10. (We) have 10 of (our party) by the sea to look
11. after our ships 14 days-journey
12. from this island. (In the) year
(of our Lord) 1362.

The first argument against the stone pointed out that no expedition was apt to be made up of "Goths and Norwegians"; the Swedes and the Norwegians did not see eye to eye on much of anything. But there was briefly a king who ruled from both thrones, and he was much worried about the Greenland Norsemen who had — it was rumored — run off and joined the pagan Eskimos. He had got a combined force of Swedes and Norwegians together to go on a crusade to Russia; but word came that Russia had the plague, so he sent them instead to Greenland, to try to rescue the wandering Norse colonists. The records tell that the year, 1354, was a bad year for sailing.

The next part is only in bits and pieces. They landed at the harbor where Eric the Red had built his great farm three hundred fifty years before. The buildings were still standing; they had not, for instance, been burned by an invading army, and the people must have left by choice. What happened next we do not know.

It is quite possible to go by ship from Hudson's Bay through Lake Winnepeg, the Nelson River, the Red River, and that great network of lakes and rivers that lead to Lake Cormorant in Minnesota. Interested people, a few years ago, traced out a reasonable route on a map, supposing that they were coming from Newfoundland and wanted to get to Mr. Ohman's farm in Minnesota. Later, hikers and adventurers followed the route themselves. They found bits of old armor that had to be Norse, and fire steels that were used to light supper fires six hundred years ago. And, here and there along the route, they have found mooring stones — great stones with holes drilled in them to hold a boat's hawser. A Viking longship? Perhaps one day we will know for sure.

Speaking of Islands . . .

There is a legend in the city of Galway, which of course is in Ireland, that there is a sunken city on an island somewhere on the bottom of Galway Bay. Nobody knows where these stories come from, but still there is this sunken city down there under the waters, they say. And to make matters worse, the legends say that one day, just before the end of the world, that city will rise on its island, and the city of Galway will go down in its place. Now, *that* is not a nice thing to have hanging over you.

One black, stormy night in 1946, some sleepless citizen of Galway looked out across the black waters and he saw lights there, like the lights of a city. Not a sound could be heard but the roar of the storm; he could, however, see some lights — so he was sure he was not dreaming. He ran to get his neighbors. They watched but were too scared to talk. By morning, nearly the whole city had joined the vigil. With the first break of dawn, some of the lights moved. As the sun rose higher, it became apparent that the "city" was breaking up. The "city" turned out to be a fleet of fishing trawlers, caught outside in the storm. It had put in to Galway Bay to ride out the heavy seas, and now was preparing to go out on the morning tide.

But you never can be too sure about these disappearing islands.

Chapter 10
City in the Sky

U.S. Highway 66 has often been called "The Main Street of the Old West." It is also one of the main streets in the new West, being one of the transcontinental highways of our country. You could almost say that it runs from yesterday to tomorrow, as it whizzes along eating up the miles from Chicago to Los Angeles, some twenty-five hundred miles away.

Today it is a four-lane highway roaring with heavy traffic: refrigerated trucks with fruit from California for the eastern markets; auto carriers heading west with their shining loads of new paint and chrome; trucks full of washing machines, floor tiles, baby chicks, bicycles, paint, and television sets; long-distance vans moving Americans from place to place; and thousands of tourists in cars and trailers, seeing their country.

Up on a high mesa, just fourteen miles off this very modern highway, is a little Indian pueblo that has been sitting there, watching the centuries go by, for the past thousand years. We have other buildings that old in the country, among the cliff dwellings for example, but nobody lives there now. The little pueblo of Acoma (pronounced AH-co-mah) is still alive; people have lived there all that time, and are still living there. Americans are always in a hurry, and few of them have even heard of this old city on the rock. Acoma has been there since long before there was a single highway in this vast country, long before the white man came.

Sixty miles west of Albuquerque is a big factory where the

very latest in space-age equipment is made. Here at this tomorrow-point, the highway turns to yesterday and runs off to the south. You can see the road winding off to disappear in the red-gold distance. The road is fourteen miles and a thousand years long. Acoma, perched like an eagle's nest on top of a four-hundred-foot mesa where you can barely see it from below, was built about the time that Leif Erickson was tying his Viking ship to a rock in Vinland the Good. We do not know what people passed this way before the Spanish came in the sixteenth century, but the Indians watched them come and go. Acoma, thrust into the sky, has survived all the comings and goings and is still there, the oldest continually inhabited city in America. The children who come down that steep hill to catch the school bus every morning have a heritage that few Americans can boast.

Pottery fragments found in the town dump indicate that Acoma has been in existence about a thousand years. The Indians themselves have long memories and many traditions, but they are vague about time, as they do not count it the way we do. They have a legend that, long ago before they came to Acoma, they lived a few miles away on K'Atzim, the Enchanted Mesa. This is a long, narrow rock with very steep sides and it rises up out of the desert like something made by magic. Before they lived on the Enchanted Mesa, the White Shell People (which they have always called themselves) lived down on the plains below where their fields were, and where there was a beautiful lake. But roving Indians came down upon them from the north, and stole their crops and killed their people. They moved to the top of the Enchanted Mesa, and the only way to get up there was hand over hand up a trail of notches cut in the rock. At night it was a simple thing to set a guard with a pile of stones at the top of the ladder, and nobody ever got up the ladder who was not welcome.

They still had to raise their crops in the fields below and bring up both food and water in pots and baskets carried on their heads on that hand-over-hand trail. You had to have good balance to be a citizen of K'Atzim. You also had to gamble on getting your harvest in and stored away upstairs before robbers swept in off the desert and stole it.

One day when everyone but the very old people and the babies had gone down to bring in the harvest, tragedy struck K'Atzim: a great earthquake shook down the side of the mesa where the ladder was cut. There was no way for anyone to get to the top any more, and the ones on top could not come down. The tribe gathered, wailing, at the foot of the cliffs and waited until all the voices from the top of the rock were still. Then, sad at heart, they took their harvest and went away to build another home, on top of the rock of Acoma. And there, for all these years, they have stayed.

There are a great many things we do not know about the Acoma Indians: for one thing, where did they come from in the first place? They have always called themselves White Shell People, but — aside from fossil shells several million years old — there are no shells, white or any other color, in the New Mexico desert. One of their tribal legends is about a whale; this is not whale country. Their word for "sunrise" is a descriptive word meaning "sun coming up out of the sea." What sea? People who have made a special study of these Indians say that they can be traced back to the Florida Keys where, of course, there are many white shells. At some point in history, they must have made friends with the men from Tyre, because there are Phoenician words in their language. (There is also that curious carving of the Ten Commandments, partly in Phoenician, forty miles from Acoma.) Other Indian tribes give evidence of having crossed the land bridge from Asia at the Bering Strait, but the White Shell People seem not to have any connection with these migrations. Also, they do not seem to have come from Mexico.

It is possible now to process the artifacts that are found in ancient diggings and test them to find out how old they are. Matter that has ever been alive — bones, wood, fossil plants, baskets — can be accurately dated by the carbon-14 process. Pottery cannot be tested in this way because nothing in it has ever been alive, but we know a great deal about all pottery by now. It is possible to get a quite accurate date on every piece. Acoma pottery, rebuilt from shattered bits in the rubbish dump, must always have been very beautiful, and examples of it have been found far from New

Mexico, proving that it was a popular trade item. It is mostly black on white, with trimming of rust color, and most of the designs are of graceful birds and plants. You see this ancient pottery in the museums and wonder how they found time to make it all so beautiful.

The thing that makes Acoma different is that if you go today up the twisting mule trail to the top of the rock, you will see women making exactly the same kind of pottery today, just as if a thousand years had never gone by.

The pueblo is built on solid rock; the streets are rock, and not a blade of grass can find root in it. The houses were once three stories high, with ladders leading to the upper floors so that when you pulled up the ladder for the night, there was no way anyone could get in. The houses are built of sandstone and adobe, pale gold in the daylight, shading to gold in the sunset. (This was probably one of the "golden cities" seen by the Spaniards.) The top of the rock is about sixty acres in all. It is a very colorful place, especially in the fall when strings of red chili peppers hang like Christmas garlands drying on the fronts of the houses.

Acoma Indians weave and wear garments of coarse woolen cloth and also make Indian blankets. They have many ornaments made of fur and feathers, and their dances are colorful. For the fiesta, or feast, of St. Stephen, September 2, Acoma Indians from all over the country come home to celebrate in the pueblo. Many young people have to go away to find work, but they come home for the fiesta if they can.

The great Church of St. Stephen which looks out over the mesa top was one of the largest mission churches in the Southwest. This is more remarkable when you know that every handful of material for building the church had to be carried up on the heads of the Indians. Some of the adobe walls are nine feet thick. Big beams that were cut thirty miles away and dragged home by teams of Indians were swung up to the mesa top by a sort of pulley invented by the Franciscan who was directing the job of building. The church was decorated by the Indians, and there were pictures of St. Stephen and other saints painted on buffalo hides instead of canvas.

Once the church was finished, in 1627, the Indians carried up baskets of dirt on their heads to make a cemetery. They certainly earned their rest, those Indians who sleep in that cemetery in the sky.

Only once in a thousand years was Acoma beaten. Coronado was so impressed with the fortress on the rock that he made no attempt to attack it. But in 1599 a group of Spaniards came exploring. The Indian chief, a warrior by the name of I-Give-Him-Pancakes, felt that the strangers were too demanding in their requests. He attacked the Spanish leader with a club and killed him. The Spanish retired quickly to headquarters and returned with more men and two brass cannons, which they had dragged with great trouble over the sharp volcanic rocks that made up this part of the desert. They turned the cannons on Acoma and some of the Indians, terrified, jumped off the cliffs and were killed. Peace was finally restored after a great many people had been hurt, and the Spaniards went home to write up reports about how unfriendly the Indians were. One of the Franciscan Fathers smuggled out a message to the Spanish governor: "The Indians of this province are all orderly and timid, peaceful, and have offered no resistance." He added that most of the Indians had been injured and enslaved, and the whole thing had been cruel and unjust. One Indian, named He-Who-Kicks-People-Off-Cliffs, was not too friendly, but then, some of the Spanish were not very friendly either.

Someone visiting Acoma in 1848 reported that there were many snow-white geese near the lake, and that the Indians raised turkeys, chickens, cotton, and watermelons, besides the usual Indian crops of corn, beans, and squash. Also, he said, they made a specialty of training birds. The lake is dried up now, and of course the waterfowl are gone.

There is now a steep zigzag path that leads up the rock (laid out, it is said, by the Franciscan's burro) so that no one ever needs to use the rock ladder with the handholds. Sometimes at fiestas, the young members of the tribe race up the stone ladders, just to prove that they are as smart as their ancestors. Only a few families — about fifteen — now live on the rock full time. But hundreds come back for the fiesta of St. Stephen and the summer fiesta of St. John the Baptist.

This is the only place in our country where men have lived, and worked, and died in the same location for so long a time; the old pueblo of Walpi in Arizona is its nearest rival. It is a living picture of peoples and families, going on from generation to generation, treasuring the history of the old and hoping the best for the new.

One thing that visitors to Acoma must remember: this is *not* a national park belonging to the American people as a whole. This is a private village where people live and have a right to their privacy. You should no more walk into one of these houses than you would walk into strangers' homes in your own town. Young people of Acoma earn their spending money acting as tourist guides to the pueblo, and in their company you can see it without offending anyone. Permission should be asked for sketching or taking pictures.

There is nowhere else where you can stand at the edge of the mesa and look out at the world that Acoma has watched for a thousand years. "On a clear day, you can see forever . . . and ever . . . and ever . . ."

Chapter 11
Gold, Frankincense, and Myrrh

> Now when the queen of Sheba heard of the fame of Solomon . . . she came to Jerusalem with a very great retinue, with camels bearing spices, and very much gold, and precious stones. . . . The king had a fleet of ships of Tarshish at sea with the fleet of Hiram [king of Tyre]. Once every three years the fleet of ships of Tarshish used to come, bringing gold, silver, ivory, apes, and peacocks.
>
> —*1 Kings 10*

> All which learned men and painful travelers have affirmed with one consent of voice, that America was an island, and that there lieth a great sea between it, Cataia, and Grondland, by which any man of our country that will give the attempt, may with small danger pass to Cataia, the Moluccas, and India.
>
> —*Quoted by Sir Humphrey Gilbert (1582) from "an obscure narrative about a voyage made by Ochter [Arthur?] in the time of King Alfred of West Saxe in 871"*

The search for the Northwest Passage had its start, strangely enough, in the Gospel of St. Matthew with its story of the three wise men from the East who followed a star to the stable of the Infant Jesus and gave Him gifts of gold, frankincense, and myrrh. Matthew, like all the Scripture writers, left a lot of things unsaid. He did not mention in which country of the East the three visitors lived. Their fabulous crowns, the beautiful silks of their clothing, even the richly decorated boxes in which they had carried their gifts — all these were marvels to a poor people who had never dreamed of such things. People who had seen them, or, better still, had only heard about them, told tall stories about the fabulous riches of the three strangers.

One could not ask the wise men themselves where they came from and what kind of a country it was, because — as it says in the Gospel — they were warned about the wickedness of King Herod, and went home to their country by a "different route." They disappeared into the mysterious East to be talked about for a thousand years.

Scholars pored over the sacred books and soon ran across Solomon the king, who lived many hundreds of years before the time of Christ. Solomon's ships had traveled far, bringing back "gold, silver, ivory, apes, and peacocks" from the unknown land of Ophir and the wealthy city of Tarshish. No one had any really clear idea where these places were: somewhere East, without a doubt.

Christian Europe was in a bad way during the last century of its first thousand years. True, the so-called Dark Ages were on their way out, but there was a stubborn idea among a lot of people that the end of the world was at hand. Many unhappy people firmly believed that at midnight, December 31, 999, the world would come to an end in a cloud of smoke. When January 1, 1000, arrived safely, they could hardly believe it. Everyone began breathing normally again. Norwegians, who had been sailing their longships among the icebergs, finding first Iceland, then Greenland, sent a shipload of converted pirates to preach Christianity (if they could find anybody to preach it to) and also settled down on the coast that would one day be called Normandy, after them. Before the century was out, the First Crusade was called, and fighting men from all the Christian countries began streaming down to the Mediterranean to save the Holy Land from the Turks.

The First Crusade did not exactly save the Holy Land, but it did a lot for the European market. The Crusaders came home with all sorts of things from the rich East. Men had seen Constantinople, Baghdad, and Jerusalem, and they had stories to tell for a lifetime. The German Knights from the horde that had followed Barbarossa brought back what they claimed were the relics of the three kings. A new cathedral was built in Cologne to house the relics, and all Europe was talking again about the land of the wise men and its great wealth.

One after another the Crusades were fought and lost. From each one, the men came home telling of strange places and products and the wealth of the East. Things moved so slowly in those years that it was sometimes more than a century before one could get action on anything. But the Crusades kept the pot boiling.

In 1270, the brothers Polo and the young son of one of the brothers set out to find the land of the three wise men. Cathay was forbidden land to all Westerners, and if the Polos had not been Venetians (who are the cream of Western traders, and as such respected by the Chinese who can outtrade anyone), they might not have come back alive from this dangerous trip. Young Marco stayed twenty years at the court of Kublai Khan and came back filled with ideas for his people. He suffered the fate of many an honest man who has had an unusual adventure: nobody would believe him.

The merchants wished they could believe him, as he told them just what they wanted to hear. You could, of course, always trade with the Greeks and the men of Tyre, who bought the wonderful goods from the Easterners. But these people took a large share of the profit. It would be so much simpler if only the men of the West could trade directly with those warlike peoples who brought the goods by camel train from far-off Cathay. *That* was where the money was. There was no use to pay ruinous rates to the men in the middle. Men from Venice, Marseilles, and other Western trade centers should go out there and —

Just at this point, the bubble broke. The Crusades failed,

dreadfully, and the Holy Land was lost to Christianity, perhaps forever. Then the Turks took Constantinople and closed the gates to Eastern riches against the whole of Western Europe. All the lovely luxuries that Europe wanted were out of reach of everyone.

There was just one thing left to them — the sea. And who knew anything about the sea, except that you would fall off it if you went too far?

The Portuguese, pushed by Prince Henry the Navigator, made the first nervous journeys down the west coast of Africa. They came hurrying home with news that they had found the place where dead sailors go, a place in the ocean boiling like a witches' cauldron, which no decent Christian could pass. Prince Henry, who never was able to go on any of the eventful journeys himself, spent his time designing better ships and calming sailors' nerves. He designed the caravel, the ship that made world discovery possible. And one happy day, thanks to his financial backing, encouragement, and sheer stubbornness, a ship under Vasco da Gama rounded the Cape of Good Hope and pointed its prow north by northwest. With shivering sailors praying around him, Vasco da Gama found the back door of India and opened the route to riches for the West.

Thereupon, to the envy of everyone else in Europe, Portugal took over the rich spice trade with the Moluccas. They had found the "land of spices" mentioned in Scripture, and they expected to find Ophir any day now — unless the Spanish got there first. The two items of news made the rounds of Europe together, though they actually happened a few years apart; the sailor from Genoa called Christopher Columbus had, it was said, found the other side of India, and Spain was about to get rich, too.

Since he was convinced that he had discovered India, Columbus quite reasonably called the dark-skinned natives Indians. We are still calling them by this mistaken name, though it took only a little while to discover that what he found was not India. India was undoubtedly in that direction, but there was a large island in the way.

Columbus's problems with the earth had nothing to do with its roundness; most people, by that time, believed that the world was round, though there is still, as of yesterday, an International Flat Earth Society whose members claim it is not. At any rate Columbus had a poor idea of the size of the earth, and he thought — from the distance he had traveled — that he had gone much farther around the globe than he actually had.

Columbus was not looking for a new world; he wanted the old one (India or China, it did not matter which — they were probably the same place anyway), and he died with a sad heart, without any idea of what he had found or how famous he would one day be.

The opinion was, in the Christian countries, that God must certainly have provided a way around this tiresome island. There must be, somewhere, a passage that cut right through this big island and brought them to the door of the Indies where they would all get rich. If ever there was a thing made out of a wish, this was it: a passage to India. The idea caught on like measles. What started with "If only there were a passage . . ." was quickly shortened to "There is a passage . . ." and everybody in Europe was talking about it. Someone told the Spanish that it was called "The Straits of Anian" — Anian being a place in Japan at the other end of the passage. Spanish ships, nosing along the "island" coast from Hispaniola (Haiti and Santo Domingo) southward, found the land always falling away to the south and east. The passage, the voyagers reasoned then, must lie to the north and west. Now they had a name for it: the Northwest Passage. It sounded very practical, and hardly anyone dared to doubt its existence. All they had to do now was find it.

Two things happened at about the same time to give encouragement to the search. One was the publication in London of a book with an exciting title: *A Verie Late and Great Probabilitie of a Passage, By the Northwest Part of America in 58 Degrees of Northerly Latitude.* It was written by one Richard Hakluyt, a Welshman, and printed "at London for Thomas Woodcocke, Dwelling in Paules Church-Yard, at the Sign of the Black Beare, 1582."

This was one of the first books printed in English after the invention of printing and it had a great influence. Hakluyt said he had "heard it from an excellent learned man of Portingale, of singular gravitie, authoritie, and experience," that he had found the passage in 1574.

England felt a particular interest in this idea, because their king, Henry VII, had sent John Cabot off into the unknown nearly a century before this, armed with a royal paper that stated bluntly that everything he found belonged to England. (Cabot was a Venetian.) Cabot had found a place only eighteen hundred miles from Bristol where there were "bigge fysshes" so anxious to be caught that they could be dipped up in baskets. There was fine lumber, too, on the land he passed as he went, one after another, into all bays and inlets that might turn out to be a passage but did not. England wanted more out of the deal than codfish, and the ruder members of the wealthy class made fun of Cabot's "Codfish Canal."

At about the same point in history, an old Greek sailor named Apostolos Valerianus, whom the Spanish called Juan de Fuca, turned up in the port of Venice and told a wild tale to some traveling Englishmen. He himself, he said, had commanded a Spanish ship a few years earlier when they found the Straits of Anian from the western end. But Spain would not even pay him a pilot's wages, and he had come to see if he could sell his idea to the Venetians, who had a sizable navy. He claimed he located the western entrance to the passage somewhere between latitude 47 and 48 degrees north, and he described the opening of the passage in great detail. There were terrible seas outside the entrance, as if dragons were on guard. Right at the gateway was a stone pillar that looked almost as if it had been hand-carved. And straight ahead as far as you could see, there was open water eastward.

Poor old Juan de Fuca has come down in history as a liar and a dreamer. But the strait that so many years later was named for him *is* located near latitude 48 degrees north. Outside the strait are some of the most terrible seas on earth when a storm is blowing. And there is a rocky pillar at the entrance of the passage which a later explorer said "looked as if it came from Egypt." No one who had not seen the place could have described it so accurately. But, alas, it did not cut clear through America; it led only into Puget

Sound. Juan de Fuca was mistaken, but it is unfair to call him a liar. The pillar named for him tells us that he told the truth as far as it went.

Prompted by these two promising leads, the search began in earnest. Up until the middle of the nineteenth century, some maps still had "Ophir" marked on them somewhere. Hope dies hard.

Every country with ships and money set out to find the passage. French and Portuguese, as well as English, aimed at the St. Lawrence River and its cold and rocky mouth. People, when questioned, told them wild stories and they believed what they wanted to hear. In 1534, Jacques Cartier named the La Chine rapids for China, which he was sure was just up the river a little way. Three Cortoreal brothers, one after the other, captained Portuguese ships into the foggy northeast coast and were lost in the stormy seas. Some people called the strait "The Strait of the Three Brothers."

Martin Frobisher, for the Muscovy Company of England, went around Newfoundland and found the entrance to Hudson's Bay. He wrote home happily that he had America on his left and Asia on his right. Two more voyages failed to improve his geography, but he brought back an Eskimo, complete with kayak, and England was duly impressed.

Dutch and English and French and Portuguese — they all sailed off into the frozen North and never came back, but no one would abandon the search. In 1609 Henry Hudson, for England, got into the enormous bay now named for him, and thought it was the Pacific Ocean. Terrified by the grim frozen land and the frightful seas, his crew mutinied and left Hudson with his young son to die in a small boat with no oars and no food or water. Today you find memorial stones, here and there in the grim North and down along our New England coast, in memory of these men. Not one of them says, "He found the Northwest Passage"; they give us a greater message: "Here was a brave man."

The Hudson's Bay Company spent a million pounds in trying to find the Northwest Passage. In fact, their original charter was given for the purpose of "the discoverie of a passage to the South Sea," which they never found. This charter gave to the

Hudson's Bay Company almost three quarters of the newly discovered continent. While Balboa generously claimed "heaven and earth, air and water, etc." for Spain, the "Gentlemen Adventurers of England" laid claim to "the whole trade and commerce of all these seas, straits, bays, rivers, creeks, and sounds in whatsoever latitude that lie within the entrance of the strait called Hudson's Strait, and all that is not actually possessed by the subjects of any other Christian state. . . ." All the leading European nations had big ideas at the time and were very generous to themselves in dividing up this immense new land. But the fact still remained that unless they could find that mysterious passage, it was a mighty long way back to Europe around Cape Horn.

There were a number of harebrained schemes for settling the new land; it would make a nice halfway house to India once the passage was found, if there were a snug colony on that grim coast where travelers could rest. One plan was the notion of Sir Humphrey Gilbert, a young English knight of the time of Queen Elizabeth I, in the exciting days of Sir Francis Drake and Sir Walter Raleigh. Gilbert set out to raise money and the ships to set up a private colony, as the queen was not one to give out money for such things. One bad (or at least, impractical) feature of their plan was to send out to the new country all the very poor and those in debtor's prison "who were not quite bad enough to hang" — these being all city people from the slums of London who would have no idea at all how to live in a new land. However, it took so long to get the permissions from the queen and other officials, that their money ran out. Some of the gentlemen adventurers died, and the whole thing choked to death on government red tape.

On the other side of the world, Spain was desperately trying to find the western end of the passage. Cabrillo, a Portuguese sailing for Spain, had started the parade in 1542, and got as far as San Diego Bay. Centuries before Los Angeles invented smog, Cabrillo took a tired look at the muggy waters and named it, "The Bay of Smokes."

Balboa had claimed the Pacific Ocean for Spain:
"Heaven and earth, air and water,
from the Pole Arctic to the Pole Antarctic."

That pretty much covered everything, but it was a long way home to Spain; they needed that passage badly. Every year or so for many years, bulky, uncomfortable little Spanish ships would make the long haul up the silent coast, always winding up in freezing Arctic waters that went everywhere but east. Burying their dead in the great ocean, they would struggle back to Mexico with their sick crews and wait for another summer. And then, when anybody did discover something, the record of it went home to Spain to be lost in the royal archives. A discovery made in 1602 was not followed up until 1792. The marvel is, with a system like that, that anything at all got done.

The North Pacific coast from San Francisco up to Alaska is a hard place to go looking for anything. Redwoods love the fog, but sailors do not. One Spanish ship off the mouth of the Columbia River saw the fog part like great theater curtains and reveal a silver path of water leading off to the east. The clouds closed up and they never saw it again, nor did the sharp-eyed Captain James Cook who passed it twice. These enchanted places appeared and disappeared until everyone connected with the search was a little crazy on the subject, but they still believed in the passage — it *had* to be there, somewhere!

Verrazano, for France, found Chesapeake Bay in 1524 and reported joyously that it was the ocean they were looking for. He anchored near Staten Island in his wanderings around the Hudson's mouth and remarked on the beautiful country. The bay where he said, "Any great navy could ride safely without fear of tempest," now holds the Brooklyn Navy Yard, and a great bridge named for him arches over the sound that he admired so long ago.

In 1795 a gentleman by the name of Davidson, who had personally explored what was thought to be the eastern end of the passage, declared once and for all that there was no passage at all. No one heard him. He wrote newspaper articles about it, which few people read. The passage was two hundred years old by this time — how could anyone dare to say that it was not there? If it was not *there*, it was somewhere else!

By this time, there were new plans afoot: a land expedition under the direction of Thomas Jefferson, president of the new and brave United States of America. Needing to know what he had bought in the Louisiana Purchase, he set up the Lewis and Clark expedition to find out. Besides this, he had other plans for them. The two big fur companies, British and Canadian, were rivals for the Chinese market. The Canadians were anxious to work with the Americans, to use American waters for crossing the continent. They sent Alexander MacKenzie to search in the frozen North for the headwaters of a great river that came out in United States territory. He found the river later named for him, but it came out in the Arctic and was impractical for transport. It was thought that Lewis and Clark could find the river Oregon, and save everyone trouble.

President Jefferson was a scientist, interested in everything on earth. In those days, when so little was actually known about the country, he had probably the clearest idea of anybody of what they would be apt to find in the West. And Jefferson was one of the last solid believers in the Northwest Passage; his theory was a clever one even though it did not work out. He had read all that was written about the centuries of search, and he knew that nobody was going to come upon a hidden harbor and a long, straight canal reaching from ocean to ocean. But when he sent Lewis and Clark to go up the Missouri River to its source, he was convinced that they would find, on the same watershed, the headwaters of another great river, the Oregon. This would flow into the Pacific as the Missouri did to the Atlantic. He had read somewhere that there was not more than a twenty-mile portage between them. And there would be your passage: up the Missouri, down the Oregon. A Boston schoolteacher had said that the whole trip could be made in a comfortable carriage, though he had never made it.

The really weird part of all this is that there *is* a place in the Rockies called Two-Ocean Pass, where Two-Ocean Creek meanders along for a while and then divides. The western end joins the Columbia; the eastern comes down at last to the Mississippi. A trout who likes to travel could (at least in theory) go up one river and down the other, but nothing much bigger than a trout.

Lewis and Clark toiled up the "Big Muddy," up to their armpits in freezing water, going farther and farther away from the known world into the unknown. They found unbelievable natural riches and greatly widened the horizons of our world, but they had to come home and report that the twenty-mile portage was a myth, and there was no such thing as a place where you could step from an east-flowing river to one flowing west. There was not — at least in the river system that linked the various parts of our country — any passage.

But the enchanted passage was still causing confusion. Alexander MacKenzie came down the Fraser River and had to portage because of an accident. He came out on a river which he thought was the Columbia (other countries were still calling it the Oregon); it was the Bella Coola River. The same winter that Lewis and Clark camped at Fort Clatsop, the Canadians built a fort at the mouth of the Fraser River, thinking it was the Oregon. David Thompson came upon the Columbia and did not recognize it. He named it the Kootenai.

In spite of all the disappointments, it was only a few years until someone came up with a new idea. It was Henry Hudson — poor, unhonored pioneer left to die among the ice floes — who had discovered and insisted on talking about, a current that pulled ships against the wind and — he thought — might go over the North Pole. Perhaps there was open water over the pole itself; nobody had ever been there to see. And maybe *that* was where the passage was hidden all this time! All at once, everybody was interested again. England offered a prize of ten thousand pounds for anyone who would find the passage.

In 1818, Sir John Ross and his party began the procession of brave men, bundled in their warmest clothing, who aimed to pass by ship or dogsled across the pole. He failed to make any significant discovery.

Sir John Franklin and his party of one hundred twenty-nine men disappeared into the icy mist and several rescue parties were lost trying to find them.

A party led by Robert McClure was first to make the trip and survive. They walked, so the matter was not settled whether or not there was a ship passage.

The first ship to make the passage from Atlantic to Pacific was a battered old Norwegian herring boat captained by Roald Amundsen, who finished the journey on August 13, 1905. No one, least of all Roald Amundsen, claimed that this was a handy way to get from the Atlantic to the Pacific, but he had proved one thing — there *was* a passage there. His little ship, the *Gjöa*, had made it through.

Juan de Fuca's world is gone now. Most of the gold is carefully put away in Fort Knox and other such places, and it is no longer possible (if indeed it ever was) to go along the beach picking up pearls. The ships that ply the oceans now are not usually looking for Chinese silks and gold. But countries are still rivals for world trade, and ships are the answer to commercial problems; today, it is oil.

It was only natural that modern adventurers would try to see if they could get a modern oil tanker through the passage; it would cut more than eight thousand miles off the trip if they could, and time is money. So they fitted out an enormous tanker, the *Manhattan*, the biggest in the world at the time, and sent it north. Steel plates on the hull and the special curve of the bow, which would run it up on the ice and break it with the tanker's weight, were expected to handle the ice problem. With the help of the *John MacDonald*, a Canadian icebreaker, the *Manhattan* got through. But it hardly put a dent in the icy barrier that has kept men away from the poles for all these years. If even the mighty *Manhattan*, which is so big it takes miles to slow to turning speed and has all the modern gadgets for keeping warm and well fed, had a hard trip, we can imagine the terrible suffering of the early explorers in this icy land. Oilmen trying to work out transport problems inside the Arctic Circle would tell you that all the modern improvements in the world do not make this the fun way to travel to the Indies.

Today oil is power, and the nations of the world are all busy trying to get their hands on the world's supply in order to make sure that the "right people" have it. In the time of Alexander the Great, who lived before Christ, the thing the countries wanted most for their armies was a herd of elephants — war elephants, trained for battle. It was an idea that Alexander picked up in India, and it really made an army — people were utterly terrified of the huge beasts, and whole armies would run rather than fight them. So Alexander set about importing elephants from India to Suez. And on the way they had to pass through several countries where, quite soon, people began watching the shipping, so that the elephants only went to the "right people." The Middle Eastern countries where the sorting out was done are known to us now as Iraq, Iran, and Syria. It does not all seem to change very much.

We may smile at the simplicity of the early explorers, but we, like them, are still looking for instant wealth — for ourselves.

Chapter 12
Manila Galleon

Gold ships had been sailing from Manila to Acapulco for twenty years when the *Santa Ana* ran into the scourge of the Spanish seas — the fledgling British navy. "Drake" was the only English name the Spanish knew, and they blamed him for everything that went wrong with the galleon trade. They thought of him as a magician and claimed that he had a mirror in his cabin in which he could see Spanish treasure ships — a very early type of radar, we would say. But in spite of everyone hissing "el Drago!" (Spanish for "the Dragon") and cursing the luck of Francis Drake, it was not Drake who took the *Santa Ana*, but Thomas Cavendish.

The *Santa Ana* was neither the biggest nor the fastest ship in the Spanish gold-carrying fleet; but loaded for the Mexican Fair of 1587, it carried the richest cargo ever shipped out of Manila. The voyage had been long and nerve-wracking, full of troubles and discomforts. Sebastian Rodríguez Cermenho, the pilot, was happy to see the rocky coast of California slipping past and to know that in a couple of weeks — with luck — he could get the enormous cargo safely into the hands of the owners and his sick people to land where they could get well. He was expecting to see another Spanish ship, which had been sent north from Mexico to look for good harbors, so it gave him great joy to hear the lookout announce that three fast little ships were coming up on them from the northwest.

Cermenho watched as the ships came closer. Not until the strangers ran up their flags, and the red lions of England pranced

141

in the breeze, did he realize what was happening. The awful truth hit the Spanish crew and left them speechless: *someone* had the boldness to sail into the Pacific, which every educated man knew was a Spanish lake! And there was not the least doubt what they wanted, either, as the first shots crossed the bow of the doomed galleon.

The Spanish were shocked at such rudeness on the part of England. So sure were they of owning the great sea that *Santa Ana* did not even have a cannon on board! Hand arms were speedily issued and a running battle began, rather like a big dog attacked by three small poodles. After four hours of gallant but hopeless defense on the *Santa Ana,* a cannon shot felled the galleon's mainmast and English trumpets signaled victory. Cavendish and his fellow officers boarded the Spanish ship, and the chaplains asked — and received — mercy for the captured Spaniards. Cavendish took the pilot and all the clergy aboard his ship as hostages. Then he set about seeing what kind of a prize he had captured.

He soon saw why the Spanish had fought so desperately to save the ship. There was booty beyond their wildest dreams; it took six days to unload the treasures, including "600 pesos in golde; silkes, sattins, damasks, 22 *arubas* of musk for the making of perfume; divers other merchandise, and a great store of all manner of victuals, with the choyce of many conserves of all sorts for to eat; a great quantity of pearls, and sundry sorts of very good wines." The mail chest they threw into the sea.

The one hundred ninety people from the *Santa Ana* were put ashore. Among them — according to tradition — were two men of whom history was to hear later: Sebastián Vizcaíno, the explorer of the Pacific coast, and Juan de Fuca, whose theories would set all Europe searching for the Northwest Passage. They were provided with food and with material to build a small boat. Having sacked the ship, Cavendish had it set afire and left to burn. He made an attempt to talk Cermenho into going on with him (good pilots were hard to find), but Cermenho assured him that he had a previous engagement — returning to Spain to explain to the king how he happened to lose the treasure ship. Cavendish took over the Spanish charts and hurried on across the Pacific; he did not want anything to happen to his cargo and felt that he was safer dodging the Portuguese around the tip of Africa than braving both Cape Horn and the Spanish Main.

Finding the *Santa Ana* was almost pure luck for Cavendish. He had known next to nothing about the mysterious gold ship until a French captive, on one of the ships he had taken, told him that the galleon not only came this way, but that it was due in any time now. So the three fast little ships (the type that Englishmen were beginning to build in quantity) went after the galleon, and could hardly believe their luck when they found it. The bishop of Manila, when he heard about the *Santa Ana*, said in great annoyance, "An English youth of twenty-two years, with a wretched little vessel of a hundred tons, took our beautiful ship, and he went away laughing!" This is an excellent description of what probably happened.

The "wretched little vessels" of the Englishmen had sailed boldly around Cape Horn and into the great Spanish lake eight years before Cavendish took the *Santa Ana*. Drake was not after the Manila galleon then, because at that time he had never heard of it. He was on the trail of the silver-laden ship from Peru, which proved to be well worthwhile when he finally captured it off Panama the same year. His prizes included "13 chests of coined silver, 26 tons of silver bars, 80 pounds of gold and several boxes of jewels."

From another captured ship he gathered in a load of China silk, some fine linen cloth, and a great many of the newfangled dishes that people would call "china" because of their place of origin. With a fat prize like this, he preferred to take no chances with the Spanish guns in the Caribbean; it was a long way to London whichever way he went, but he decided to make a run for it with the Portuguese around Africa.

So Drake had been the first to come back to London with plunder from the Indies. Queen Elizabeth knighted the skillful pirate for his accomplishments but — oddly enough — she was not interested in the fact that he had planted the English flag and claimed a land that had white cliffs like the cliffs of Dover, a land that would some day be called California and would be worth a great many times his precious cargo. Perhaps she was put off by his remark that it was very foggy where he careened his ship to repair it (either Drake's Bay or Bodega Bay, north of the Golden Gate). Coming from London, who needed any more fog?

She was much more interested in Drake's plans for relieving the Spanish of their gold. He had a great many ideas, some of which he put into practice, such as capturing and misleading the first mule of a two-hundred-mule silver train bound for Nombre de Dios (Panama), and leading it firmly into the English camp for loading on a hidden English ship. He even tried to figure out a way to get into Acapulco Harbor, which was sheltered by great cliffs and carefully guarded with cannons, in order to sink the gold ship at the dock. No wonder the Spanish suspected Drake of the most bizarre wickedness and blamed all their bad luck on him.

The Spanish had worked hard setting up the Acapulco-Manila trade, and they were in no mood for sharing with the English — of all people. We do not, even yet, have complete records of those early years; some records have been buried in the Spanish Royal Archives for four hundred fifty years, and some will probably still be there, undisturbed, at the crack of doom. We do know that when the first Spaniards stumbled onto the storybook harbor of Acapulco, there were Chinese junks bobbing at anchor in its beautiful blue bay. Questions revealed that there had always been Chinese junks there, as far as anybody knew. They came for the abalone. It was probably this fact more than any other that sent the Spanish ships westward across the biggest ocean in the world.

The Portuguese navigator, Ferdinand Magellan, did not finish his voyage around the world; he was killed in a skirmish with the natives in the South Pacific island, and his ship went home without him. It returned to Europe by the Portuguese route around Africa. This choice of routes left a curious gap in Western knowledge of the Far East. The Spanish had found a source of great wealth in the Philippines, where Manila would shortly grow up at this crossroads of all the Eastern trade routes.

There was, however, one vital thing they did *not* discover:

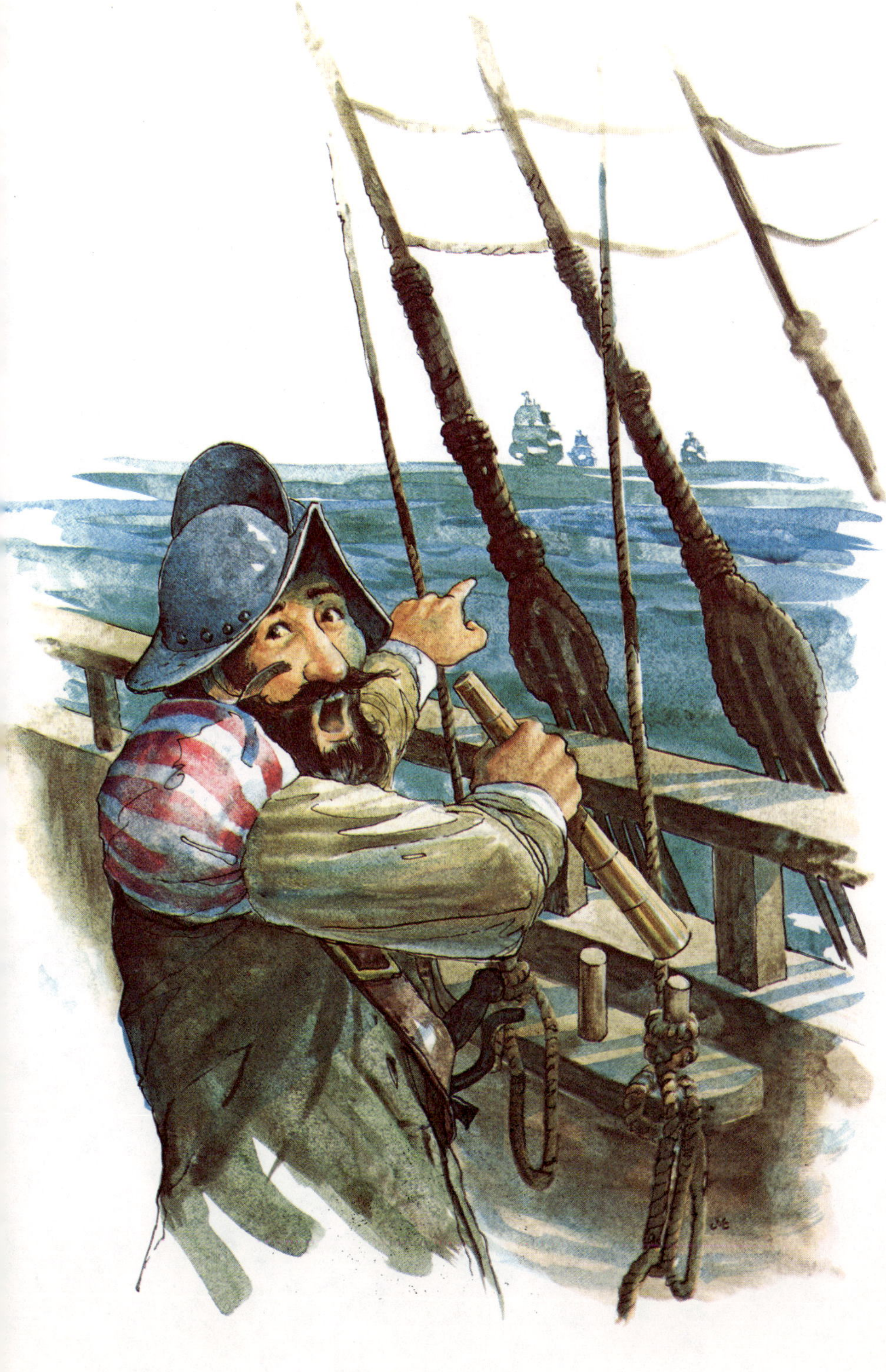

A lookout aboard the Spanish galleon SANTA ANA reports the approach of three vessels. The Spaniards are dumbfounded to learn they are English vessels.
(See pages 141-143.)

others who followed them found to their sorrow that they could sail west on the great ocean on what seemed to be a smooth highway of the sea — but they could not get back. The winds and currents that made it so simple to go from Mexico to the Philippines were dead set against them on the return trip. Ships struggled with the terrible seas, tacked impossible distances trying to defeat the steady winds, were blown off course, damaged and sunk — but they could not get back to Mexico. Because of the slowness of travel, it was several years, with one expedition after another sailing off into oblivion, before anyone understood the problem.

One of the most experienced of Spanish sailors, Juan García de Loaysa, took a fleet of six ships to the Philippines in 1525. Only a few of his men survived the years of suffering and frustration of trying to get home again. One who did survive was a young sailor named Andrés de Urdaneta. That part of the world, the Spice Islands in particular, was the possession of Portugal, and the Portuguese were not in a sharing mood, either. They attacked any Spanish ship that tried to use their sea lanes, and saw to it that the rich trade from the Moluccas went straight into Portuguese pockets. Andrés managed to get work on Portuguese ships around the Spice Islands and finally, after eleven years of trying, got himself aboard one of the ships headed for the West. After some years in Spain, Andrés returned to Mexico, but he had had enough of the greed and hassle of trading, so he went into a monastery and settled in for a peaceful old age. Here, years later, the king's officers found him and begged him to head a new expedition to the Far East.

Andrés did not want to go. It had been nearly forty years since he sailed with the Loaysa expedition across the Pacific, and he was now the only living man who had ever been there. He was happy where he was. But he knew the problem of ships going out to the East and not being able to get back. Never guilty of doing anything in a hurry, Spain wanted to check on Magellan's discoveries (of forty-eight years before), but Andrés was more concerned about the homeward route. He finally agreed to go, but refused the command.

The ship was the *San Pablo*, and it sailed from Acapulco in

1563, with Miguel López de Legaspi in command. The westward passage was easy; all they had to do was to steer into the path of the northeast trade winds and stay there. Legaspi reached the Philippines in 1564 and busied himself founding the city of Manila and setting up the framework for a line of trading ships that would sail, treasure-laden, from Manila to Acapulco, then to the Spanish Main and home to fill the king's empty cupboards. It was a beautiful plan, but nobody yet had figured out how to get back across the Pacific.

Legaspi did not give much thought to the homeward route; he was not going home. So he turned the command over to his nephew, Felipe de Salcedo, who could probably cope with the problem if he had Fray Andrés to advise him. Unfortunately, since he was not sailing the ship himself, he gave them an unseaworthy old tub and kept the *San Pablo* for his own errands. Shorthanded, the miserable old ship sailed out of Manila with Andrés as pilot. Once outside the islands, they turned north. The Portuguese, gifted sailors that they were, had found the "great circle" route on the Atlantic, and Andrés had a theory that there was probably a similar route in the Pacific.

The story of that voyage is a classic of human endurance. The ship began leaking before it was out of sight of land, and the weather got colder as they went north. The sailing master died and most of the crew went down with scurvy. Fray Andrés took the wheel and kept on bearing north. At last, at latitude 36 degrees north, he felt the sweep of westerly winds and slipped into the long-sought path across the seas. They had come two thousand miles, fighting contrary winds. Now they simply turned eastward and ran before the wind until a strange coast came into view. They rode the northwest gale down the American coast to Acapulco. In four months and two days they had traveled ten thousand miles over uncharted ocean. Fourteen of the crew were dead, and when the ship finally slid into the harbor of Acapulco, no one even had the strength to drop the anchor. In fact, only two men on board were able to stand up: Andrés at the helm, and Felipe the captain.

They had found a way to get across the Pacific eastward, but as a practical route for a heavily laden galleon it left a great deal to be desired. We ask now, why did they not come by way of the Hawaiian Islands, and the answer is curiously simple: they never found them. So for two hundred fifty years the gold ships traveled the hard way across the Pacific, hoping for harbors that nobody ever found.

The first treasure ship, the *San Pablo*, sailed from Manila as soon as Fray Andrés's route could be explained to the captain. The last treasure ship sailed into history in 1815, after Spain's great colonial empire had crumbled. The ship was known to Mexico as "the China ship," and its westerly path, "the China road." To Manila it was "the Silver Ship," as it brought coined money from Mexico.

Over the years, four gold ships were captured by the English, the richest of which was the *Santa Ana*. The Japanese took two more. The records show that at least ten ships never made port. Somewhere on that long, rocky coastline that runs from the Strait of Juan de Fuca to the tip of Baja, California, there must be the remains of who-knows-how-many richly loaded galleons, sharing their beds with the creatures of the sea, probably just safely out of reach of the breakers. Only now are the treasure hunters beginning to dive for the sunken ships in the Spanish Main, which is a small area compared to the vast Pacific coast. But there are sunken treasures somewhere on that coast.

Some of the wrecks we know about. The *San Augustín* went aground in 1595 near Point Reyes in California. A little plaque beside the highway tells you that it happened here. You look out beyond the pounding surf and you can imagine the great bulky galleon, anchored out beyond the rocks while the captain and his party come ashore to look for a harbor where a crippled gold ship could put in for repairs and fresh water. The pilot, Sebastian Rodríguez Cermenho, was one of the best in the business, and he did not believe in endangering his ship while he went exploring.

However, they had their orders — every incoming galleon should search for harbors. His crew, furthermore, needed both food and fresh water. Some one hundred thirty tons of rich goods for the Fair of Acapulco were riding uneasily out there — not only fine silks and beeswax, but some of the new-style dishes that were the rage among the rich. While Cermenho and his party were dealing with the Indians about food and taking on water, a sudden storm came up. The *San Augustín* freed her anchor and swung onto the jagged rocks that lie just under the surface of the water. The rocks tore the bottom out of the ship, which sank almost at once — cargo, crew, and all. When the captain and his party returned, it was too late to save anything. Cermenho, the same unfortunate pilot who had lost the *Santa Ana* to Cavendish, had to go back to Spain again and explain himself.

Galleons for the gold-ship trade were usually made in the Philippines, where there was magnificent hardwood for the taking, and thousands of people with clever hands to do the building. Some of the galleons were lost because of poor design; people were always experimenting, trying to design a ship that would carry more goods. Often the ships were overbalanced by poor loading, or by greedy overloading. The temptation to skim off some of that lovely gold was always there, and even though Spanish customs officers were one hundred percent suspicious and equally ruthless, people did sometimes manage to bring in contraband — usually by not listing the whole cargo.

One of the tales told about those years concerns a ship that had listed cargo worth half a million dollars. For some reason, the ship was wrecked on the rocks just short of the harbor of Acapulco, near enough that the customs officers could preside personally over the salvage of the wreck. When something over a million dollars' worth of goods had been rescued, the crew members began quietly disappearing; this was a smart idea, as it happened, since the captain and all the officers got ten years in the galleys for their part in the plot. Another time, the Manila customs official was giving the ship his last survey and he noticed that the anchor had been freshly painted. He gave it an idle kick, and his boot left a scar of sparkling gold on the black anchor!

But in spite of all this, the trade went on; it is unique in the history of the world because of the distance and the dangers which hedged it in on every side. Ships expected to lose half their crews with scurvy; several ships lost the whole crew and drifted for months, and in one case, years, before meeting another ship. Early in the trade years the great ship *San José* drifted in below Acapulco with everyone dead on board, its treasure untouched.

The galleon brought all the riches of the world to the people who were, for the first time, able to buy them. Many a wretchedly poor young man came out from Spain and made his fortune from the apparently boundless riches of Mexico and Peru. Rough army living gave way to cities of great houses run by slaves. It was a bad country for women and children in the early days, just as our own rough frontiers were at first. Trade with the Orient brought luxuries that pleased the women and gave prestige to their menfolk. These things could be bought for gold and silver, and the gold sent on to the king, who preferred the money anyway.

The Acapulco-bound ship, "a floating gold mine," always brought silks — magnificent Oriental silks either printed or with rich embroideries. The Chinese had perfected the making of beautiful fabrics that every woman wanted — gauze, crepe, the flowered silk of Canton called "Springtime," velvet, taffeta, damask, and heavy brocade. What was even more eagerly sought, most of the ships carried silk stockings for the ladies — not, of course, the sheer luxuries of modern times, but a rare sort of luxury to women living on the frontier of European civilization. China also sent bed coverings and tablecloths, and jewel-like china dishes for the table. Carpets and fine cottons came from India; rugs were imported from Persia. Uncut gems and gold for coinage in Mexico City were always part of the cargo. One galleon listed "80,000 women's combs; fans of ivory and sandalwood; jade items; brass bells and finely-decorated boxes." Portuguese ships sailing to the Far East around Africa brought Flemish lace and many other European luxuries that had come halfway around the world to the Acapulco Fair.

The galleon of 1573 listed "712 pieces of Chinese silk, 22,300 pieces of fine gilt china and other porcelain ware." On the other hand, one disappointed boatload of pirates discovered that their prize carried only "hennes, hogges and rice," and another was full of quince marmalade and white mules for some officer's carriage.

On the trip back to Manila the ship carried not only coined silver (which was legal tender almost everywhere in the world) but also Mexican chocolate, quinine from the Peru ship for malaria sufferers, and such items of European ware as the Spanish in Manila might need.

The Spanish were nothing if not businesslike in getting their loot home to Spain. They scheduled the ship from Peru so that it would arrive near the time of the Manila galleon, which usually came in around Christmas or the beginning of January. The China ship had much farther to come and was in much greater danger, both from the sea itself and from those shadowy pirates — Dutch, Japanese, the tricky, lucky Englishmen, and perhaps even the French. Therefore the plate (silver) fleet from Peru was timed to the galleon's schedule. Then a great fair could be held in Acapulco with the combined riches of far-off kingdoms. Acapulco, a ghost city the rest of the year, would ring with music and laughter — and fighting — and the clink of gold being exchanged for the beautiful things from far away. Gold — and this included priceless art treasures stolen from Aztec and Inca cities, which were melted down into ingots — was much simpler to send to Spain than a full load of bulky cloth and dishes.

The Peru galleon brought mainly the rich silver ores from Potosí. From Callao, the port of Lima, to Panama, it took two to four big ships to carry the silver which had come down on an endless chain of llamas during a hectic two weeks of loading under heavy guard. The Peru galleon to Acapulco brought other precious metals and jewels, and the badly needed quinine for malaria sufferers in this kingdom of hungry mosquitoes. A large trade came from Guatemala to Acapulco, bringing in European imports that came by way of Veracruz, black pearls from La Paz in Baja, California, pearls from Cartagena, and emeralds from Bogotá rounded out the riches that were now within the grasp of many.

Today in America, even the smallest town on the highest mountain can, with the help of a mail-order catalog, reach out to buy almost anything you can think of. A town of ten thousand will have stores and supermarkets displaying goods from all over the world, and we take it for granted. It is hard for us to imagine a life-style where our world ended right outside our own doorstep, and we were dependent on our own hands to create anything we wanted. Spanish colonials, trying to build themselves a European home in a hostile land, had few if any conveniences. To the people of all nationalities the gold ship was a bridge to another world, and they met its wonders at the Fair of Acapulco.

In the history of world trade, Acapulco is a landmark. Here for the first time Asia, Africa, North and South America, Europe, and the islands of the Far East were linked. When in later years the trail from Santa Fe in New Mexico and the trail from St. Augustine in Florida were linked with the old Spanish road to Mexico City, the new people, the Yankees, joined in, and almost the whole world was pulled together briefly for the Fair of Acapulco.

The Acapulco Fair was not the only one, though it was the noisiest, most dangerous, and most exciting — and then, of course, there was first pick at the China treasures. The entire network of Spanish treasure ships, from all over the New World, gathered eventually to sail in a well-protected fleet from Havana. Several fairs were held on the Atlantic side of the isthmus before the fleet sailed for Spain. But the Acapulco Fair was the important one.

The gold ship and its fortunes were like today's stock exchange in that everyone prospered when all went well, and everyone suffered when it did not. Watchers up along the coast, in what are now quaint little fishing villages where tourists roam, waited for the first sight of the incoming galleon. It was hoped that its troubles were over, once it got safely past the stormy waters at the tip of Baja, California. Indians soon learned that a reward awaited the first man to bring the welcome news that the gold ship was in sight.

Cannons from the fort at Acapulco welcomed the incoming galleon. All the bells in town were rung and people sang and danced in the streets, hardly sober enough to deal with the long trains of laden mules and the richly garbed groups of wealthy merchants, both Mexican and European, coming in for the fair. Packtrains carried such down-to-earth items as coops full of hens and squealing pigs which would enrich the farmers and fill the hungry fairgoers' stomachs. Silver coins minted in Mexico City were under heavy guard; these were part of the cargo for the ship which would sail in March for the Orient. Also meant for the outgoing galleon were long lines of prisoners, roped together. They would serve their sentences clearing land and building the new city of the Far East, Manila.

The population of Acapulco, normally around four thousand, shot up to nearly ten thousand during fair time, which was ordinarily held from the tenth of January to the twenty-fifth of February — depending, of course, on the galleons. Since one of the most acute problems was that of feeding such a mob of visitors, much of the incoming freight was food. Most of the rich Spaniards from the colonies were on hand for the year's greatest event. They came in great style, their horses and mules decked out in flaming ornaments set with mirrors and pom-poms, and themselves dressed in rich fabrics that had come from the last fair. There were no air-conditioned tourist hotels in Acapulco then, and the mosquitoes had their own fiesta on the imported merchants. What is more, Acapulco had frequent earthquakes. Nobody stayed a day longer than was necessary, but one could pack a great deal into two weeks.

Eventually the shipping company learned that every incoming galleon would have a load of very sick people on board; it was a long time before someone persuaded them to import limes (vitamin C to us) to cure the scurvy. After that there would be muleloads of limes among the incoming freight. Also, as the years went by, the outgoing galleon took Mexican chocolate which was exchanged for Chinese tea. The galleon carried anywhere from twenty to fifty missionaries headed for Japan and China — and martyrdom (as both countries killed off the friars as fast as they came). Finally the galleon captains, sick of bloodshed, simply refused to take any more friars. For many years, all these varied people and products made up the glitter of the Acapulco Fair, which was like a medieval tapestry, so rich in colorful detail that it is hard not to get a clear picture of it as it was at the height of its importance.

Products changed as new industries were developed in Mexico and other countries of Spanish America. Pottery from Guadalajara was eagerly sought after because it was both beautiful and durable. A Spanish friar, recognizing fine pottery clay deposits near Puebla, sent to Spain for potters. Chinese potters from a wrecked ship were brought in to add their know-how, and a couple of Portuguese who knew how to make the lovely *azulejos* (blue picture tiles) joined in. The result was the world-famous Talavera ware, which is still prized after four centuries.

Missionaries to Mexico brought in grapevines, and many plants from their homeland that were new to the Indians. They also had that European ability to organize things that produced such fine results. Europeans on the whole discovered that Indians did not organize very well; they were much too apt to go fishing or hunting when their white neighbors had planned for them to plow and plant fields, and other hard labors. The friars, who either had more imagination or better luck, soon organized great haciendas — we would say plantations — where the Indians, as well as being cared for and having the constant pageantry of church festivals, soon were producing flour, sugar, walnuts, dates, pomegranates, figs, and oranges that could be shipped to the Far East.

All these exotic goods joined the packtrains leading to Acapulco and to the Mexican Fair at Saltillo, where cattle, pottery, as well as peasant crafts and fabrics, were sold. Vanilla, indigo, and cochineal took their place on the galleon's manifest for the Far East, and all of these things helped the economy.

The trade in slaves was forbidden by law; but like a lot of forbidden things, it was profitable, so it went on, horrible as it was. In all justice it should be remembered that this was not a Spanish monopoly; Drake's English friends made a fortune in slaves which they bought from the Portuguese. Any country that could manage it was taking stolen bites from the forbidden pie.

Through the years of the galleons, the legends gathered. Many of them centered on Drake. Drake could, in all, have spent little more than ten years tormenting the Spanish in the New World. He made three trips to the West Indies, scattering dismay wherever he went. After he had taken Cartagena, Spain's pearl port, and sacked it completely, he refrained from burning it to the ground only because he was in a hurry.

At the last minute he got so angry that he would have started all over again, except that his ship was already loaded with loot, and the climate was so terrible at Cartagena — not to mention the clouds of starving mosquitoes — that he just wanted to get out to sea, away from the insects. The thing that made him so angry was a letter he found in a house they were stripping, in which the writer referred to Drake as a "pirate." This was probably the nicest thing that the Spanish ever called him, but he was greatly insulted. An English gentleman, a *pirate!*

After leaving Cartagena, he did put back into port, and the citizens of Cartagena prepared for the worst. But all he wanted was to borrow their ovens so the cooks could bake a supply of biscuits. They would be a long time at sea. With Drake, you just never knew.

One rumor had it that Drake was French, and his father was a shoemaker. (He was born in Plymouth.) He was said to have brought five French ships into the Pacific, and they were *out there*, waiting for the galleon. He was also said to have stolen six hundred thousand ducats from the plunder of ships, and buried them in France. After the sack of Cartagena, word got around that twenty thousand Englishmen were on their way to take America away from Spain. As a matter of simple arithmetic, someone should have realized this was impossible. Drake had his troubles, too; he lost seven hundred fifty men in his war against the Spanish. And once his luck was out — clear out, when he missed the entire Spanish treasure fleet as it went blundering up through the Florida channel, headed for Spain — he missed it by only a few hours.

Later, a Dutch sea captain was to have the luck that Drake had missed on this occasion: he took an entire Spanish fleet, crippled by a hurricane, and went home to Holland with his ships so full of treasure they could hardly float. With this unexpected windfall, Holland paid off all its debts and made the captain a national hero. The Dutch, who depended almost entirely on fish for

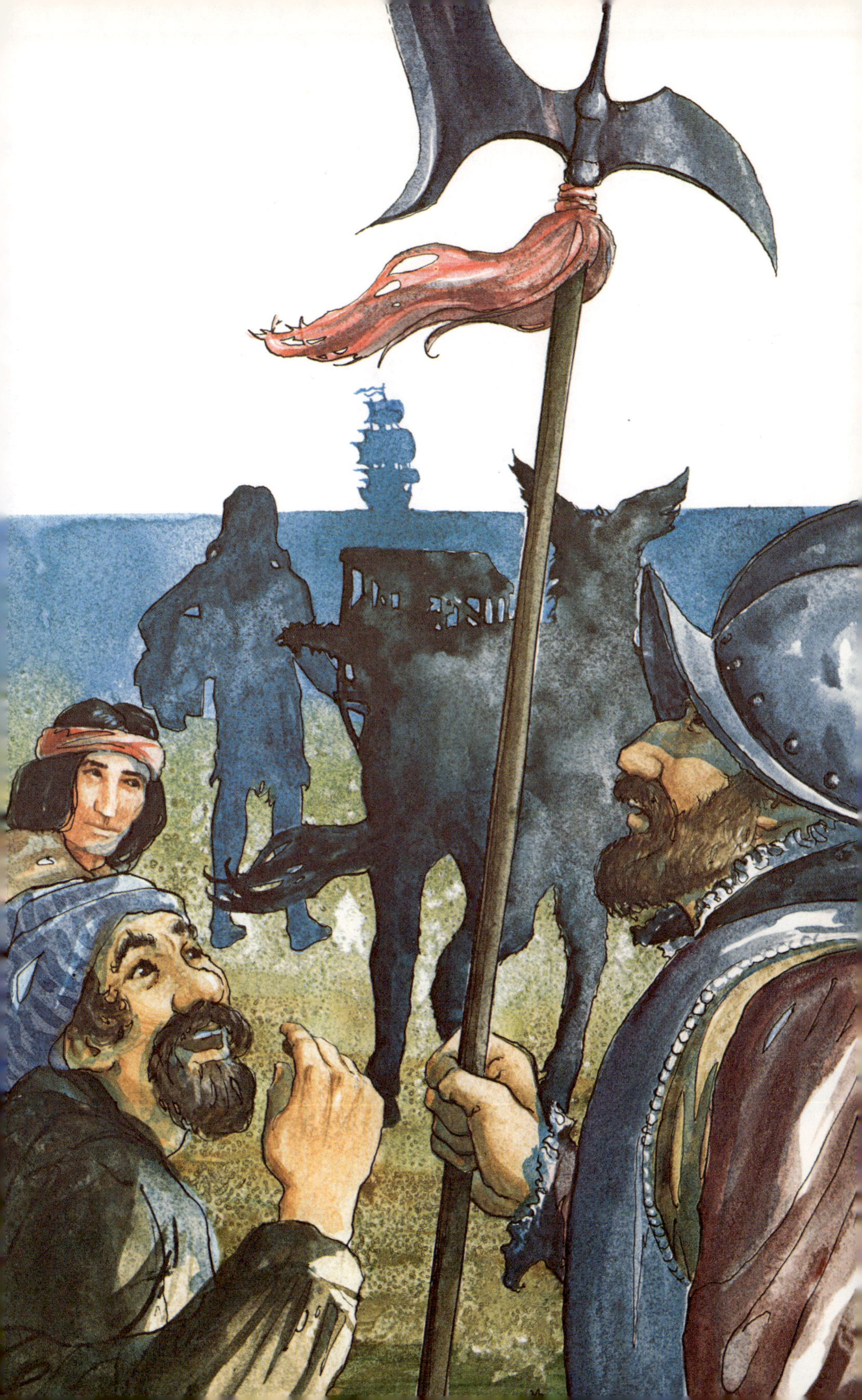

**A treasure-laden Spanish galleon
is eagerly awaited in Acapulco,
Mexico.** *(See pages 153-155.)*

their economy, absolutely had to have salt; and Spain had recently cut off their salt imports from Portugal and left them no choice but to sail clear to South America for it. Sending out two hundred fifty salt ships a year across the stormy Atlantic did nothing to sweeten the Dutch temper, and they did not really feel sorry that Spain had lost a whole fleet.

After they had learned to carry guns, the treasure galleons fought off Portuguese, English, French, and Japanese pirates, and other ships that carried several flags in their lockers for occasion. Years after Drake was dead, the Spanish still shuddered at the thought of the wicked little English ships with the cleverness of Drake, waiting out there at the world's end for a loaded galleon to come in sight.

The Spanish, as we mentioned, were not very forthcoming with their information. If they admitted the loss of ten galleons, we can safely suppose that they knew of at least twenty, which is about average for public admissions. We have American records, vague but interesting, about the following ships:

- A galleon sunk near the mouth of the Quinault River in Washington State, probably in 1570.
- A galleon wrecked in the Strait of Juan de Fuca, 1596.
- A galleon wrecked off Nehalem Beach, Oregon, 1679. There is a tradition of Indian witnesses, concealed in the nearby woods, who watched a small boat come ashore and strange men dig a deep hole to bury a heavy chest. (This is pure classic "Treasure Island," but that is what the record says.) They then killed one of their number and threw him in on top of the box, and closed the hole, and rowed away.
- A Spanish merchant ship, not a galleon, wrecked on Clatsop Beach, Oregon, in 1725.
- The *San Sebastian*, off Santa Barbara, 1754.
- The *San Carlos*, in San Francisco Bay, 1797.
- The galleon *San Francisco Xavier* failed to reach Acapulco, though there was some evidence that she had got across the ocean. Her cargo: gold and beeswax. Near Astoria, Oregon, there is a cave with what appears to be either a spongy

sort of rock, or petrified beeswax. Since each flat stone is plainly stamped "IHS," the chances are that it is beeswax, meant for altar candles in Spain.

In 1604 the two gold ships, *Jesús María* and *Espíritu Santo*, spent two weeks fighting terrible seas to get around Cape Mendocino in northern California. They came so near to not making it that one wonders how many others ran into the same rough waters and did not make it. Cape Mendocino was a landmark for the incoming galleons — it was the point where they turned south — and all of them came that way.

The Japan Current, that "great black river in the sea," will bring ships — and almost anything else that floats — around the great circle and dump it on the shores of Washington and Oregon. The remains of nearly one hundred Chinese junks have been found along this coast, and it is now a beachcomber's paradise for clear glass fishnet floats from Japan and fantastic driftwood from all the Western Hemisphere. When we consider the risks of that long voyage, and the condition the crew must have been in when they first sighted land, we realize that there were probably many ships, desperate for water and fresh food, that would put in anywhere along the coast that gave any hope of being a passage. Since everyone was searching for the Northwest Passage, we can regard with suspicion any waterway opening in an eastward direction — among them the Strait of Juan de Fuca, the little bay that is called Grays Harbor, the Columbia River, and various little island-hidden bays like Drake's Bay in California.

The most logical of all is the strait named for Juan de Fuca; on clear days, looking in from a calm ocean, you can see nearly two hundred miles of water leading almost straight eastward. A damaged galleon, seeing clear water ahead in the direction it was hoping for, would hardly be able to resist going in. Storms come up quickly at sea, and the strait can be deadly in a storm or heavy fog. Such a galleon would probably pile up on the West Beach of Whidbey Island, where the big breakers come roaring in off the Pacific with nothing to stop them for three thousand miles.

Perhaps someday, somebody will go and see.

The Legend of Drake's Drum

Sailors are superstitious, they say; most people are. Many perfectly logical people carry a "good-luck piece," or wear a "lucky garment" when they travel. Sir Francis Drake's good-luck charm was a drum, which in his day was used to give signals in both army and navy.

He took it with him everywhere, and when he was dying, halfway around the world from Plymouth, he made his friends promise to return his drum to his hometown. Then, he said, if England was ever in danger from a foreign power, someone should beat on the drum and he, Drake, would rise up and come to fight for England.

The drum, it is said, sounded by itself when Napoleon was brought to England on his way to exile. It sounded again, they say, at the beginning of the Great War in 1914. It beat its sad tattoo at the sinking of the *Royal Oak*, the pride of the British navy in World War II.

No one has reported that Drake rose at any of those times, but the legend has been carried on to the present time. It is probably one way of letting us all know that Drake was a very patriotic Englishman, willing to give his life for his country.

Chapter 13
A New Mexico in the North

>Passed by here the officer Don Juan de Oñate from the discovery of the sea of the South on the 16th of April, 1605.
>
>Here was the General Don Diego de Vargas, who conquered for our Holy Faith and for the royal crown all of New Mexico at his own expense.
>
>— *Samples of messages found on Inscription Rock, New Mexico*

>Find buried treasure, relics, for fun and profit! Exciting, rewarding, family hobby! The NEW GOLDMASTER, complete, only $169.50! $29.50 down and balance $10.57 per month!
>
>D-TEX Electronix treasure locator: $19.95 up!
>
>— *Samples of modern-day advertising*

When the Spanish came into the Indian Southwest, they hoped to conquer it peacefully since, they felt, the Indians ought to be grateful to be taken over by civilized people. It was not to be that way; it took them one hundred fifty years of hard fighting and harder traveling over dangerous country on the other side of the world from Spain. Nothing could have kept them at so thankless a task but the lure of gold. To give them their due, they did try to convert and educate the strange people they met; but the Indians had worked out quite a good life-style of their own. They did not especially want to be either converted or civilized, if the greedy invaders were any example of Christian citizenship. It never ceased to puzzle the Spanish that the Indians did not want what the white man had to give.

When Cortez took Mexico City, it was five times the size of sixteenth-century London. Taking it was no easy job for a few travel-weary Spaniards and a mob of assorted Indians who did not like the Aztec government. The city sat on islands in the middle of a huge lake which was the caldron of an extinct volcano, well fortified against land attack. So, crazy as it seemed to attack a city on a mountaintop nearly two miles high, that was what Cortez did. He had two prefabricated boats made (in case you thought "prefabricated" things were a modern invention) and carried up the mountain in pieces. Then he put the boats back together again and attacked the city from the water.

Once they had taken the city, the Spaniards went about looking with great surprise at the beautiful buildings and works of art. The Aztecs were savages who killed victims by the thousands in their temple. But not even Spain had such beautiful buildings, bridges, and gardens. And gold — gold was everywhere!

Montezuma at this moment made one of the most outstanding mistakes in all history. There was an old Aztec legend about a "fair white god" who had once come to them from over the seas and taught them all the arts and sciences they knew. The fair god had gone away again over the water, promising to return in the Year of the Morning Star from the sea where the sun rises. The Spanish had appeared just on time and from the right direction, but some of Montezuma's advisers were already saying that they were not gods. Trying to do the best he could for his people, not to anger the gods — if they truly were gods — Montezuma gave the fatal order. He had his bankers unlock the treasure house and bring out a great wheel of gold that was made like the sun, and a matching silver one for the moon. They brought out jewels of all kinds, and priceless robes made of feathers, and embroideries — and gave them to the Spanish so that they would go away and leave them in peace!

After this nothing could stop the plunder of Mexico and of all the places the Spanish were to explore in the New World. The doom of New Mexico was sealed twenty years before it was found, by the hint of gold. The Apache, Geronimo, said many years later: "I do not know why the white man prizes the yellow iron. It is too soft for weapons and it cannot be eaten. Yet they will kill to get it." The Coronado expedition, which opened up New Mexico to the men from Europe, was powered by the hope of gold, as a car is powered by gas.

Coronado was not the first Spaniard to travel in this vast country which is now our American Southwest. Parts of the country were seen, first of all, by four Spanish sailors who survived a shipwreck on the coast of Florida. Cabeza de Vaca was the leader of the group, and one was a tall black man by the name of Estevanico (Steve), who brightened up a very grim journey with songs and laughter. They went nearly two thousand miles across Texas, New Mexico, and Arizona, hoping to strike somewhere on the west coast of Mexico where there might be Spaniards. When they did finally meet some of their countrymen, they tried to take Estevanico as a slave. When the governor of Mexico heard that there was another great country to the north, he sent an exploring party under a Franciscan, Fray Marcos de Niza (Mark of Nice, a Frenchman) with Estevanico as guide.

The Zuñi pueblo of Hawikuh in New Mexico still remembers a legend told long ago to Zuñi children which tells what happened to this expedition: "It is to be believed that a long time ago, when roofs lay over the walls of Kya-Ki-Mi (Hawikuh), when smoke hung over the housetops and the ladder rounds were still unbroken in Kya-Ki-Mi, then the black Mexicans came from their abode in everlasting summerland. Then and thus were killed by our ancients, right where the stone stands down by the arroyo of Kya-Ki-Mi, one of the black Mexicans, a large man with chili lips. Then the rest ran away, chased by our grandfathers, and went back towards their country of everlasting summerland."

Turned back when Estevanico was killed by the Indians and the others "chased by our grandfathers," Fray Marcos reported that they had seen golden cities, seven of them, but only from a distance, as they were afraid of the Indians. As these stories were retold, not only were the seven cities made of gold, but there were jewels set around the windows and people ate from silver dishes, though it is hard to see how they found this out from a distance.

It is easy enough now to criticize Fray Marcos for letting his imagination run away with him, but before you do so, you should drive the road from Santa Fe to Pecos in the late afternoon on a clear day. As you come around the corner, there, two miles away, the ruins of Pecos mission glow red-gold in the afternoon sun. The adobe of this country, which is used for bricks, shines copper-gold from afar. To nervous Spaniards peering from behind rocks at the strange little city, they *expected* it to look like gold, and it did. The little matter of moving the seven cities from an island in the Atlantic to the middle of the New Mexico desert did not bother them. Spaniards — and everybody else — believe what they want to believe.

The Coronado expedition was sent to explore what Fray Marcos had described, and there never was an expedition like it, before or since. Heading out into unknown country where water was rare and there were no roads but the buffalo trails, three hundred Spaniards and eight hundred natives of Mexico agreed to go. Soldiers, explorers, adventurers, colonists, dreamers — they had everything. There were three Spanish and one Portuguese women with their children, many Indian women with their families, five Portuguese men, two Italians, a Frenchman, a German, and a Scot by the name of Thomas Blake. In addition there were six Franciscan friars, also two of their young students, an Indian and a Negro, who acted as interpreters. There was a walking pantry of cattle, sheep, and hogs, and fifteen hundred horses and mules.

Horses had been gone from the American prairies for nearly

ten thousand years. They came back with Coronado, moving into the mainstream of our history to stay for centuries. This was Pueblo Indian country, and Pueblo Indians were farmers who did not even suspect that horses and farms belong together. But when the time came that the Pueblo Indians revolted against the Spaniards (then one hundred fifty years in the future), other Indians, who knew exactly what horses were for, came in and stole the horses that — like the gift of fire so long before — would revolutionize their way of life. Apaches and Comanches took to horses with great delight. When the long train of covered wagons started across the prairies in later years, the whole prairie country was full of mounted Indians — courtesy of Coronado.

The expedition left from the west coast of Mexico in February of 1540. It must have been a colorful sight to those who watched them go off into the unknown, with banners waving, trumpets blowing, and everyone cheering. Many of the Spaniards were young and penniless. They wore their brightest clothes and put up a brave front, telling everyone that they would make their fortunes in the new land and come home covered with glory, with pockets full of gold. Some of the soldiers had old-fashioned coats of mail, some had iron helmets or bits of European battle dress, and some had already discovered buckskin jackets. Coronado, a young man of thirty, was dressed in gilded armor and a plumed helmet. Some carried swords; some, crossbows, pikes or spears; others had Indian arms; and a very few had guns. Half a dozen cannons brought up the rear of the procession.

Their route lay along the coastal lowlands, following the Indian trails up through Sinaloa and Sonora; there are still nearly a thousand miles there where no wheel track marks the way. In some places the jungle was so dense that they had to hack out a path for the horses. In one place the ground muttered and smoked with volcanic pools like those at Yellowstone; one Spaniard remarked that there was a very thin floor over hell in this region. How they got the herds of cattle and pigs past this, history does not tell us.

Coronado deserves better than history has given him. He was, for one thing, kind to his Indians, at a time and place where others were not. He angered the young Spanish noblemen by making them handle their own baggage instead of expecting an Indian to do it. "He treats them just as if they were people!" they grumbled. Also, he had planned ahead for food and supplies to be sent by ship up the Gulf of California; this was very farsighted thinking in a day when a geographer could write: "New Mexico extends from the north to the strait located between Nombre de Dios and Panama, turning west within sight of the continent of China, with a narrow strait of ocean . . . which the geographers . . . locate on the maps by guesswork, for we do not know the true facts."

Another bit of geographical guesswork tells us that "the land between China and Norway is very far up." Neither of these opinions, nor the fancy maps with monsters drawn around the edges, would be much help to a leader trying to get so many people and animals across the desert alive.

The first Indian people they met were at the Zuñi pueblo of Hawikuh, which Fray Marcos had thought was one of the seven golden cities. As the hungry Spaniards approached the mesa where the pueblo was, they could see smoke signals going up from the tops of nearby mesas. They were much impressed with the Indian signal system and they soon had a chance to sample the Indian way of fighting, for the Zuñis had no intentions of letting the strangers into their city. Never having seen horses before, they thought that the horse and rider were one terrible creature, a fighting monster much stronger than any man. Also, the iron-headed men had thunder sticks that threw death at the Indians.

Even with this advantage, the Spaniards had a hard time conquering Hawikuh. Coronado himself was wounded in the fight, and to his credit it must be said that he made no attempt to punish the Indians. He asked only for food and housing until he was well enough to travel.

Once on the road again, they came to Acoma, which looked down at them from the top of a rock they were not at all anxious to climb. The horses' hoofs had been cut by the bad walking on the desert, which in that area was volcanic rock like broken glass. Everybody was hungry again, but the leaders of the expedition agreed that the city of Acoma was the strongest fortification they had ever seen, and they left it strictly alone except to buy some food. They moved on into the valley of the great river which the Mexicans called "Great Wild River of the North," which we call the Rio Grande.

The Rio Grande Indians were friendly, and the expedition settled down for the winter in a pueblo called Kuaua near where the little pueblo of Bernalillo now stands. Here, for its first real trial, were two very different peoples who must work out their problems together. America is proud now of its "melting pot" of nations, but the melting itself has never been easy. Language was only one of the barriers to understanding one another. We know some of the history of Europe and the influences that made the Spanish what they were. We know little or nothing of the great Indian civilizations that came and went over the centuries, shaping the Indians in quite a different pattern than the Europeans. Certainly today, meeting the friendly people of the golden Southwest, we can admire the wonderful people who, after four hundred years, have grown out of the union of two very different peoples.

Two such different points of view as the Spanish and the Indian had are hard to imagine. Even in little things they were miles apart. Spanish soldiers, like all European soldiers of the time, fought their battles in orderly ranks, marching in formation like a drill team. It had never crossed their minds that there was any other way to do it. The Indians, on the other hand, invented what we today call "guerrilla warfare," and success, to them, meant staying invisible. It seems never to have occurred to the Spaniards that they, in their bright uniforms, made wonderful targets; they did not even see the Indians who attacked them.

Which Indian, looking down from some dry mesa top on the brightly dressed Spaniards, first thought about the beautiful red pants, no one will ever know. But some smart Indian took a second look at the red wool pants that made part of the Spanish uniform, and the wheels started turning in his head. Probably he looted a pair of these pants from the fallen soldiers, and took them home to his wife who, delighted with the beautiful red coloring, happily raveled out the wool thread to use in her weaving. One could guess that every Indian wife sent her warrior off to battle with instructions to bring back a pair of the beautiful red pants for mama's weaving. Today, if you buy an Indian blanket that is very old — and very expensive — you will see in it the threads of that beautiful wool which was once, not very wisely, a part of a Spanish uniform.

The main problem in red man and white living together was, of course, gold. Gold had brought the Spanish — and a great many other white Europeans — across a stormy ocean in miserable and uncomfortable ships, with all the horrors of bad food, sickness, mutiny, and shipwrecks to make it worse. The hope of getting rich had made bearable the miserable journey from Mexico. Starvation and thirst and Indian arrows could not stop these men, if only there was the hope of gold at the end of the road. Only today are we beginning to understand that gold was worthless to these Indians. They simply had no use for it, beyond making a few trifles of jewelry to wear; the Incas and the Aztecs, far to the south, had made beautiful use of the metal, but Indians north of Mexico did not. They had never heard of money, and as far as jewelry was concerned, they preferred shells, any day.

Coronado's men were told to look especially for gold: gold mines, gold made into dishes and ornaments, gold in a public treasure house like Montezuma's. They talked to the Indians in sign language about the gold they must have. Their talk sparked no answers. They talked about "treasures," the sort of thing that people hid away and guarded. It does seem to us that if they had looked around them, they would have seen for themselves that Indian "treasures" were not anything they wanted — feathers, bones, shells, and the like. Roving tribes kept nothing that could not be carried with them when they moved. Even the Pueblo Indians' idea of riches was a fine necklace of blue shells from the Gulf of Mexico, with bear claws or sharks' teeth for a little trimming, or some bright feathers from Mexico to wear on special days. In fact, Mexican Indians who traveled with Coronado carried live parrots which they planned to trade for turquoises in the Rio Grande country. But the Spaniards did not understand this; they were sure that any human being would want to own all the gold he could get.

During this first winter in New Mexico many of Coronado's men went out searching for mines. They needed crude sulphur to make gunpowder, and they hoped to find the gold that — surely — the Indians had hidden away. It is hard to explain this in sign language to someone who has no taste for gold and has never seen a gun before, but they tried. And one group of Indians finally agreed that, yes, they had a treasure: in a hole in the rocks, in the mountains. They would show it to the Spaniards if they would promise not to tell any other Indians about it. The soldiers went with them cheerfully through cactus thorns, over great rocks and waterless wastes and rough, dangerous country. It took a long time to get there, but they were busy spending the gold they were going to find and went on very gladly. Finally, the Indians told them that they were coming near the hiding place, and made them promise again that they would never tell any other Indians. The Spaniards swore they would never tell *anybody* where it was, and they could hardly contain their excitement when the Indians led them to a hidden cave mouth and started down a tunnel.

The leader pointed out to them that here on this wall was where you get the good dark red for wartime: you mix it with a little bear grease just before you put it on your face. If you were getting ready for the winter dance where you painted your whole face black, this was a very good black. There in the ceiling, high up, was a streak of good yellow. This colored earth was rare and valuable. The tribe had guarded their secret since the time of their grandfathers, and they did not want any other tribe in on it. But, they urged their paleface friends politely, "You are our friends. Help yourself to the face paint."

The soldiers were luckier in finding the crude sulphur that Coronado wanted, and with it he made the first gunpowder in the New World. When he tried it out, the Indians fell on their faces and howled because they thought that the end of the world had come. The same reaction came from most of the world when — almost exactly four hundred years later — the United States tried out the first atomic bomb at the White Sands military proving ground, forty miles, as the crow flies, from Coronado's camp.

Moving on, with the arrival of spring, Coronado's party came to the edge of the buffalo country and the powerful pueblo of Pecos. (How the Spanish got "Pecos" out of *Cicuiq* is hard to say.) This pueblo was built on a rock that would be easy to defend and hard to attack. Rumor had it that Pecos had five hundred warriors. Coronado kept his conversations with the Pecos people on peaceful subjects.

It was at Pecos that Coronado met the man they all called "the Turk," the wheeler-dealer who would move this tired and hungry band of Spaniards clear to Kansas in search of the seven golden cities. The Turk was a born salesman, and he convinced the Spaniards that the wide gold bracelet worn by one of the local Indians was from Quivira, which was out *thataway* and he could show them. And yes, of course, he knew about the seven golden cities: they were *thataway*, too. By now, all the Indians in New Mexico knew that the Spaniards were slightly crazy on the subject of golden cities.

It is always possible that the Pecos Indians paid the Turk to lead the strangers out onto the endless plains and, as the saying goes, get lost. But the Turk had a scheme of his own. He was a slave, from the country of the Wichita Indians, and he wanted to go home. The whole tired, groaning mass of men and beasts started moving again, over the plains to find Quivira.

Not far out of Pecos they met the buffalo, and it cheered them up immensely. Had not Marco Polo talked about cows with bumps on their backs? These must be Marco Polo's cows, and they must be just coming into India — or China. While ordinary folk put in their time planning what they would do with all that wealth, the hunters put in a good supply of buffalo meat. The young men of the group tried catching and riding the strange beasts, which proved very hard to do. The buffalo might look clumsy, but they could turn on nothing and be gone before you knew it. They would not drive and they would not be ridden, and Coronado finally had to forbid the sport because so many young men were hurt, and he would need every soldier he had if there were trouble at Quivira.

Just where in Kansas, or Nebraska, Coronado finally decided that the Turk was lying about the golden cities, we do not know. But somewhere in that vast, flat country he turned back and returned to the Rio Grande.

His men had seen a remarkable amount of country, but no cities of gold or anything else. One of his exploring groups came upon the great gash in the earth that we call the Grand Canyon, and for several days tried to climb down to the river to cross it. Someone wrote that "rocks that from the top look to be only the size of a man, turned out to be bigger than the Seville cathedral." The suppy ship he had sent up the Gulf of California had never reached him. His people were hungry and discouraged. Coronado gave the word: they were going back to Mexico.

The Franciscans decided to stay and work with the Indians. A few families and some of the single men stayed, too; but the soldiers and the rest of the party turned their faces to the south, which was very far away.

The sheep had it the worst. Cows and hogs had long since been eaten up, but a poor, tattered band of sheep came straggling back from Kansas and were only spared another thousand-mile hike when Coronado decided to leave them as a mission flock at Pecos where Fray Luis planned to begin his work. This small flock of far-traveled sheep was the beginning of the New Mexico wool industry.

Fray Juan went to the old pueblo of Isleta to begin his mission, and after a few months he went to the Wichitas on the plains of Kansas. Within a year, both of the Franciscans had been killed by the Indians.

Pecos pueblo (Cicuiq) had been a thriving little city for probably five hundred years before the Spaniards came. It was a prosperous trade center between the plains tribes and the farmers of the river. The Indians raised the usual corn, beans, and squash, and traded for buffalo and other luxuries. When the Franciscans came, they seemingly would not stay dead. Fray Luis rests under a stone cross near the great church which the Indians built under direction of the Franciscans. If you killed one Franciscan, there would come another in his dusty gray robes, plodding up the trail from the south, to replace him. The friars brought wheat, rye, oats, peaches, and grapevines, and taught the Indians how to care for sheep and chickens, and how to build the outdoor beehive-shaped ovens that the Moors brought to Spain in the seventh century.

The pueblo is gone now. A hundred years ago, all the surviving members of the tribe moved to Jemez pueblo, whose people are related to the Pecos. You can trace the outlines of the great pueblo and the bones of two churches, one on top of the other, which are being dug out so that visitors can see them and scientists can study them. Each year on the fiesta day of the pueblo, the Jemez people come and give a buffalo dance in memory of Pecos. There are still legends about Pecos, many having to do with buried treasure, which is supposed to be in a cave guarded by a giant rattlesnake. Nobody ever seems to have found it, but you still hear about it.

Isleta, where Fray Juan began his mission among the Indians, has its own legends. Fray Juan, when leaving Kansas with Coronado, promised the Wichitas that he would come back to them as soon as he could. He did go back, and they killed him. Some time later, the Isleta Indians, having a couple of years of bad weather and scant harvest, decided they would go and bring the Franciscan home. They carved a coffin out of the trunk of a cottonwood tree, with a curved lid wired on. They carried it to Kansas, put the Franciscan in it, and carried it back to Isleta where they buried him under the floor of the church.

Unfortunately, he would not stay there. The coffin kept coming up, every twenty or twenty-five years, and breaking up through the packed dirt floor of the church. You will find all kinds of wild stories about the times the coffin came up, and they simply cannot all be true. But there are written records going back to 1790, kept in a little leaden box in the coffin. Some people say it is "ground water" springs — *Isleta* means "little island" — that brings the coffin up. Three other Franciscans and sixty-seven Indians buried under the floor do not come up. But he has, several times in recent history; a newspaper took pictures of him in 1960. The Wichitas say that he is simply trying to get back to Kansas.

The Isleta Indians say that he comes up to walk around the pueblo now and then, to see that the white man is not hurting the Indians. Today there is a polished wood floor in the church. No one knows the answer to the puzzle, but it makes a fine ghost story in these practical times.

The reward of $10,000 offered for finding Quivira has never been collected. We have a national park monument at the little pueblo of Quivira east of Albuquerque, and it is a fascinating place to visit but could hardly have been what Coronado was seeking. It is one of a group of Indian pueblos — Abó, Tenabó, Quarai, Chililí, Manzano, Tabira, and Quivira — that have been called "the cities that died of fear," because they were abandoned by the people who lived there. We do not know why, nor even exactly when, but they left their rooms as if they expected to go on living there — and never came back. With this sort of spooky background it is not surprising to find that they are full of legends, mostly of buried treasure.

Chililí, of which today there is nothing but a stone wall and a number of diggings, is the place where the legend of the Gypsy lives. He came into town, driving a wagon with six white horses, it is said, sometime early in the nineteenth century. He had an old map showing the location of the treasure, and he asked the people who still lived around the neighborhood to go in partnership with him to dig it up. They did the work and he went around encouraging them. The day came when they discovered a huge old chest in the ground, but it kept falling to pieces when they tried to lift it out. The Gypsy sent someone to Albuquerque to buy a good solid wooden box, and in the meantime gave a great party with all his helpers, to celebrate their all getting rich. When they had slept off the party, they woke to the fact that Gypsy, treasure, and six white horses had long since departed, leaving them with nothing but sore muscles and a hole in the ground. You must be careful driving along those roads at night, because the team of white horses may loom suddenly out of the night, with the Gypsy standing in the wagon, whipping the horses; at least, that's what they say.

Even longer-lived are the tales about the lost mines that are supposed to lie waiting for some lucky finder in the mountains of New Mexico and Arizona. Then there is the "Mine With the Iron Door," which you can locate by standing just at sunset on the steps of the mission on the fiesta of San Miguel (September 29) and watching just where the sun goes down. *Which* mission will depend more or less on who is telling about it. The "Lost Padre Mine" is supposed to alert searchers by the little blue flames that flicker along the ground at the entrance. The "Naranja" (Spanish for "orange"), where the bells ring far away, is supposed to be an old mission cut off from the rest of the world by a fall of rock which closed a passage through the mountains, leaving only room for a deep, rocky river. Once in a while, even today (they say) oranges from the mission grove come floating down the river, though neither the mine nor the mission has been in operation for two hundred years. Both these places have legends of an Indian coming into town once a year with a bag of gold which he gathered "where the white man's money grows," but no one was ever able to follow him back there.

The most popular of the lot is the "Lost Dutchman Mine." People here and now have given up good jobs to go searching in the Superstition Mountains for this long-lost source of legends. This is the really bloodcurdling spot in our gold mine literature, as people who hunt for the "Lost Dutchman" are supposed to end up with their heads cut off. Who cuts them off is not at all clear, but there are more spooky stories than you can imagine, telling about someone who knows someone whose head was cut off; no one ever really seems to know any of the victims.

The original mine grant was supposed to have been given to Don Miguel Peralta of Mexico by the king of Spain, in 1748. He and his family worked the mine and drew out a huge fortune before the land became United States territory. His grandson is supposed to have brought up trade goods, which he sold to the Anglos; then he would load the mule train with gold and return to Mexico. The system worked fine until the Apaches discovered that the Mexicans had mules. They killed all but a couple of the Mexicans, dumped the gold down a crack in the mountain, and ate all the mules. At about this time, the Peraltas sold the mining rights to two German prospectors; Americans of the time called all Germans "Dutchmen" because Americans were never very strong on pronouncing foreign-language words, and "Deutsch" (German) was just plain "Dutch" to them. This is how a Spanish mine came to be called for the two "Dutchmen." After a short time, both the men were found murdered. So the mine became the "Lost Dutchman."

Nobody had much luck with the mine; some say seven people (others claim seventeen) had their heads cut off when trying to find it. As of now, the legends are so badly mixed with those of the Adams mine, which also had two partners who ended up headless, that it is hard to tell which belongs to which.

In the 1860s an enterprising man consulted a lawyer and showed him a fascinating old paper that indicated that he was the rightful heir of the Peralta mine. The property at that time would have been worth some one hundred million dollars. The document looked very real, but someone with a suspicious mind had it examined, and it turned out to have a watermark on the paper from Appleton, Wisconsin. The hopeful heir turned out to be a horsecar conductor from St. Louis.

Hundreds of books have been written about the lost mines and buried treasures of the Southwest. On a law of averages, *some* of the stories must be true. They do at least tell us, quite clearly, that very few people ever find gold, though a great many are looking for it.

Coronado's historian said it very nicely in his records: "Even though they did not find the gold for which they sought, they found a place to look for it."

And it is a lovely place to look! A place where you will find many other things, much more lasting than gold.

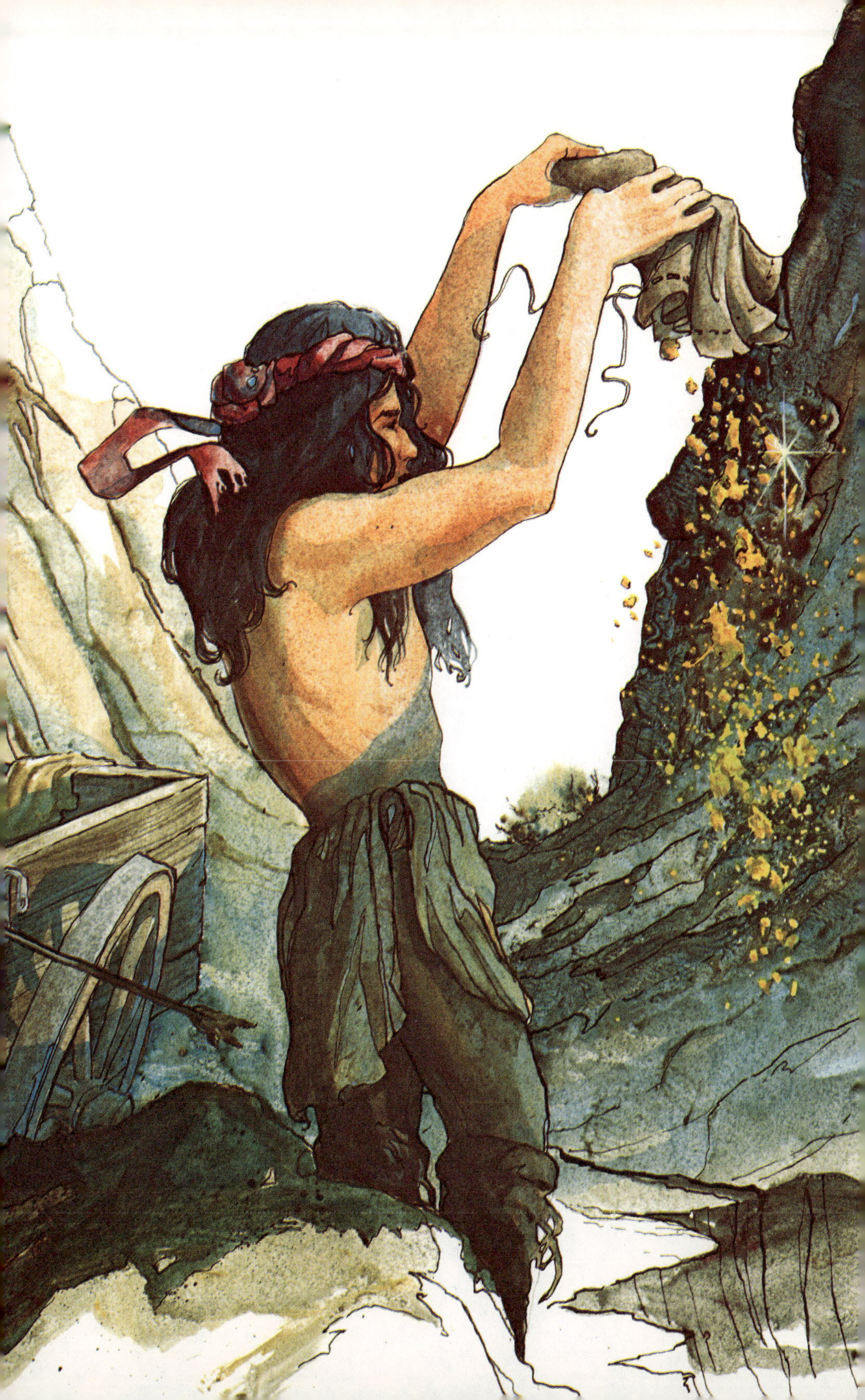

Does the Lost Dutchman Mine
really exist somewhere in
the Superstition Mountains?

Chapter 14
Time Capsule

At first there was only the sea.

— *From a Haida Indian song*

December: Moon when the gray whale appears. March: Moon of the finback whale. May: Moon of the salmonberry. November: Moon of winds and screaming birds.

— *From a Makah Indian calendar*

If you will study a globe of the world — and for this, it must be a globe, not a flat map — you will see that the spot farthest west in the United States, south of Alaska, is a tiny bump on the Olympic Peninsula of Washington State. It is too small to have a name on a globe, and even on quite a large highway or geographic map the only name you will see is Lake Ozette. On this spot, thrust out into the Pacific on their small peninsula, the ancestors of the Makah Indians lived. We would not know anything at all about this village if it had not been for a great tragedy.

One fine summer night more than three hundred years ago, the side of the sea cliff that towered over the village gave way and went into a rumbling slide. Loosened by heavy spring rains and perhaps started by a small earthquake, a great mass of mud broke loose and rolled down, gaining speed as it went, and the sounds of the sea hid its noise from the sleeping people. The avalanche of thick mud swept down over the village and buried it deep, just as the city of Pompeii was buried by the eruption of Mount Vesuvius long ago. And, like Pompeii, the village was still in one piece when found. It was like a time capsule that had been buried, centuries ago, so that we could learn about their times.

We do not even know the name of the village, for all traces of the vanished people had faded from the memories of living Indians. A few years ago, when part of the shore was washed out in a big storm, someone found the corners of buildings and other man-made things, and called in the archeology department from the state college to see it. For the men who are digging the village out of the mud, bit by tiny bit, it is the greatest treasure ever found in this part of the world. When it is all cleared out and set up as an exhibit, it will be a window on a world that we know very little about, and it will be unique in the whole country.

The site is called "Ozette" after the nearby lake. There is not even a road in to the place, only a four-mile hiking trail, and a helicopter to bring in supplies. The college has built a dormitory there for the teachers and students who are learning the fine art of digging up our yesterdays, and they cheerfully live under very rough conditions and hike the long trail in, usually in the rain. There is the ocean, of course; the Makahs never traveled any other way, but most white people are not nearly as handy with a canoe as the Indians are on this wet and windy coast.

A small number of Makah Indians still live nearby. Two centuries ago the tribe numbered around five thousand and they were one of the most powerful tribes in the Pacific Northwest, related to the Nootkas from Canada. Now, like so many Indian tribes, they have dwindled down to a few hundred. The discovery of the buried village gave a new spirit to the modern Makahs, who are watching the dig with great interest, as anxious to learn about their ancestors as we are. Some of the younger members of the tribe are being trained so that they will be the experts who can explain this unique museum to visitors.

This was a whaling village, in existence hundreds of years

before the trim ships from Nantucket and New Bedford sailed around Cape Horn and up the long Pacific coast after whales. Anyone who will paddle out thirty miles into the stormy Pacific to do battle with the biggest creatures in the world certainly rates our attention. One wallop of that powerful tail could cut the canoe in two, and the man who threw the harpoon did not have a long-range harpoon gun as we have now; he had only his strong arms, and he had to be all but standing on the whale to be sure of a hit.

The gray whale which, the Indians noted in their calendar, passes by their village in December, makes the longest yearly trip of any mammal on earth, a migration that takes eight months and adds up to ten thousand miles. The path in the sea which they always follow comes closest to land just here, where the little peninsula juts out into the ocean. The village site must have been chosen for just this reason, for it could save several miles of heavy paddling to be that much nearer the whale's path. When the long-ranging grays came through in December, and the big finbacks in March, the Indians arranged to be right on the spot to catch their big strong brother of the sea.

The days are long gone now when the eight-man canoes were launched to the sound of singing and went far out into the mist, out of sight, while women and children and old hunters watched from the tops of the rocky little islands that fall away from the cliffs. This was a time of both prayer and worry, for everything must be done properly or the great ones would not come at the call of the master hunter. Sometimes, if the weather was bad, or the chanting was not exactly right, the big ones would swing away from the coast and pass far out to sea. How many brave men faced death in this contest with the strong one of the sea? It was true: this was the way to glory for hunters who were lucky enough to kill their whale. But many canoes never came back to the families who watched the misty seas waiting for them to return. They were strong men who lived in this village, strong people who were brave and reliable.

Each time a new tool or weapon is found in the mud pack, we find out a little more about the people who used it. Most of these things would crumble away to dust as soon as the air hit them, but archeologists have found ways of treating them with chemicals that will keep them from falling apart. The tools and other finds are washed free of the mud with a water hose, which is less apt to damage old fibers and materials. This is hard work for the young archeologists, but there is always the possibility of turning up something really exciting.

At one point a wooden club was found in the mud. The top of the club is a carved head, which looks very much like the stone heads that stand around the cliffs of Easter Island. If you will look again at the globe of the world, you can see that Easter Island — a tiny dot in the Pacific Ocean thousands of miles away — is just about the only bit of land between Ozette and the continent of Antarctica. Do you suppose that, long ago, far back before the memory of man, someone made that long, long journey? Ozette may someday tell us.

Another strange thing that was found at the Ozette site is a whale's tail carved out of red cedar and decorated with sea otter teeth. It must have been part of the religious preparation for the whale hunt. Perhaps it was a plea to the spirit of the great one, asking him not to lash at their canoe with that terrible tail.

Harpoon points are plentiful and they are well made and sharp. It must have taken a powerful arm to thrust a harpoon through the whale's rubbery wet suit and the thick layers of fat, to wound him fatally. Parts of whale skeletons and the barnacles that always seemed to grow on the gray whale's hide have been found in the dig, and they give proof that the men succeeded sometimes.

Whalers were very special people: those who actually hunted the big one made a long preparation for their hunt. Certain prayers must always be said or sung, and each man must free himself of any bad habits or it might spoil the whole hunt. Indians had very strong feelings for what we now call conservation. They did not believe in killing except for food, and they felt that if any village was greedy and wasteful in killing, they would suffer hunger later for their sins. Before the hunt, songs were sung to invite the great one to come to their harpoon. A good whaling master was said to understand the language of whales and be able to talk to them. It was he who apologized to the whale for having to kill him.

The Makahs were sea people, like all the Indians of this watery country. They were not headhunters like the Haidas from the Queen Charlotte Islands, off British Columbia; but they were a strong and warlike people who were held in awe by tribes around them who lived a quieter life-style.

This North Pacific coast is a heavily forested land, even yet, and in the tribal days before the white man came, the forest and the sea made up their world. The big red cedar trees gave them logs for their canoes, which would be hollowed out with primitive tools and much prayer. The Indians were a polite people, no matter what history says about them, and they had a great reverence for life of any kind. They apologized to a big cedar tree when they went to cut it down, reminding its spirit that they were going to change the tree into a form where it would not have to stand still any more, moved only by the wind; they would make it into a great canoe that would go out on the water to challenge the great gray brothers of the sea. They even sang a song to the cedar when they took bark or roots to use for baskets, clothing, or mats. The cedar song addresses the tree as "fire-giver, life-giver." Baskets now being dug out of the mud at Ozette have survived to prove that the Indian was wise in trusting his friend, the cedar. Even cooking boxes were made of cedar planks and sewed together.

There were many other trees in this dense forest: the yew tree gave tough wood, used for wedges to split logs; the alder, strong and firm, was used for tools. Spruce, hemlock, and fir were used to build their houses and to burn in their fires. Even crab apple, the bad-tempered tree of their myths, was good for many things. We are finding out these things and many more as the dig gets deeper and the treasures are examined.

There were many advantages to the village in this location, aside from being close to the whale's path. In July, when the salmonberries gleamed orange in the leafy woods, the waters would be full of salmon; and at different times four other kinds of salmon filled the waters with flashing silver, and the Indians ate well. The Pacific flyway, by which most of the western birds migrated, went right overhead; so twice a year great flocks of geese, ducks, and other game birds came. The woods were full of berries in the summer, and there were always deer and bear to hunt. There was never any need of anyone going hungry on this bountiful coast. Because of this, the Makahs never farmed and never domesticated animals.

Very early in their history, the Makahs added beachcombing to their life-style. That "great black river in the sea," which we call the Japan Current must have had "On to Oregon" as its motto, like the covered wagons of a later day; absolutely everything that would float turned up, sooner or later, on the shores of the Oregon country. Deep in the mud at Ozette, puzzled scientists keep finding blades and spearpoints of metal. Because of the way the metal was made, it cannot be traced to early trading ships, and it is thought that the metal came, a long time ago, from Japan, which had processed steel by the year 800. It is at least possible that a Japanese ship, storm-battered and perhaps crewed by dead men, was swept up on the beach a thousand years ago, and stripped of its metal by some smart Makah who saw possibilities in it. The village, as far as we know, must have been there at least twelve hundred years.

Quite a few known, and a great many unknown, ships were wrecked on the rocks of this lonely coast over the last thousand years. One was a Spanish merchant ship that drifted in around 1725. Watchful Makah sentinels saw it driven in by the storm, making no fight against wind and weather. They judged that the crew was probably dead, or someone would be trying to save the ship. In the night they could hear it breaking up on the rocks, but there was no sound of human voices.

One cannot be too careful about ghosts, so they kept their distance. A strange discovery was made by a woman of the tribe who had gone down to the beach to gather driftwood for her breakfast fire. She was completely puzzled by what she saw. Two Spanish sailors had managed to get in from the shipwreck, and they were trying to get warm at a beach fire. They were heavily bearded after months at sea; the woman could not understand this, as Indian men did not have any beards at all. She ran back to the camp and reported to the chief that she did not know whether they were men or bears; they wore clothes, but they were very furry. And whatever they were doing with the fire, they were making something white that jumped. Robed in his best and carrying his staff of office, the chief and his advisers approached the visitors. "They are not bears," he pronounced, once and for all. What they were doing, he could not tell either. The answer? They were popping corn, that being the only food they could reach in the wrecked ship!

The Makah chief promptly took them prisoners. One of the men proved to be the ship's blacksmith. He led the Indians to the wreck where they salvaged all the useful pieces of iron and other metal, which he showed them how to make into tools. A hundred years after this wreck, a Makah Indian whose last name was Soto proudly related, to any white man he could find, that his great-great-grandfather was one of those washed-up-by-the-sea people who came from another world.

Quite a few wrecks in later years were trading ships, and some had cargoes of trinkets meant for trade with the Alaska natives in exchange for furs. The Makahs went joyfully into the salvage business and traded with all the nearby tribes, using the white man's trade goods.

In 1808 the tragedy of the *San Nicolas* was played out on their shore. The *San Nicolas* was an American ship that had just been sold to the Russians, who were hoping to move south from Alaska and set up farming colonies. The captain was one Nicolai Bulagin, and he had with him (unknown to the ship's owners) his bride of a few weeks, Ana Petrovna, who was eighteen years old. They had a beautiful voyage down from Alaska, but off the Strait of Juan de Fuca they ran into a hurricane. It was a new ship and well manned, but three days of hurricane battering all but shook it apart, and it piled up on the rocks near Cape Flattery. The survivors had barely got themselves to land when they were surrounded by Indians.

The Makahs took them to one of their villages and there, after feeding them and letting them have a night's sleep, they took away Ana Petrovna and the seven Aleut women who had survived, and brought them to another village. They then offered to trade with the Russians: "You give us your guns and we will give you these women we have imprisoned." Nicolai, frantic to get Ana back, tried to convince the other Russians to do this. They refused to give up their guns, so the Indians refused to give up the women.

The Russians camped for one miserable winter on the Hoh River; no one was around to tell them that this was the wettest spot in western America, a place that is known now throughout the world as the "Rain Forest," where trees hang heavy with wet green mosses and the underbrush is like an underwater garden. When spring came, they made another attempt to rescue the women, but by now it was plain that Ana preferred living with the Indians; she did not want to go back to her own people. The Indians took all the Russians prisoners and made slaves of them. Nicolai died in a village on the seacoast, and Ana — who had been traded off to some other Indians — died in the forest, trying to escape. Just one Russian survived, to be ransomed by the Boston ship *Lydia*, to tell their story to the world.

If we knew more about these Indians who were mighty whale hunters long ago, some of our own scientific studies of today might be made easier. For instance, we are just getting around to the study of whales as creatures, and not merely as a commercial crop. There is a branch of marine biology called cetology (whale study) in which men are trying to translate the language of whales and dolphins into something understandable to earthbound creatures. Dolphins navigate by bouncing sound waves off objects, much as bats do in the air. (Sometimes a smart ship captain, lost in the fog in this northwest land of islands and dangerous rocks, can get his position by bouncing echoes off cliffs.)

We do not know what whales and dolphins talk about — unlike the old whale masters of Ozette, we do not understand their language — but we do know that they can send messages over great distances at sea. Dolphins can make more than thirty different sounds. This may surprise us, but it would be no surprise to a Makah whaler, who knew that his great brother of the seas is very smart, and also very sensitive to man's remarks about him. It was considered very unlucky to criticize the mighty ones of the deep. Who wants anything that size mad at him?

Whales are not fish, a thing that not all people realize; they are warm-blooded and they breathe air. Both the gray whale and the big finback, which ruled the Makah world, are baleen whales; that is, they have no teeth, but a sort of bony strainer called "baleen" through which tons of small sea life are taken in as food. The killer whale, which lives all year in these waters, has a fine set of teeth; he does not hesitate to attack a whale much bigger than himself. This is perhaps the reason that the whale one sees in so many carvings among the Makah and other canoe Indians is a killer whale. Perhaps they felt he was a good patron for hunters who were going out to do battle with the mighty ones. They never hunted the killer whales.

The dig at Ozette has brought up more than forty-five thousand pieces of what are called artifacts — examples of things that were used, long ago, for many different purposes. These include hundreds of baskets, textiles, ropes, net made from nettle fiber, and other household and hunting gear. The dampness has ruined some of it, but there is enough left to give us a clear picture of a long-gone people. With looms copied from those found in the houses, students have learned to weave cloth as it was done by the Makah women before Columbus set foot on our shores. Other students studied the reeds and roots that were used in basketmaking, and learned to make them the same way. Patterns were woven into the mats and baskets to make them beautiful as well as useful. Others studied how blankets were made with cattail fluff and dog hair. When it is all free of the mud and set up for us to see, we may be very much surprised at how civilized these people were in the days before gadgets.

Give a white man a piece of land, and right away he wants to change it. He will cut down the trees and plant other trees somewhere else; he will dig ditches, dam creeks, and channel rivers to flow the other way. Beavers are trapped and killed, and without God's small engineers, there is nothing any more to control the water flow, so there are floods. Fires start from carelessness. Before very long, the beautiful land that Grandpa owned is not worth anything much, so people dump old wrecked automobiles on it and there goes America the beautiful. If the Indians could teach us to love the land as they did, they would do a great favor for us. Indians were the first real ecologists, and perhaps the whole work of Ozette, when it is finished for us to see, will be respect for the world, its oceans, and its creatures.

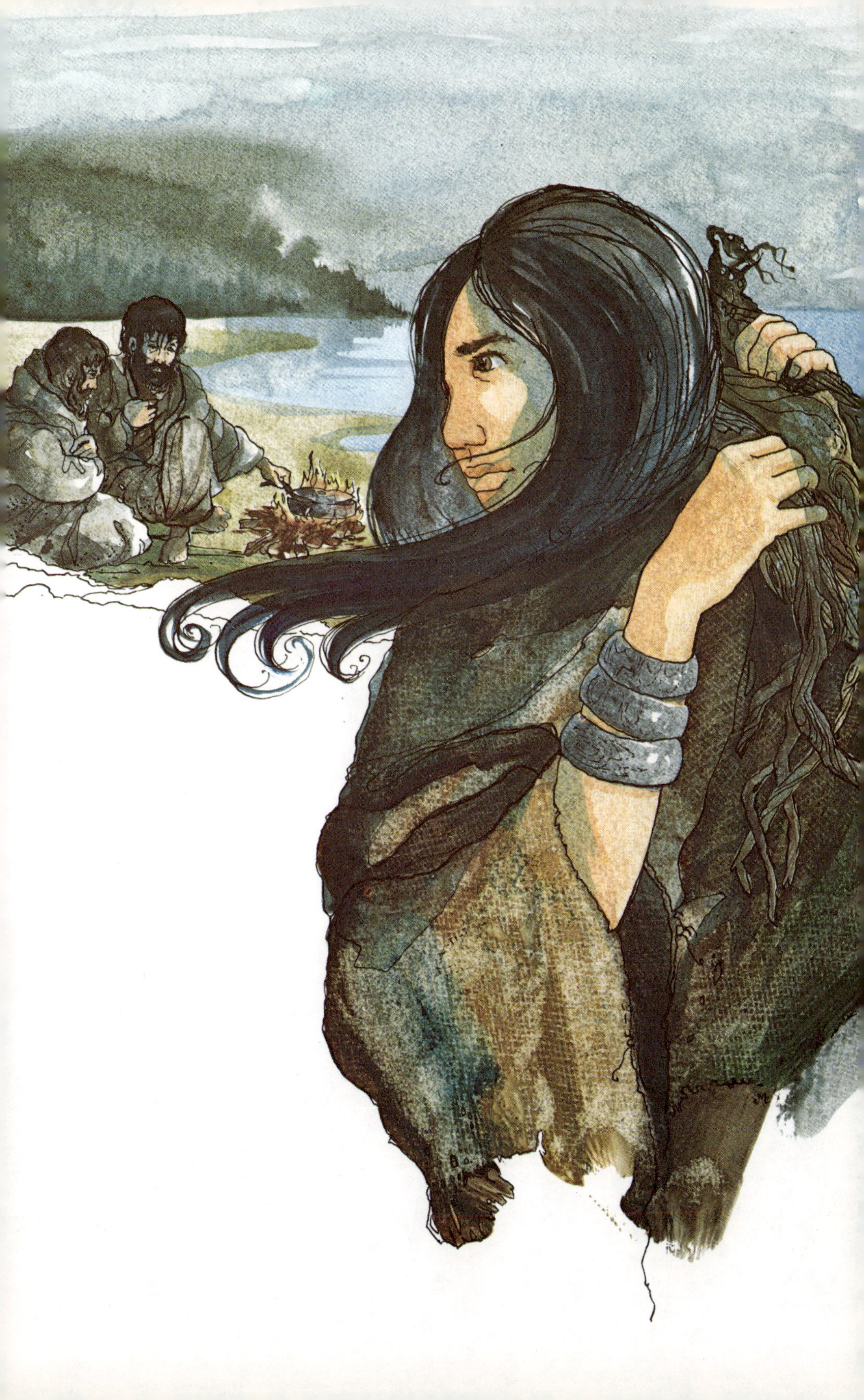

A Makah Indian comes upon two shipwrecked sailors huddled around a fire, preparing the only food they could salvage from their ill-fated vessel. Their meal? Popcorn.
(See pages 184-185.)

Chapter 15
The Great Land

Alaska has, to begin with, a coastline of 26,000 miles, more than twice as long as all the coastlines of the South 48. . . .

—*From a tourist folder*

Back a few yards from the beach the forests are as trackless as the sky, while the mountains, wrapped in their snow and ice and clouds, seem never before to have ever been looked at.

—*From John Muir's "Travels in Alaska"*

When Alaska became the forty-ninth state of the Union, it also became the largest and coldest piece of real estate that the American people had ever dealt with. More than a century ago, Lincoln's cabinet made fun of Secretary of State Seward for promoting the purchase of this huge "wasteland." The cabinet members variously called it Seward's Folly or Seward's Icebox and laughed at the idea that it would ever be worth the seven million dollars that Russia was asking for it. "What will we ever *use* it for?" asked the same people who could not see any sense in owning the Grand Canyon or the state of California. What a pity they could not have lived to see!

To members of the cozily warm states of the "Lower 48," Alaska was always the dead end, the frozen, lifeless North, a place without a reason for being. To the Russians it had always been the "Great Land," the land of promise. As for the cold, no place in Russia was much warmer.

One of the early expeditions searching for the Northwest Passage was sent by England to go north around Europe. Only one ship out of three survived the rugged voyage, and those expedition members who made it met the Russians at the White Sea. They saw the fortunes in furs that the Russians were handling and made plans to set up trade routes with them that would bypass the Hanseatic League (which had a monopoly on European trade), even if they had to go by way of Spitsbergen, which is the hard way to go anywhere. Soon the Dutch merchants got in on the business and tapped the land route to India which Russia had kept to herself for centuries.

Now that they had a steady market, Russians began moving toward Siberia, where the furs were. Pushed by the terrible tyranny of the government, they streamed into Siberia where, if it was colder, it was at least farther from the capital. They followed the old salt trails that were the only roads in this almost endless country. A man named Stroganoff set up a saltworks and became very rich shipping salt back to the capital. He used his money to finance fur trading, and crowds of penniless and persecuted people fled to join his business.

Whole families came along, whole villages — all moving like a glacier toward the new and untrapped fur lands north and east. Some people stopped along the way and carried on the business of shipping Mr. Stroganoff's salt — and furs, and walrus ivory — back over the endless miles to the rich people of the capital. When the czar discovered that Stroganoff had hit on a splendid money-making scheme, he sent troops of Cossacks — superb riders and ruthless fighters — to kill off any natives that might get in the way. They were also supposed to keep Mr. Stroganoff from getting too rich, but the czar could always be bought off with the magnificant furs they were getting.

At last the great moving wave of humanity reached the Arctic Sea, and here they had to fight. The powerful Chukchi natives who lived on this coast had no intention of handing over their land to the Russians or anyone else. They fought valiantly, but there were more Russians than natives, and the Russians had better weapons. The Chukchi went down to defeat, but even in this situation they showed business ability. There was this great land, they said, across the frozen sea. It could only be seen on very clear days. It was a land full of furs, of fossil ivory, of tall trees reaching to the sky. Like the Indians of the Southwest who told the Spaniards that the seven cities they were looking for were off in *that* direction, very, very far, the Chukchi sold the Russians on the idea of crossing the frozen sea and looking for their promised land. That far away, they reasoned, the czar could never find them.

The Russians had never built ships, and their first attempts were pitiful: open sailboats with planks held together by leather thongs. In terrible hardships, in the killing cold, without compass or any knowledge of navigation, they somehow got across the open water and landed near Kamchatka. They found natives who had warm houses and plenty to eat. Life was good here in this land of much game and great forests. Siberia, across the water, was bleak and bare; Alaska was the land of promise. It had taken the Russians two hundred years to reach it, and nobody knew how many hundreds had died on the way. It was some time before word drifted back to St. Petersburg (as Leningrad was then called) that in the great land to the east you could get fabulously rich and be far enough away from the czar that he could not take it away from you.

It was Czar Peter the Great who first began to tap the riches of Alaska. He first sent out an exploring party under Vitus Bering, a Dane. "Ivan Ivanovich Bering" was sent "to open commercial routes to Japan and America" and to make various exploratory trips "in the interests of science." He was chosen by the czar because "he had been to India, and knew all the approaches to that country." Second in command was a Russian, Alexei Chirikoff; the party also included an Englishman and a Dutchman. There were carpenters, surgeons, surveyors, astronomers, instrument makers, two artists (this was in the days before cameras), three German scientists, a chaplain, and six Russian Orthodox monks — in all, five hundred seventy men with their wives and children.

Crossing the American plains in a covered wagon was a luxury trip, compared to this journey into the frozen North. The expedition planned to be gone six years, but it took six years to cross Siberia alone. They arrived at the frozen seacoast in a state of great misery. Here they put up rough shelters and set about building two ships, the *St. Peter* and the *St. Paul.* Chirikoff in the *St. Paul* sighted Alaska in 1741, but the sailors sent to shore to claim the land were killed by the natives, who had already learned to hate Russians. Bering's ship, damaged, put in at one of the Kuril Islands, where he died during that first terrible winter. When spring came, the survivors built another ship out of the remains of the wrecked one and set sail for Russia. Most of the expedition had died, and the rest were in such fearful misery that we cannot even bear to read about it. But the hold of the ship carried one thousand sea otter skins and the pelts of two thousand blue foxes, and the world would never be the same again.

The cargo sold for 122,000 rubles, and the news spread across the country like a prairie fire. As soon as men could build ships, some of which were little better than rafts or clumsy boxes, a steady invasion of Russians, half-mad for furs, bore down on Alaskan waters. Many of the ships were wrecked in the treacherous seas, or simply fell apart and went down with all on board. But the few ships that returned made immense fortunes, and there seemed to be no end to the furs.

Cruelty to the natives and greed prevented the building of any permanent settlements. In forty years the Russians had stripped the land of furs; they found the islands where the fur seals breed and stripped them bare; they did the same to the Pribilof Islands. China and the Russian aristocrats were the market for these magnificent furs. But the fur trappers were rapidly wasting the wealth of their promised land and there seemed no way to stop it. It was true, the czar could not reach them in Alaska, either to help or to punish them. St. Petersburg was eight thousand terrible miles away over savage and nearly roadless country. It may as well have been on the moon.

The more responsible men among the merchants tried to set up some local government and decent rules for hunting. Nobody wanted any government. That was exactly why they had left St. Petersburg, and the fur trappers were rough men who saw only a chance to get rich. At last it became evident that the Russians would have to organize for self-defense; by this time, the natives were in a rage at the Russians, and were ready to kill them and burn their buildings at every chance. There was a constant state of war, and conditions finally got so bad that all anyone could think about was getting food on a day-to-day basis. In a country full of game, with waters full of fish, such a problem should never have come up, but the trappers wanted only to hunt for furs — and get rich, quick.

It was the thought of other countries cutting into the fur monopoly that finally brought action from the czar. Spain, Sweden, England, and that young American upstart of a city, Boston, sent ships to nose out the fur trade. Spain had sent ships north year after year, trying to find the Northwest Passage, and claimed Alaska by right of discovery. Ships from England and Boston, disagreeing on everything else, agreed to ignore the Spanish claim. There already existed an "East India Company" in England, Holland, France, Denmark, Scotland, Austria, and Sweden. The czar gave a charter to the Russian East India Company to cut a piece of this rich pie before it was too late. He sent an ambassador, Nicolai Rezanov, to see if he could straighten out the dreadful mess in Alaska. Russia bought two beautiful new ships from the British, who were much better at building ships than they were. Armed with all kinds of permissions — and gifts — the new Russian navy, with Rezanov in charge, was sent on a "round-the-world trip" to let folks know that Russia was a world power. Their main object was to break open the sealed kingdom of their next-door neighbor, Japan, who refused entry to any ships but the Dutch.

Rezanov had recently lost his wife and the trip promised to keep his mind off his sorrows, but Japan proved to be too tough a nut to crack. The Russians were kept in jail for five months and their gifts were rudely refused. Finally, humiliated and angry, the new navy sailed away, warned never to come back. At the Hawaiian Islands, King Kamehameha told them that Sitka had been burned to the ground and the Russians would starve — that is, if the natives did not kill them first. Rezanov set off for the doomed colony.

Even the most terrible descriptions could not do justice to what Rezanov found in the Russian colony in Alaska. If anyone ever suffered from bad management, or no management at all — they did. Everyone was poor, dirty, cold, and sick. The woods were full of firewood, but they were freezing. The place was filled with game, but they killed only for the furs — that was where the money was. Sitka had been rebuilt by the time Rezanov arrived, but the natives soon burned it down again. They told him that over a million seals had been killed the year before. The warehouses were jammed with rotting furs, not cured properly, so that they were completely worthless. Rezanov commanded that the killing of seals was to stop completely until they could work out a system that would keep them from destroying both the seals and themselves. This, of course, brought on howls of rage against Rezanov, this St. Petersburg dandy who had never killed a seal and now tried to tell *them* what to do.

The Russians were not fond of the trim little Boston ships that sailed boldly into waters that both they and the Spanish claimed. But they were very glad to see the *Juno*, under Captain John de Wolff, who had a fine new ship loaded with both food and trade goods (mostly English cloth and ironware). Rezanov bought the ship, cargo and all, and hired part of the crew while the rest of them scattered to hunt for furs. Food from the *Juno* kept them until the worst of the winter was over; but there was another winter coming, and Rezanov knew by this time that Alaska was not the place to raise vegetables for the starving and impractical colony. He took the ship, still full of trade goods, and sailed south to trade for food with the Spanish of California.

Sir Francis Drake had planted the English flag on one of the points of land north of the Golden Gate and claimed it as "New

England" in the name of Queen Elizabeth I. In 1791, England sent Captain George Vancouver to check on this land and see if it was still available. Vancouver, a polite and genial gentleman, stepped carefully around Spanish and Russian claims to the West Coast, but apparently did not worry very much about the Bostonians, who had won a little revolution against the mother country a few years ago and now were sailing around as if they owned all the seas. It was, of course, some little time since Drake had been in California — around two hundred years (in case you thought the Spanish were a little slow about things). Vancouver kindly gave Rezanov a copy of his charts and sailing directions. These they followed carefully down the long, stormy coast. They found the Columbia, which by now had been discovered and named several times, but could not get across the bar. After sailing back and forth for several days, they gave up and went on south.

The Spanish had first built their presidio (fort) in upper California because word had reached them that the Russians were about to invade them. This had been several years ago, and the presidio had grown into the beautiful, timeless, peaceful landscape, as if it had always been there. They were always getting letters from the king, reminding them not to be *too* polite to the Bostonians, and above all, not to buy any of their goods — instead, *buy Spanish*. There was said to be a ship belonging to General George Washington on the high seas, and it might do them harm. They had carefully questioned Captain Vancouver, who said no, his ship did not belong to General Washington. When the *Juno* appeared out of the mist and anchored, safely out of reach of the presidio guns, men were alerted, but pleasantly — company was coming! It was a lonely coast; you hardly ever saw anybody but the Indians, and it would be lovely to have a little news from outside. Young Luis Arguëllo, proudly acting in his father's name in the commandant's absence, set his sombrero on straight, buckled on his father's sword, and galloped down to meet the little boat that was coming ashore.

Rezanov, trained to the formality of diplomats, hated to do things in such a haphazard way. He sent the two men who knew the most languages — Davidow, a Russian, and Von Langsdorff, the German doctor. He watched the little boat with anxious eyes; what if Spain and Russia were at war? It had been so long since he had any word from Europe, Napoleon might be doing anything. Perhaps the Spanish would fire on his ship if they tried to come in closer, and there would be no food for Sitka. This was a rash, undiplomatic way to meet a foreign power, but every man on the ship was hungry and Sitka was soon to be starving. There simply was not time to be diplomatic.

While Rezanov watched the small boat through his binoculars, the men he had sent were trying to find a common language with these oddly dressed strangers. The young man in the bright-colored cape and the enormous hat was wearing the biggest silver spurs they had ever seen, and a very fancy sword. He looked to be about fourteen years old, but the guard around him looked alert enough. They tried French, and the young man answered in what was obviously Spanish. Von Langsdorff tried Portuguese and German; Davidow, Russian. Suddenly the Spanish party wheeled their horses and galloped off, returning almost immediately with a Franciscan friar in gray robes. Von Langsdorff tried Portuguese and German on him without success, and Davidow spoke up in French. Then the priest asked them in Latin, "Who are you and why do you come?" — and the doctor understood Latin. He and the priest took over the conversation, which ended with everyone shaking hands and smiling.

The Russians got back in the boat and started for the ship, and the horsemen rushed off toward the presidio. "They want to see my papers," said Rezanov to his officers. "I hope they don't fire on the ship. The Spanish are very formal," he told himself unhappily. "They must know this isn't the proper way to do things." As the boat drew near, he called out anxiously, "I suppose they demanded my papers right away?" and Von Langsdorff said no — they had only invited them all to breakfast.

Rezanov put on his dress uniform, which hung on him like a sack because it had been so long since they had had enough to eat. He was very formal and colorful in his uniform as he stepped from the small boat to greet the young Spaniard. Fortunately, he knew a few words of Spanish, and this pleased the boy greatly. It was explained to him that the commandant was away on business, and his eldest son was acting in his place, and loving every minute of it.

Rezanov was offended that nobody — nobody at all — asked to see his diplomatic papers. They only kept pouring him cups of Mexican chocolate. Rezanov was not the only member of the party who was upset. Concha, the fifteen-year-old sister of Don Luis, was furious with her brother. The first presentable man who had *ever* come to California, and here she was in her everyday dress, because her brother did not have the sense to tell her there would be company for breakfast!

Ambassador Rezanov, who had been having second thoughts about making a settlement on the Columbia, began to dream of somehow getting his hands on this lovely, lazy country where there was always sunshine and plenty to eat, and people took time for dances and fiestas and did not need to worry about tomorrow. When it became evident that Concha had fallen in love with him, the chances for Russian expansion began to look brighter. In spite of the strict Spanish rules against buying foreign goods, he sold his entire cargo of cloth, ribbons, and tools; no laws on earth could stop the women from buying when they found there was something to buy. The weeks went by so pleasantly that the Russians did not want to go back to the cold North.

A dispatch from Mexico told Rezanov that Russia was at war with Napoleon and had lost twenty-one thousand men at Austerlitz. St. Petersburg was in revolt and the government was in deep trouble. He had to go home. Before he sailed away, he became formally engaged to Concha, who promised him that she would wait for him while he went to St. Petersburg and make arrangements for their marriage. It was a twenty-thousand-mile round trip, but Concha did not know what that meant. They still show you the point of land from which one could first see a ship sailing from the north, the point where Concha waited — for more than forty years — for her Russian sweetheart to come back.

It was not Rezanov's fault that he never came back. He returned with a cargo of food to the Sitka settlement and mentioned that he thought California was a better place to raise vegetables than either Alaska or the Columbia. Someone told him that those miserable Bostonians were already on the Columbia, building a fort. (The Bostonians who were building a fort were Lewis and Clark). He told them there was a good chance of setting up a colony in California, perhaps at the place Drake had claimed for the English, as England was much too busy with Napoleon to worry about California. Then he set out for St. Petersburg, and somewhere on that seven-thousand-mile trip across Russia, he was killed in an accident.

In a few years' time, Russian ships, complete with dozens of Alaskan natives with their skin boats, arrived off Drake's Bay. The Russians bought the site for their settlement from the Indians for three blankets, two axes, three hoes, three pairs of trousers, and some beads. The new settlement they called "Rossya," for Russia; it still has the name of Fort Ross. Here they built gardens where food could be raised for the hungry colonists in Alaska.

The Bostonians were busy with another war with England, and Mexico was plotting a break from Spain. Rossya grew and gained fame. California was full of fine redwood lumber, and the Russians understood building with wood; they could never quite get used to the adobe mission style of their Spanish neighbors. They planted a rose garden and an orchard and set out a vineyard with vines from Peru. They built a little Russian church with onion domes like those in their far-off homeland, and the ancient Russian Easter music floated over the Marin hills. Women came from St. Petersburg, and at one time the colony numbered two hundred. The Alaska natives skimmed about the California waters chasing seals until they died of disease or homesickness; there were no big, friendly icebergs in California waters.

There were also earthquakes — a whole year of uneasy tremors just after the Russians came. There was the year when grizzly bears killed four thousand head of cattle and all upper California had the jitters about them. Farming was hard work, even in this golden country.

The Monroe Doctrine rang the death knell of Russia in America. Just before the discovery of gold in Sutter's Creek, the Russians moved out. Finally in 1867, the United States bought

Alaska from Russia for $7,200,000, which amounts to about 2¢ an acre for one of the richest pieces of territory we have.

One of the Russian remnants in Alaska is the Russian Orthodox Cathedral of St. Michael in Sitka. Originally built from the wreck of a ship named the *St. Michael*, the church is still a sharp reminder of its Eastern background. Damaged by fire several times, it is still a living memory of a far-off time and people.

California's Fort Ross, high above the Pacific, is a tiny wooden fort looking more like a movie set than anything else. Its museum has exhibits that tell of the good years and the bad ones (like the year they killed and ate two hundred thousand sea gulls) and of a people struggling to build a home in the wilderness. The trip to see this place is well worth the effort, and it *is* an effort — unless someone has recently done a lot of work on the road one must travel to reach it.

Nothing else is left of Russia's "great land of promise" except for a few Russian place-names around San Francisco, where there is a typical little onion-domed church on Russian Hill. All this colorful background, the happy and the sad, became part of us when Alaska was made our forty-ninth state. More and more in the future, people will be traveling to this place of great beauty and opportunity, and one should know the history that helps to make it what it is.

Chapter 16
The Battle of Glorieta Pass

Today, if you should drive along the winding New Mexico road between Santa Fe and the old ruined pueblo of Pecos, you would find nothing but peace. There would be birds singing in the nearby woods as the road wanders comfortably up to Glorieta Pass. There are few people to disturb the birds. Not even tourists come in great numbers.

Most people do not think of the Civil War in terms of the Southwest. Yet in this quiet place, where only once in a while you can hear the far-off wail of a Santa Fe diesel or the hurrying swish of cars going somewhere else, a battle of that tragic war was fought. It was not a major battle, of course, and whether the battle was lost or won, and by whom, has never been too clear. Yet there was a cannon placed against that rocky hillside where a standing rock made shelter for a gun. Men died behind that barricade of stone; soldiers came slipping and sliding down that dry, grassy slope to attack. And under the waving grasses there, an unknown number of young soldiers lie in their last sleep under the wide New Mexico skies and the nearby stars.

The South was losing the war in 1863 when someone had the desperate idea of sending a small army from Texas to secure New Mexico and then go on to take California. All the Confederate ports were blockaded by Union ships, and California had ports they badly needed. The plan was just crazy enough that it might have worked.

Today the state of New Mexico is a Cinderella envied by

many of her sister states, but a hundred years ago it was an arid wilderness full of angry Indians and swarming with things that bit and stung. The territory included present-day New Mexico, Arizona, and part of Nevada — a huge chunk of land that nobody knew anything about. Several Senators had already pleaded with Congress to give it back to the Indians and spare the white man his having to live there. The South was more imaginative; it wanted the California ports, the California gold, and the Nevada silver. (The Southerners, unfortunately for them, proved to be entirely right in this: Nevada silver helped to win the war for the Union.)

Young West Pointers on their first tour of duty were sent to the great Southwest — officially, to survey it (since nobody knew how big it actually was) and to set up military laws (since there was nothing else in the way of law and order). A few dismal little forts had been built to defend the white man against the Indian, and to house the cavalrymen with the black hats and yellow bandannas that spend so much time on our TV screens. As a defense against the Indians, the forts were not much help; the Indians were mobile and they struck where they pleased, while the fort had to stay where it was. Troopers were always riding out to head off a massacre, and arriving too late.

All the young officers who were later to be the great names in the Civil War — William T. Sherman, Philip H. Sheridan, Jefferson Davis, Robert E. Lee, and many others — served their early years in the Southwest, many in Arizona-New Mexico. Some were stationed in Texas, where they took part in the attempt to set up a camel caravan route for carrying the mail across the desert. Camels were imported from Arabia, and Jefferson Davis, future president of the Confederacy, was responsible for seeing that three caravans a week would set out from St. Louis, headed for Los Angeles.

It all makes hilarious reading and a funny movie at this safe distance, but it was not funny at the time. Army life in the great Southwest was grim and dangerous work, isolated from the civilized world. The only thin line back to the world they knew was a stagecoach that left El Paso once every two weeks with connections to the States. There is hardly a place left on our planet today that is as remote as the Southwest was in the 1860s.

When the war began, men with Southern sympathies resigned their commissions in the regular army and went South to join the Confederacy. This meant, among other things, that the forts in this vast territory were left dangerously short of men. The Indian problem was not with the peaceful Pueblo people farming the river valleys, who in general simply ignored the white man. The problem was that horde of mounted Apaches and Navajos, "the best light cavalry in the world." Being natives of this wild country, they knew every inch of the desert and the trackless mountains. They were people who had a real grievance against the white man and were quite well able to do something about it.

Just before the Civil War started, the situation became much worse. Americans captured the great Apache leader, Cochise, and instead of dealing with him as the chief he was, they whipped him and insulted him. He made his escape, swearing that he would destroy every American between the Rio Grande and the Colorado, and he almost did.

In the midst of this trouble the guns fired on Fort Sumter and the war began. The Indians did not know that the white-eyes (as the white man was called at times) were fighting a war with their own kind in the land where the sun rises. They watched the blue-clad troopers ride away from the forts and told each other comfortably that they had finally frightened the white-eyes into going back where they came from — and good riddance, as far as the Indians were concerned.

Mangas Coloradas was chief of another band of Apaches who had been working peacefully with the new stagecoach line that a Mr. Butterfield was trying to set up from St. Louis to Los Angeles. Mangas Coloradas promised not to bother the stagecoaches, a promise he kept faithfully until a very stupid army officer massacred an Apache camp full of women and children. Then there were *two* angry Apache chiefs to deal with. The new stagecoaches had to flee through Apache Pass at the dead of night, since it was well known that Apaches would not attack at night.

It was not a good time to start a stagecoach line in the Southwest, but Mr. Butterfield was a very stubborn man. He bought two thousand horses and two hundred fifty stagecoaches and sent crews ahead to build stations where the drivers could change horses and take on food. Right away the Indians got the word: some crazy white-eyes were bringing in hundreds of lovely horses, which they hitched to a tepee on wheels and sent off into Indian country with only two men to guard it. The Apaches happily ran off the horses, leaving coach and drivers where they fell. Eventually, someone told Mr. Butterfield that he should get mules: no Apache would be caught dead riding a mule. He traded in the few horses he had left and bought two thousand mules. His informer was right about the mules: no Indian would ride one. But they had developed a taste for mule meat, so they ran off the mules and ate them.

Into this jumble of misunderstandings came a new note, this time from the West. California was inclined to Southern sympathy, but one General Carleton, a devout Union man, had trained twenty-five hundred Californians for the Union army: two regiments of infantry, a battalion of cavalry, and a battery of artillery. Since there did not seem to be any other way to get there, they set out to walk to the war, at least until they encountered a boat going in the right direction. Word reached the Apaches from their westernmost scouts that a mighty army of white-eyes was moving up the Gila River valley, going east, and they had a lot of guns. Cochise and Mangas Coloradas, still puzzled by the troopers' withdrawal from the forts to the east, decided that this was probably some clever new tactic on the part of the white man to take away the Indians' land.

The chiefs thought it over and sent scouts to fill in all the wells east of Tucson. Then they settled down behind the rocks in Apache Pass and waited for developments.

The Californians were in great misery; it was a dreadful march to begin with, and they could not find the wells that were marked on their maps. The heat and dust were terrible. Since no one had seen signs of any Indians for weeks, they were completely off guard as they came straggling up to Apache Pass. They did not even have an advance guard, and the entire twenty-five hundred men would probably have been massacred (by a small group of superbly trained Indians), if it had not been for the merest chance. A young recruit, glancing around nervously, thought he saw motion behind one of the rocks. He drew up his rifle hastily and fired at random, and the bullet hit — of all people — Mangas Coloradas. There was mad confusion, as the Indians came surging out of the rocky shelters, howling and shooting with deadly aim. But before more than a few soldiers had been killed, the Indians suddenly melted away before their eyes. Word had got to them that their chief was injured, and they drew around him and hurried him off to a place of safety, leaving the terrified soldiers to their own fearful thoughts.

We read of the eastern regiments that fought in the war in the great battles, men from Maine and New Jersey and Michigan and New York who covered themselves with glory at Gettysburg, Cedar Creek, or Chickahominy, and will be remembered forever. But the men of the far western regiments, all volunteers and most of them very young, should not be forgotten, either. The simple problem of *getting there* was so great. One of the young Texans, setting out on the long road from San Antonio to San Francisco, spoke for them all when he said, "Next war I'm going to, I'll pick one easier to GIT to!"

The army men who stayed in New Mexico for the Union had two wars to fight at once, and of the two they probably felt much more concerned about the one with the Indians. As a matter of fact, New Mexico seceded before Virginia did, and there was much Southern sympathy in the territory. Colonel Edward Canby was left to hold New Mexico for the Union when his superior officer went South to join the Confederacy. His letter to headquarters, pointing out that the Indian situation was extremely bad and he needed men to replace those who had left for the regular army, crossed a letter addressed to him from headquarters, ordering nearly all his remaining men back East. Colonel Canby, it said, was to raise two volunteer regiments in New Mexico. Immediately.

The white population of New Mexico did not make up one

regiment, even counting women and children. The small Mexican population was anti-Texan and therefore Union, but they were simple farmers and had just finished a war of their own. Frantic letters from Colonel Canby produced nothing but more and more disastrous letters from the U.S. War Department.

Under the circumstances, Colonel Canby did very well with his command. He could not staff all the forts, so he moved his troops to two forts that seemed most apt to be usable, and burned the others. Fort Bliss, near the Texas border, was flying the Confederate flag, and a Texan, Lieutenant Colonel John Baylor, arrived to take over. Baylor fixed his eyes on the army storehouse at Fort Fillmore. Fillmore was hard to defend, so Canby hurried — but not quite fast enough — to move the supplies to a safe place. Baylor's troops, out scrounging for supplies, met Canby's men at a moment when they were all suffering from illness and heat exhaustion. They surrendered without a fight, and Baylor drove off the beef herd, the cavalry, and four pieces of artillery. Then he took all the hand arms, declared that Arizona was one of the Confederate States of America, and set all the prisoners free so that he would not have to feed them.

If Canby had his troubles — and he did — so did Brigadier General Henry Sibley, who was given the job of recruiting in Texas for the army to go to California. Sibley must have been an optimist; he claimed that his brigade was composed of "what is probably the best material for an army that the world affords."

His troops included the Davis Rifles; a company of cavalry under a character named "Daddy Green" and one led by Powhatan Jones; a company of Germans who did not speak English; and a mounted infantry. They drilled at a field north of San Antonio — in the morning as infantry, in the afternoon as cavalry. The men had all manner of weapons: squirrel guns, bear guns, Minié muskets, common rifles, navy revolvers, double-barreled shotguns, lances with nine-foot shafts, and four mountain howitzers. They wore no special uniforms, and nobody thought to tell them that it could get cold in the New Mexico mountains. Women relatives of the young soldiers, wiser or more imaginative, begged heavy clothing and bedding for their boys. The volunteers rode gaily off to war on a sunny morning, singing "The Texas Ranger." They faced seven hundred miles of rugged wagon road before their first stop, Fort Bliss.

From Fort Union, Colonel Canby was sending a desperate message to Washington: "If we are to hold forts, send arms. Send warm clothing. Send pay officer." He did get an answer to this one. It said: "Raise third company of volunteers."

The Texans had yet to find out what Colonel Canby already knew: that no paymaster so far had survived the trip through the Indian country. Nobody had been paid for months and was not likely to be. The Texans had planned to live off the land, but no one would accept Confederate scrip and the Mexicans would not even sell to them for gold. They were all cold, hungry, and homesick, and both pneumonia and smallpox were in their camps.

The first battle in the Southwest between the North and the South took place at Valverde, where the victory — if any — must be credited to the weather. Both armies were so completely miserable, it is a wonder they could fight at all, but the battle was long and bloody and left a great many men wounded. The Texans froze in the mountain weather, their baggage wagons bogged down in the miserable muddy trails, and there was no water fit to drink. To add insult to injury, a terrible Southwest sandstorm blew up and for two days they were pelted with sand and gravel that felt like tiny bullets.

Baylor's men captured the cannons, so they claimed the victory. They occupied Santa Fe and Albuquerque and took over supplies that had been stored there for the Indians.

If you look carefully at a map of the southwestern United States, you will think that the Battle of Glorieta Pass simply could not have happened. This is enormous country: the distances are almost unbelievable even today, when trains, cars, and buses can take you anywhere. Yet, in spite of that great distance, Colorado, Kansas, and California sent out troops to help the Union to hold the country! It is a very long hike from Denver to Santa Fe, yet a young officer named Chivington led a band of "Pike's Peakers" to the help of Colonel Canby, and saved the hour. A volunteer regiment of New Mexicans under Kit Carson had brought word

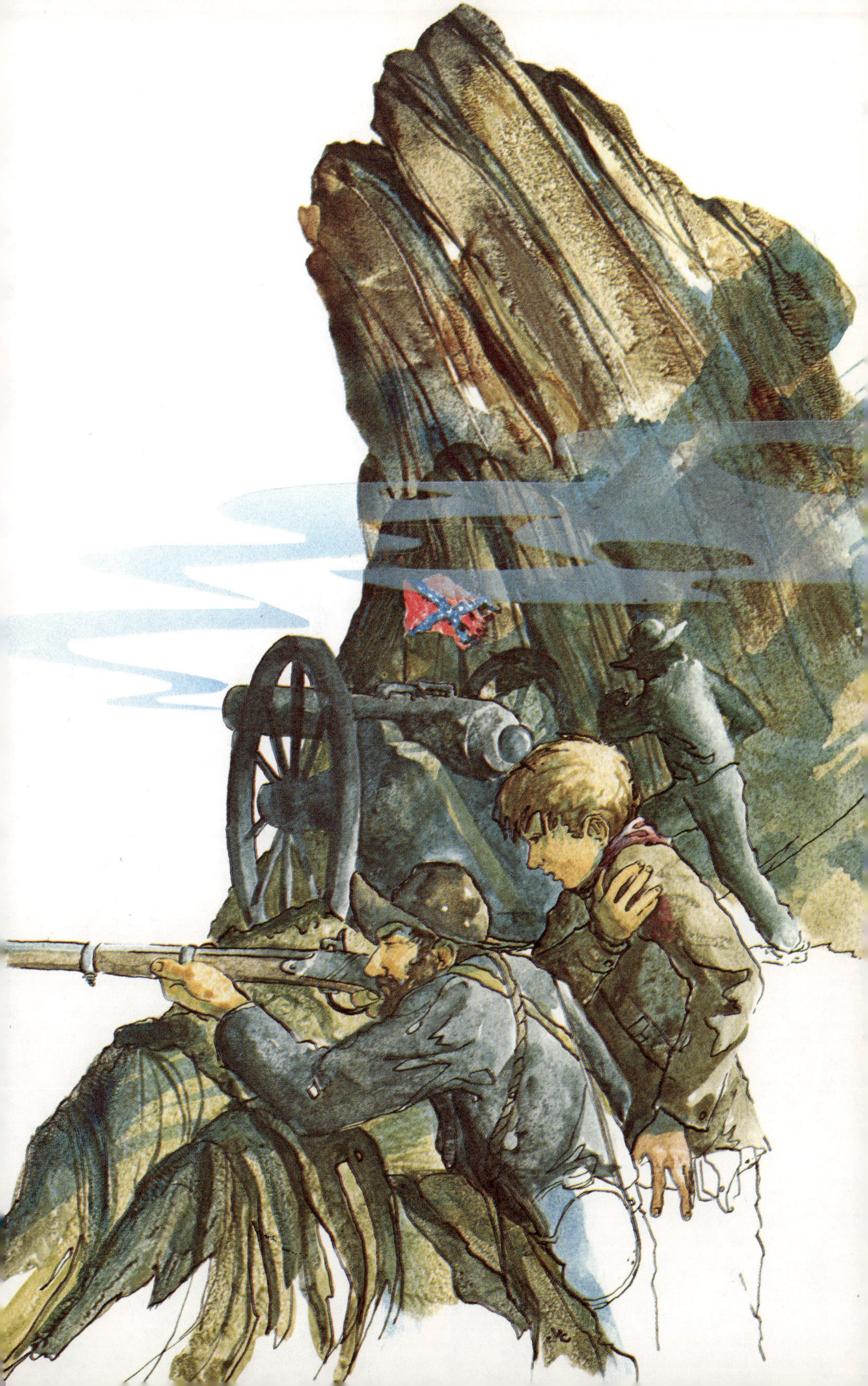

Confederate soldiers fight in
a futile attempt to gain control
of the territory of New Mexico.

to Canby that the Colorado men were on their way, and — if they got past the Apaches — they would be a great help. They were.

When the battle lines were finally drawn up at Glorieta Pass, the two armies were equally miserable in this jagged land of ridges and rocks, and it was a dreadful place for a battle. Canby had around thirty-eight hundred men after the Coloradans arrived, and Sibley around twenty-five hundred. Chivington was the hero of the hour: he and his mountaineers went up a steep bluff and around behind the Confederate lines, where they took their baggage train.

Without stores of food and ammunition, the Texans had to give up. The battle was over — over forever for the dead of both armies strewn around the rocky hillside.

The Confederate burial detail had to borrow shovels from the Union army to bury their dead, and medical corpsmen of both armies took their wounded to Santa Fe, where Colonel Canby's wife had charge of a hospital that cared for all of them. The Confederates had lost all their buglers, so Union bugles got them all up in the morning. At night, the two battered armies sat, one on each side of the narrow Rio Grande, and sang the lonesome songs of home, and wondered whether they would ever see their families again.

The Coloradans made sure that the Texans got back to Texas, by pacing them along the opposite side of the river, carrying their wounded as best they could in jolting wagons. For a while, they pulled the heavy cannons, but they finally could not move them on the roadless riverbank, so they buried them and left them there.

Colonel Canby has been criticized for not taking the whole Texas brigade prisoners, but he could neither feed nor house them in such a wilderness. Probably the Texans were grateful to get back to the warm South.

California, over which the trouble all started, was still uncommitted. The commandant at the San Francisco presidio had resigned his commission and gone south at the beginning of the war. Southern Democrats were trying to make California a slave state. By the time of the New Mexico battles, California was toying with the idea of joining the Pacific Republic, which was proposed by Oregon Democrats in 1851. One of their quarrels with the U.S. government was over postage: east of the Rockies a letter cost 3¢, west of the Rockies, 10¢. Legislators protested that the West Coast was farther away than Europe. Washington, Oregon, California, and the Idaho Territories were angry about it.

It seems unbelievable today that people could have written such things about Abraham Lincoln as the papers printed in those uneasy years when states' rights, slavery, and such annoying things as postage were being fought over in Congress. The *Oregon Weekly Union* of Corvallis brought out this gem of slander in September 1861: "[Lincoln] has trampled on the Constitutions, he has gagged the press, he has caused the sanctity of the home to be violated and made a mockery of private rights; under his despotic rule, quiet, peaceful citizens who did not happen to agree with the view of the abolitionist government in control of affairs were dragged from their homes and imprisoned on slight and flimsy suspicions; weak and helpless women, hitherto protected by a chivalrous America, were now made the victims of Mr. Lincoln's persecution. And, first of all, an espionage system was being introduced which threatened to surpass the whole evil structure of spying and informing for which Europe had become notorious."

From which we could learn that (1) you cannot always believe everything you read in the paper, and (2) things — and people — look different after a hundred years have gone by. History teaches us to look at things with our long-distance glasses on.

Chapter 17
The Beautiful Ships

> Yonder is the sea, great and wide,
>   which teems with things innumerable;
>   living things both small and great.
> There go the ships,
>   and Leviathan which thou didst form to sport in it.
>
> — *Psalm 104:25-26*

> You know what sort of a course a ship is doing by looking back along her wake. Well, here is a part of America's wake; you can look back here and learn.
>
> — *Carl Cutler (Curator, Mystic Seaport, Connecticut)*

> There's a tall ship to windward
> Sailing fast and free,
> All along the coast
> Of the high Barbaree.
>
> — *From a dreadnought chantey*

Speed is so much a part of our world that we have to go very far back in history to see where it started. Our Western history is tied up with the wheel; our whole world of business, pleasure, and sports runs on wheels. And, because things change so rapidly, the wheel may be gone within your lifetime. The experts say that it is on its way out, to be replaced by air pressure, nuclear power, or something even newer. But the wheel, no doubt about it, was the mother of speed.

In 6000 B.C., the fastest transportation known to man was the camel caravan. These caravans made about eight miles an hour in good weather, and this beat walking any day. They also took care of baggage. Horses were a little faster, or perhaps just a little less cantankerous to handle. Somewhere along the line someone invented the chariot, probably around 1600 B.C. On level ground in good weather the chariot could do ten miles an hour. Unfortunately, there were no roads, so the Romans — a practical people — went down in history as road builders. These roads were better for marching armies than for jolting along in a springless chariot, especially at the daring speeds reached by the young charioteers. A good, fast clip was around twelve miles an hour, which Julius Caesar's men thought was very modern and progressive.

Ivan the Terrible, who is not often quoted, made at least one wise remark: "The oceans are God's road." Indeed they were the only ones for a long time. Ships progressed from dugouts to galleys rowed by slaves, to big ships carrying sails of various kinds, to steam, to nuclear power, and to the fast little hydrofoils that rise by air pressure and skim across the waves.

The oceans are still the world's most-traveled roads. This is in spite of two strong competitors — steam-powered machines and air vehicles. Steam came into use in the mid-nineteenth century, with smoky little engines chugging along noisily, making a great deal of clatter, at around fourteen miles an hour. Speed was the watchword of the gadget-making Yankees who first built the railroads, and gradually the speed went up to almost a mile a minute. Nobody thought it could possibly go higher. Now we have lightweight aluminum trains skimming along on overhead tracks at up to one hundred twenty miles an hour and — wouldn't you know it? — railroads are going out of style.

Traveling by air has been with us, both with balloons and

heavier-than-air machines, since forty years before the Wright Brothers. True, some of the early flights looked more like hops than flights; but by 1938, planes were going four hundred miles an hour and in twenty years that was doubled. In your lifetime the Apollo rockets go seven thousand miles an hour and may yet speed up. There is no doubt that flight is man's fastest way to travel.

Man has invented a great many devices for getting from one place to another. But in all these inventions, nothing has ever been so beautiful as the sailing ships. A windjammer, spreading two acres of canvas into the gusting winds and filling the sky with white motion, may be the most beautiful thing that man has ever made. Sailing ships, as a practical method of getting anywhere, have been gone for more than a century. But they are so much a part of American history that they should not be allowed to be forgotten. Port cities on both our coasts have realized this, and now make it possible for people to visit some of the famous windships that are so much a part of our adventurous past.

When you think of sailing ships, you think of the beautiful "greyhounds of the sea," the fast clippers that raced to China for tea and set up records for speed that are still unbroken: *Rainbow*, *Flying Cloud*, and *Sovereign of the Seas*, and the pride of the British tea fleet, *Cutty Sark*. These beautiful ships did not come about all at once. They have a long history.

The first shipbuilders of the ancient world were the Phoenicians, who, four thousand years ago, found their way across unknown oceans and built up a trade that was the envy of all their neighbors. The Phoenicians never went to war with anybody; war ruined trade, and they were traders. They hired out to another king to sail around Africa, twenty-five hundred years ago, a deed that for pure daring got them talked about for centuries. The Greeks respectfully called the North Star "the Phoenician Star," and shuddered at the fearful tales that the travelers had "sailed south of the sun."

Phoenician ships were galleys with two or even three rows of long oars, swung by slaves. For a thousand years nobody did much to improve the design until the second great seafaring nation came along: England of mid-sixteenth century. Out to beat the Spanish to some of the treasures of the New World, they discovered a talent for making fine, fast little ships out of their native oak. The Spanish — and the French, Dutch, and Portuguese — were greatly annoyed by these "wicked little ships," which could sail circles around any other ship, and fight like a cornered lion.

When the thirteen colonies on our East Coast decided to break from England, they discovered something else about those wicked little ships: they were blocking every American harbor, making it impossible to get goods in or out. So the first American ships were blockade-runners, built in the hidden little harbors of Long Island Sound, Chesapeake Bay, or the rocky New England coast. America, too, had a lot of beautiful wood and also a lot of very angry young men who said they could build ships better and faster than the British ones. It was a high standard to reach, but it seems to have been good for both countries: they still share much of the world's shipbuilding. After the Revolutionary War, the age of sail began in earnest. And, for some reason no one has ever explained, the designers of the beautiful windjammers, on both sides of the Atlantic, were Scotsmen. Scotland has not, and has never had, a navy. Yet Scotsmen — both on their native Clyde River and at our Boston shipyards — continued to turn out the most beautiful ships ever to sail the seas.

The most famous old ship in our country dates from this time: she is the U.S.S. *Constitution*, better known as *Old Ironsides*. Schoolchildren of America collected funds to restore the ship when it was discovered some years ago, old and battered and pitiful in some forgotten dock. Once more shipshape and ready to meet all her young friends with her tales of bravery, she is berthed at Charlestown, Massachusetts. "Decks once red with heroes' blood," as Oliver Wendell Holmes expressed it, have still the power to inspire us. It is her proud claim that no foeman ever trod her deck except as prisoner of war. She was a "fighting lady" like her younger sister, the *Yorktown*.

It would be hard to find anything more American than *Old Ironsides*. She was one of six frigates ordered by President Washington to fight the Barbary pirates of North Africa. Congress authorized building the ships in 1797, and the U.S.S. *Constitution* was built at Boston. Paul Revere supplied the copper used on the hull. She carried an acre of canvas in thirty-six sails of heavy linen. Top speed of the ship was thirteen and a half knots, better than some steamships can do. A "ship of the line," she bristled with guns.

The British were not impressed with the U.S.S. *Constitution*, but changed their minds after she left the *Guerrière*, unmasted and sinking, in her most famous battle. After that, both the British and the French advised their ship captains not to attack an American frigate when they were alone. Get help. The Americans were young and reckless, and they did not fight the way anybody else did.

During the battle with the *Guerrière*, the U.S.S. *Constitution* got her nickname. A young sailor, watching the fight with great pride, called out, "Her sides must be made of iron! Those shots are just bouncing off her!"

Old Ironsides and the U.S.S. *Philadelphia*, ships of the line, were sent to the Mediterranean with several smaller ships after the Barbary pirates. The *Philadelphia* grounded too close to the shore and had to be burned to keep her out of enemy hands. Left the only ship with heavy guns, *Old Ironsides* plunged in alone, trounced the pirates, and returned home covered with glory. No other ship will ever enjoy the fame of this wonderful old veteran.

The first American ship flying the flag in China, in the beginning of the tea age, was from Baltimore, and the year was 1785. Americans had worked out a three-cornered trade agreement with the Russians in Alaska and the Chinese of Canton. They gave food and other goods to the Russians in exchange for furs; then they traded the furs to the Chinese for tea, which they took back to the United States. A voyage took about three years.

Most of the captains were very young, some in their twenties, and the crewmen were rarely out of their teens. Cabin boys signed on at the age of ten or twelve. (There was then no vast system of free education, and this was one of the few ways in which a boy from a poor family might get to see something outside his own village.) It was a very rough life, terribly hard and dangerous work, and many young men were lost at sea or died of the hardships of spoiled food and bitter cold. At least by this time the captain knew that he must make his boys eat their daily portion of fruit to keep away scurvy. It was, if dangerous, always an exciting life. The captains, being young and daring, often raced their ships, and this was more exciting than anything that ever happened on land.

The Americans were the first to set up a sailing schedule and stick to it. It was a new thing, to be able to count on both passengers and freight leaving and arriving when the company said they would. This brought in a lot more freight and passengers for the American lines, and in the early 1800s the American ships were carrying a million tons of goods at top speeds around the world. Passengers went along on the faster ships for the fun of racing.

Westward across the Atlantic took two months, and they got the worst of the trips because, going to America, the ship was packed with immigrants. The eastward trip took only one month. All such ships carried passengers, freight, money, mail, and news. It tied the world a little closer together. Some companies swore by the dreadnought as a fast and reliable ship. Smaller, faster packet ships carried mostly mail and passengers. The big square-riggers were slower and were not out to beat anybody to the big freight jobs. Merchants who were not in such a hurry always sent their goods by square-riggers.

The first real racing clipper was built in Baltimore, and it led the way for a long line of beautiful ships. It was said that a clipper had to have "a codfish head and a mackerel tail." The hulls also looked remarkably like the war canoes carved out of great cedar trees by some of the North Pacific coast Indians. Styles had changed from the bulky "tea wagons" of the East India Company which had to be given up when the need was for slim, fast hulls that could carry great loads of canvas.

The *Sea Witch* opened the days of fast sailing: 97 days from New York to San Francisco. Later she was to set a record that was unbroken for a century for any kind of cargo carrier, sail or steam: 74 days and 14 hours from Hong Kong via Cape of Good

Hope to London. *Swordfish*, New York to China, set a record of 90 days, 18 hours. *Flying Cloud* cut this down to 89 days, 21 hours. *Flying Cloud*, considered by many to have been the most beautiful clipper ever built, once did 374 miles in one 24-hour day, but the stress on the wooden parts of the ship made it very dangerous to push her to this speed. Pushed to win, like a thoroughbred horse, it was a race with death.

At the height of the clipper age, just before the Civil War, a fast ship could charge sixty dollars a ton for freight. There was great competition between the companies who owned ships to get the best freight.

You would be amazed at the things that were sent by ship in those fantastic days. California was in the midst of the gold rush, full of people with a lot of money and very little common sense. They did not want ordinary things: they wanted luxuries — and they were willing to have them brought all the way around the Horn in a sailing ship and pay the astronomical freight. Back East, fresh oysters were sent by railroad from Chesapeake Bay to Buffalo, New York — and it was the marvel of the century. But the Boston and California Ice Company, undaunted by the thought of two oceans, brought more than nine hundred tons of fresh pond ice to cool the drinks of wealthy Californians — the largest cargo of its kind ever reported. Fresh butter from Vermont was shipped to Panama, transshipped by side-wheeler to San Francisco after it had been packed on muleback across the isthmus, and finally wound up on a Concord coach going to Virginia City, Nevada, where the world's largest silver strike was making everyone slightly crazy.

Probably the funniest freight of the lot was the bundles of laundry, sent by San Francisco bachelors to be done up in Hong Kong and returned — if at all — in two years. Every clipper sliding into Whampoa Harbor ahead of the summer monsoon was instantly surrounded by "washboats" — floating laundries, baker's boats, shops, boats with food, clothing and toys for sale, and theatrical boats — all heading for the American sailors. It was against the law for citizens of the Celestial Empire to have anything to do with the foreign devils, and some of them might lose their heads for it. But they had discovered one thing about the foreign devils on the white ships: they had lots of money, and lots of laundry.

The Chinese had never at any time, since the days of Marco Polo, wanted anything to do with the big-nosed Europeans. At first they said so politely, and then they got rude about it and lopped off Europeans' heads. But the big-noses kept coming. It was gold that opened the crack in the door: China had little gold and was forbidden to use it in foreign trade. Those crafty young Americans had furs to trade for tea. It was a proposition they could not pass up, though they did not especially want to let other people have their tea.

The Chinese claimed that the effect of drinking tea was to help in learning, to write poetry in high spirit, to talk with pleasure, to quiet one's heart, to help digestion, to conquer lonesomeness, to strengthen the brain, to purify the stomach, to lengthen one's life. Why should they hand over this wonderful thing to some foreign barbarians?

At the time of the Boston Tea Party, the question was already being argued: How much tea tax was fair? Since it was up to one hundred ten percent of the value of the tea in some cases, feeling ran very high. Very soon, British and American ships were racing across two oceans in their fast clippers, cutting the tax as they cut down on the time and the danger of spoilage. Tea merchants of New York and London insisted that their tea be brought in wooden-hulled ships, because the iron hulls spoiled the taste of the tea. Wooden-hulled ships took a greater beating from the great amount of sail put on for the racing. Fire at sea was an ever-present danger in a wooden ship, but the captain who took the chances was usually the one who got the best shipments.

Sometimes two or three American ships would leave China on the same tide, race all the way across the Pacific and down the coast of South America, around Cape Horn and come up the Atlantic within sight of each other, and dock within an hour or so. The first tea of the season brought the most money, so speed was always important. One famous race (which has been a subject for songs, poems, and paintings) was that run between two British ships, *Ariel* and *Taeping*, in 1866. Foochow to London in

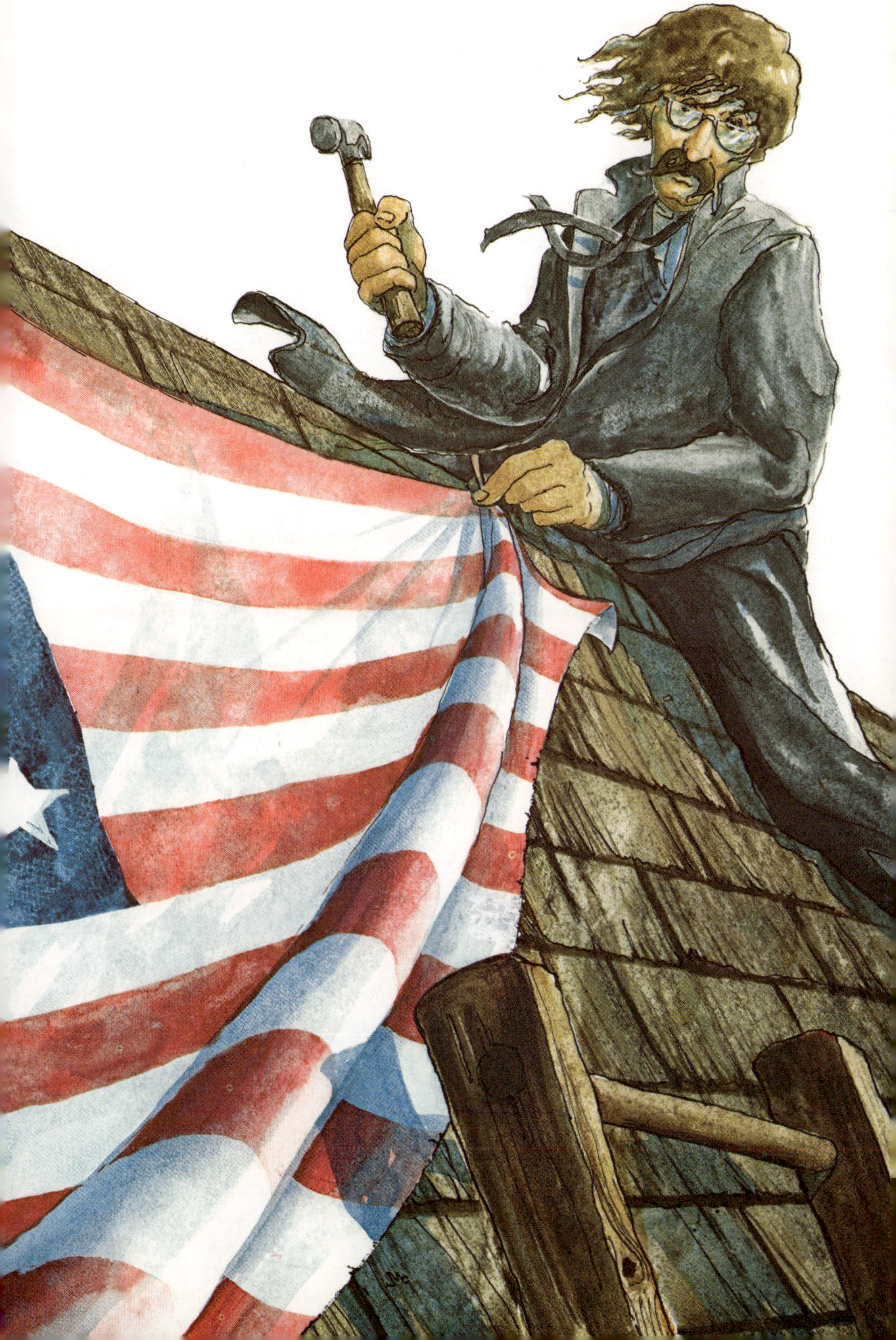

A schoolmaster, mistaking a
ship for the Confederate raider
SHENANDOAH, nails Old Glory to
the schoolhouse roof, declaring:
"No rebel is going to take
THAT down." *(See page 224.)*

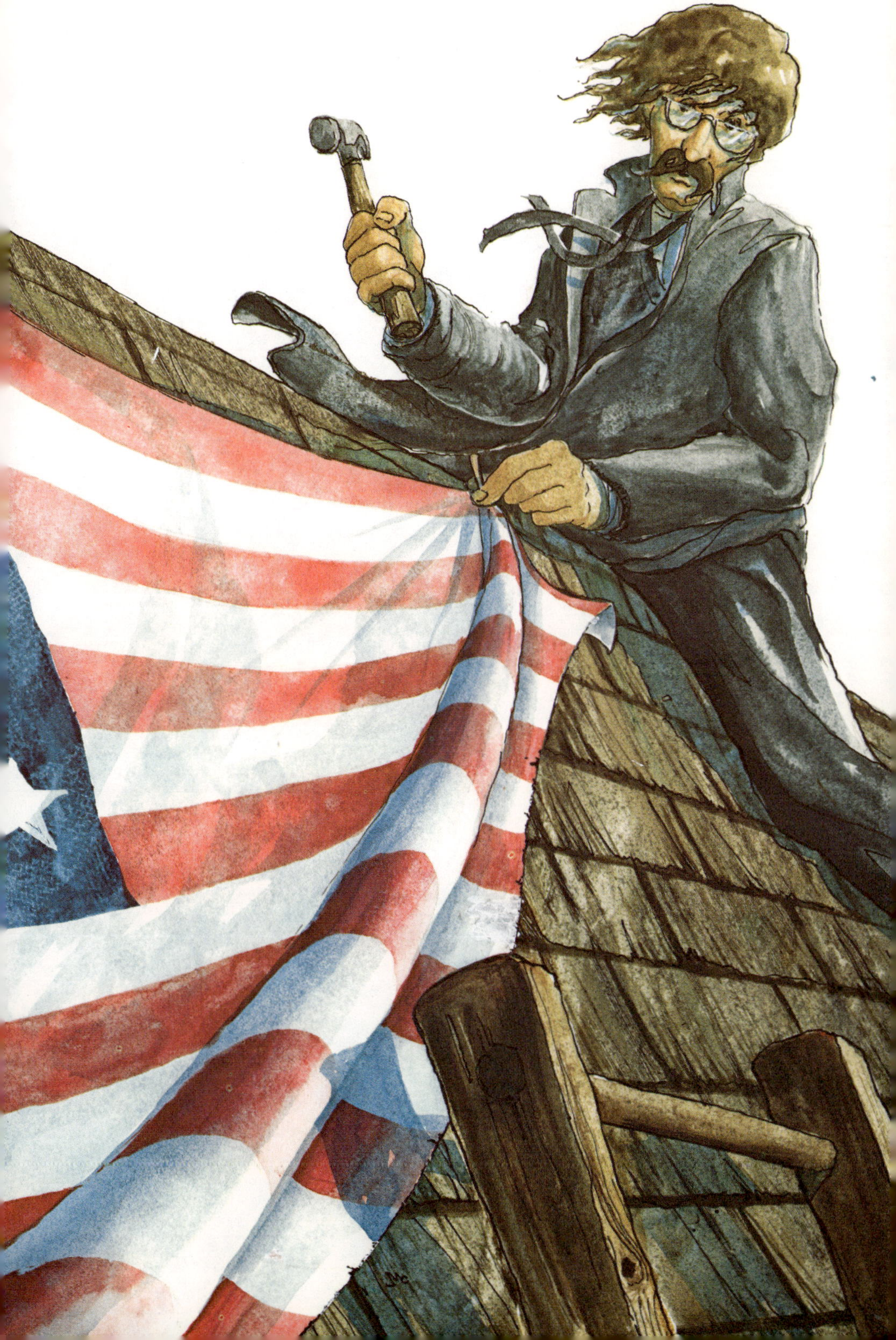

A schoolmaster, mistaking a
ship for the Confederate raider
SHENANDOAH, nails Old Glory to
the schoolhouse roof, declaring:
"No rebel is going to take
THAT down." *(See page 224.)*

ninety-nine days is a very fast trip by sailing ship. This was in the days before the telegraph, but news ran ahead of the ships as they raced up the English Channel side by side, wearing every stitch of canvas they possessed. After racing across sixteen thousand miles of ocean, they docked twenty minutes apart in London. At one time, they were more than sixty clippers in the tea trade.

Donald MacKay and his brother, Alexander, were the main American clipper ship builders and designers. They built a total of thirty-two beautiful ships. The biggest clipper they ever built never had the chance to do any deep-water sailing: the *Great Republic* burned at the dock, as she was taking on her first cargo.

Of all these lovely ships not one is left. After the coming of steam, even the fast clippers had to go into the business of hauling lumber, scrap, building materials, coal, or other slow cargo. The only black mark on the history of these beautiful ships is that some of them were used in the slave trade during the years of sail, between the War of 1812 and the Civil War.

Among the few old sailing ships that we have in repair for visitors is the *Charles W. Morgan*, now in dock at Mystic Seaport, Connecticut. This famous old ship, the only survivor of more than four hundred whaling ships of her time, had sailed for one hundred years when she finally retired. Her experiences as a whaler and as a rescue ship for disasters on the high seas makes wonderful reading. The ship has weathered fire, hurricanes, sickness, floating mines, submarines, icebergs, reefs, and quarrelsome natives. Her cargoes were generally whale oil or sea-elephant oil. The ship spent a lot of time hunting for bowhead whales in the Sea of Okhotsk, "the whaler's icebox," which is supposed to be the coldest place in the Arctic. It was used as a movie set for the picture, *Down to the Sea in Ships*.

England has saved one of her clippers — the *Cutty Sark*, queen of the seas at one time. The *Cutty Sark* was born too late; steam was already taking over the seas when she was built. However, she established several records that no steamship ever managed to beat. Made with a bow so sharp that it cut the waves like a knife, the *Cutty Sark* had an iron frame and a wooden skin. Her masts were raking and her deck was clear; she looked every inch a speed champion, and she was. For fifty-two years she sailed until most of the good freight routes were operating with steam; then she was sold to Portugal and spent twenty-seven years on short hauls of slow cargo. One day she was recognized. Under the peeling paint and the broken decking, a man who had sailed on the ship when she was queen of the seas recognized the *Cutty Sark* and immediately got to work to rescue the old ship and refit her. Her beautiful racing lines rebuilt, fresh with new paint and sails, she is at home at Greenwich, England, a national monument much visited by the children of the country she served so well.

A ship about which we know very little, but which sounds very interesting, was the *Shenandoah*, a Confederate raider which operated off the North Pacific coast from Oregon to Alaska, during the last six months of the Civil War. The ship was captained by a brave and daring navigator named Captain James Waddell. He had been in the American navy before the Civil War, and for some reason, the navy had not paid him his wages. He was very angry at not being paid, so he went to England, bought a ship, and began gathering up a crew to operate it to raid Union shipping. It would have been much less expensive for the navy simply to have paid his wages, as he managed to sink more than twenty-five ships, meaning several millions of dollars' worth of valuable goods, in the few months of the war that were left.

One amusing note — probably the only one in the story of the *Shenandoah* — concerns a schoolmaster in one of the bleak little towns on the coast of Oregon. He had heard of the raider *Shenandoah* and knew it was a three-master with one smokestack. When someone from up the coast reported that a ship of this description was bearing down on them, the schoolmaster climbed on top of the schoolhouse and nailed the flag on. "No rebel is going to take THAT down," he said. "They'll have to get me first." It happened to be another ship entirely, but it makes a nice little story.

At the time of our Bicentennial in 1976, sailing ships of several nations came to help us celebrate. They were training ships on which the country's cadets were taught to sail and to handle a windship. The visit was called "Operation Sail," and they were known as "the Tall Ships." Among them were the *Sagres* from Portugal, the *Christian Radich* from Norway, the *Libertad* from Argentina, the *Elcano* from Spain, the *Danmark* from Denmark, and the *Eagle*, a U.S. Coast Guard barkentine. The young men who train on these ships have a rare opportunity; they may be the last young men in history to learn to sail "the ships so brave and beautiful that never more shall be!"

Chapter 18
Horizons

> When the soil is gone, man must go; and the process does not take long.
>
> — *Theodore Roosevelt, 1908*

> The greatest domestic problem facing our country is saving our soil and water.
>
> — *Sam Rayburn, 1956*

> The future lies in ocean farming, not fishing.
>
> — *Captain Jacques-Yves Cousteau*

The Columbia River, which makes a great loop through a seven-state drainage in its violent run to the sea, is one of the greatest natural resources in the United States. It is also the cause of a great deal of controversy. The Columbia's flow is ten times that of the Colorado, two and a half times that of the Nile. It could annually lay thirteen inches of water over a landmass the size of California and Arizona. And it has half the hydroelectric power of the United States.

The Columbia is also one of the greatest salmon rivers in the country and the home as well of other kinds of fish. It has now reached the point where the fish fighting their way upstream have to be taxied around a series of dams that would discourage anything but a salmon. These fish are also one of the greatest natural resources of the country. And there you have the battleground of the ecologists and the commercial interests. There is only one Columbia River. Who is going to benefit from it?

This is only one of several vital questions that must be settled soon for the greatest good of the greatest number of people. Other important issues include the following:

- The continental shelf: nursery for most of the world's food fish — and full of the oil we need for fuel.
- Energy to turn our wheels and to provide power.
- Water for the world, for drinking, and for farming.
- Food for a hungry world.
- The continent of Antarctica: How shall its rich resources be shared out?
- Weather control.

The continental shelf is just exactly what its name says: a shelf around the continents. It is not the same width everywhere. Along the Pacific coast of North America it is about twenty miles wide; on the Atlantic side, north of Cape Hatteras, it is only one hundred fifty feet wide; in the Arctic it is much wider, seven hundred fifty miles across in one place. In all, it contains as much land as Europe and South America combined. It is the home and feeding ground of ninety percent of the world's fish.

The trouble is that the continental shelf contains as much of our future oil resources as it does fish. Unfortunately, we cannot just look ahead to a happy time of cooperation, with the fishes swimming peacefully between the oil derricks. Oil is slippery stuff, and one good oil spill would kill all the fish within reach, and quite possibly poison many other forms of life for a long time to come.

The best solution to this problem seems to center on Captain

Jacques Cousteau's theory that our future lies not in fishing the sea but in farming it. Controlled fish farming and the raising of other crops besides fish would call for definite areas being set aside for this work, and other areas left free for oil prospecting. The Russians talk of "peaceful coexistence," and perhaps this is the answer to the continental-shelf problems.

Ecologists insist that *this is everyone's property and belongs to the future.* Nearly ten percent of the world's continental shelf lies off our coasts. Our country has tried to set up a two-hundred-mile limit on fishing, to protect our own interests. We have probably twenty percent of the world's fish resources, but ships from ten nations have run very close to the limit from time to time. Herring, hake, mackerel, and several other commercially valuable fish are taken off our Atlantic coast by well-organized fishing operations with electronic equipment and great factory ships with fish-processing plants.

The Grand Banks of Newfoundland are still producing as many fish as they did when John Cabot reported that they could be scooped up in a basket. To people who depend on this fish harvest for the protein they need in their diet, it would be a tragedy to have this source of food poisoned by oil. Even one wrecked tanker can play havoc with a good fishing ground.

Icelanders were the first to set up legal limits around their country, and most nations (including our own) have followed this plan of a twelve-mile territorial limit and an economic zone of two hundred miles in which only a limited number of fish can be taken by foreign countries.

On the other hand, say the people who work in the field of energy, there is far more oil under the sea than under the land; all the land-based oil wells are, in fact, in the beds of ancient seas. Ecologists want the federal government to take on the task of exploring the seas for oil and govern the use of it. Oil companies claim that they have the experience and the men to do the searching. In 1976, after a greal deal of pressure from both sides, the United States auctioned off ninety-three tracts of land off the coasts of New Jersey and Delaware. Thirty-one oil companies paid 1.1 billion dollars for these and will now go ahead to explore them. It is estimated that seventy billion dollars' worth of mineral and oil was realized in one year from the continental shelf. This is about four times the value of the fish in the same area. (There is just one little thing. You cannot eat oil.)

Another of the great questions, of course, will be energy. We have come a long way since some smart farmer, a long time ago, put up a windmill to catch the wind and make it work for him. Someone else built a waterwheel to turn his grain stones for grinding his wheat. Each of these inventions, in its day, was a great step forward for man, who could save at least some of his own energy for other things while the wind and the water did his heavy work. Windmills are still powering farm work in Holland and Portugal and Denmark, where they are a tourist attraction as well as a working tool. They can also be found in the Great Plains of our own country and the dry farmlands of the West. It may be that if governments get into too big a hassle over the newer kinds of energy, American farmers may go back to building their own windmills. Using windmills may slow the pace a little, but there are no dangerous side effects of some of the solar and volcanic energy.

Solar energy is just now being harnessed for use. It is the cleanest of all the energy sources. Sun-powered heating, cooling, and transfer of light into electricity are all part of our future. It is, however, still very expensive.

Drilling nowadays is not always for oil, but for energy. Oil and the other fossil fuels are of course our main source of energy now, and there is a whole related field taking in coal, natural gas, and other products that come from the same place: the fossil remains of the dinosaur times, several hundreds of millions of years ago. New processes of converting these products are developing on all sides.

One of the newest energy systems is the nuclear power plant, which of course came about as one good result of atomic fission. An example of how this works is a big new power plant near Baltimore, which in 1977 supplied over half the electric power needed in the area. Over the next thirty years or so, it is claimed, these plants will be able to save the country some twenty-six billion gallons of oil. Their process is a combination of power systems: fissioning atoms of uranium supply the heat to convert water into steam, and the pressure of the steam turns the turbines, which, in turn, rotate a magnet inside coils of wire and generate electricity. Many of the new power systems will be combinations of methods already in use, along with the new discoveries that are being made every day.

Iceland for many years has used volcanic energy for heating water. New Zealand has more than five hundred wells tapping hot water for heat; one hotel runs its air conditioner with power from this earth-heat energy, which is properly called geothermal ("geo" for earth, "thermal" for heat). Nine other nations are working on the idea of installing this kind of equipment where there are signs of geothermal power. Teams of government surveyors tell us that the United States has enough of such geothermal areas to create as much power as that generated by one hundred forty nuclear plants. Vast formations of this sort lie beneath the Texas-Louisiana coastline. And here, of course, the ecologists have a worry: How will it be for the people (to whom these areas are home) to live surrounded by possibly dormant volcanoes? Thirty miles down, molten rock heats the water seepage, which comes back up as steam. This could add up to a very large bang if somebody pushed the wrong button.

At St. Malo on the French coast is a highly original source of energy, a power plant worked by the tides. Tides run up to forty-four feet high in this particular place, and for two hundred years people have tried to think of a way to put the tides to work. Now they have done it. The system is set up with two turbines — one complete system for the incoming tide, one for the outgoing tide. Electric power for fifteen thousand people is generated by this thundering sweep of water. At the Bay of Fundy in Newfoundland, the tides are nearly as high as they are at St. Malo, and people are studying the French system to see if it would be practical for Newfoundland. Man is very clever at finding ways to make life easier for himself. A Scotsman by the name of David Hutton is supposed to have harnessed mice to spin thread in his mill; each was said to have saved him eighteen cents a week, and he hired them out in droves. So it is not surprising that some smart man has harnessed the tides to do his work.

One of the most pressing questions of our future is the question of water. Ours is a water-rich planet, as we can tell by comparing it to some of the other planets. We *have* enough water — more than enough. It just isn't in the right places. Ninety-five percent of the world's fresh water is in the deep freeze at the South Pole, and — unless someone comes up with a much better idea than we have had so far — it is likely to stay there.

One suggestion, which is at least original, is to bring "Greenland's icy mountains to India's coral strand," as the old hymn says. This would be done by towing large icebergs from the Antarctic — or the Arctic, whichever was closer — to the places where the water was needed. The one who worked out this theory estimates that those doing the towing could handle a berg seven miles long by one and a half miles wide, using a tug the size of a supertanker. This would be a big enough berg not to melt during the voyage, which would take from six months to a year. It is calculated that the tug could make twenty miles a day, and there are no suggestions on what to do if one should run into a storm, or cross the path of somebody towing a rival iceberg to some other country. It is pointed out that at least four of the desperately dry areas of the world — the Sahara Desert, the desert areas around Western Australia and Yuma, Arizona, and Chile's Desert of Atacama — are all close enough to their seacoasts to avoid long pipelines. The iceberg in melting — when it reached port — would leave the fresh water on top of the salt water, so that it could be siphoned off to the pipelines.

It is true that water would make all the difference in the world to these bleak places. Only recently have scientists looked carefully at the Sahara Desert and realized that this place, three million miles of desert with a temperature of 130 degrees, was once a garden spot. Out in the middle of nowhere in the desert are rocks with figures carved in them, figures of people swimming! Scientists from Spain are working with the people of the Sahara on a great power project which will make use of the solar energy that is wasted on this desert and use it to generate electricity with which they can dig wells. They have already tapped an ice-cold spring a mile down from the sizzling sands above it and are making plans to restore the desert as a food factory and source of power.

Vast new food sources must be found all over the world, and our own country has been in the forefront of experimenting with ways to stamp out hunger throughout the world. In the past few years, scientists from many countries have worked together to produce rice, corn, and wheat which would give a heavy yield even in poor soil. This will mean the difference between life and death to many of the new countries of Africa and Asia and South America. Twenty years ago, no one had ever heard of fish-farming, except to help the salmon along because of the dams and for planting trout in mountain lakes. Now, all across the country, farmers have put in ponds for raising catfish, trout, and other good food fish. The world's most ambitious fish-farming project is in Mexico, where natives badly need the protein in their diet.

The place that more than anywhere else is tied in with the future is Antarctica, that cold little continent down there at the bottom of nowhere, where a warm summer's day can get the thermometer clear up to minus 25 degrees F., and the cold days can run 127 degrees below zero. We know from the research of cold and hardworking scientists that it was not always a frozen waste; it must once have been covered with the same green forests of the long-ago dinosaur country. It follows, then, that it is probably full of oil.

Twelve nations, thinking of all that lovely oil, have signed the Antarctic Treaty to guarantee that they would cooperate in keeping the continent for peaceful purposes and to police the various explorations of the countries concerned. Argentina, Australia, Belgium, Chile, England, France, Japan, New Zealand, Norway, South Africa, Russia, and the United States share hopes of finding treasures under ice that is, in places, fourteen thousand feet thick. Natural gas, coal, oil, and possible uranium have been found. Argentina has discovered copper; Russia, iron. We may need that treaty badly before we are finished.

The Arctic is mostly water, frozen ocean surrounded by bits of frozen land. The Antarctic is a continent — the long-sought continent in the Sea of the South that the Spanish never found. If the Antarctic ice cap melted, the rest of the world would be in terrible trouble; the seas would rise two hundred fifty feet and all the port cities of the world would be drowned. The only natives of this continent are the comical penguins, who waddle about like gentlemen in tuxedos, to the great entertainment of the scientists who go there to study and explore.

The penguin, like Antarctica itself, should never be underestimated. He lives in probably the coldest spot on earth, and does rather a good job of it. Penguins are like seals in the water, swimming like Olympic champions. They are slow and clumsy on land. Yet once a year, when it is time to hatch their one chick, they take off — stumbling and grunting and falling over their own feet — on a fifty-mile walk to the breeding grounds, to raise their families.

Antarctica is host to a number of studies that will affect our future. It is the base for the U.S. Navy's Operation Deep Freeze, a year-round scientific center. Scientists from forty different colleges are there studying several things, including the matter of food sources — this is not only the coldest water in the world, but it is also the richest in food values — and the weather. They are also keeping a watchful eye on an ice shelf about the size of Mexico that gives some signs of crumbling. The U.S. has now six research centers in Antarctica, including one at the geographical South Pole. They now use vehicles designed to travel over ice and snow and take advantage of all the new warm clothing of a plastic age; Admiral Richard E. Byrd, first to fly over the South Pole, was the first to winter in Antarctica. No one ever actually lives there, and no one, presumably, has ever been born there. It is still true, as Admiral Byrd wrote, "The things we can learn there will have a profound effect upon the lives of us all."

Mark Twain used to say that everybody talked about the weather and nobody did anything about it. Now, when it is possible to read an ad, "Rain for Rent," it is obvious that we *are* doing something about the weather. Since glaciers are among the most delicate recorders of climatic change, scientists are giving a lot of time to the study of glacier ice, both in the Arctic and the Antarctic where there is enough to go around and then some. Glaciohydrologists claim that it will be possible to forecast weather for centuries ahead from the glaciers; in Alaska, all the prominent glaciers have their weather watchers.

"Hurricane Watch" is a familiar term along the Atlantic coast from Florida north; "Tornado Watch" is a feature of life on the Great Plains. How many lives these weather scouts have saved we cannot say, but they have made life much safer for people in "tornado alley" and along the wild Atlantic. We must never take these things for granted; they work because people work together to *make* them work. Weather still takes twelve hundred lives a year in the United States and causes a billion dollars' worth of property damage. We are trying now to get an "early warning system" set up for each of the different weather disasters.

Hurricane Camille, in 1969, killed three hundred twenty people; it was the worst storm in modern times and might have taken fifty thousand lives if people had not been forewarned and moved out of the way. Now that predictions are getting more accurate, we have an even better chance of keeping the death toll down. When Hurricane Debbie came whistling down on us, a brave crew of men in a small plane flew into the eye of the hurricane and seeded the clouds with chemicals. It was partly successful, and the process has been improved since then.

Weather forecasting goes far back in history. The old verse, "Red sky at night, sailor's delight; / Red sky in the morning, sailor's warning," is at least as old as the first century A.D., when Matthew wrote in his Gospel (Chapter 16, Verses 2 and 3): "When it is evening, you say, 'It will be fair weather, for the sky is red.' And in the morning, 'It will be stormy today, for the sky is red and threatening.' "

Now the National Weather Service gives out five-day forecasts, and you can subscribe to rain information the way you do to a magazine. We will even go up and seed the clouds to make rain, if it is badly needed.

The United States, along with more than one hundred other nations, is a member of the World Meteorological Organization. This is a worldwide weather watch in which at least ten thousand

Americans are involved. Information comes regularly from a satellite weather eye which circles the globe every two hours and scans every place on earth twice a day. A stationary satellite twenty-two thousand miles up can see almost half the world at a glance and can spot storms and hurricanes; tornadoes are harder to see. Ghost balloons are on duty all the time; tiny sun-powered radios on them send their news back to earth. There is a twenty-mile-deep blanket around the earth holding its weather. It carries one and a half million tons of air for each person on earth.

We would like to be able to tame the storms and stop the droughts, but that is still a goal for the future. Our grandfathers would be amazed to see what we have done so far in controlling the weather.

Hailstones cause an estimated three hundred million dollars' damage annually; sometimes the stones are as big as grapefruit. The Russians are using antiaircraft guns to break up hailstorms; they report that it is helping. In Australia, the scientists shoot off rockets. We have most of our storms worked out on computers, which may give us some answers. When you remember that one thunderstorm can generate as much energy as an atom bomb, you realize what power we are trying to harness.

The Alaska earthquake of 1964 taught us the need of a warning system because of the seismic waves that run under the water and, eventually, hit on some other shore. The waves from the Alaska quake tore off a lighthouse that was forty-five feet up on a rock, and then took off under the ocean at the speed of a jet.

The Japanese call this type of wave a tsunami, and it is terrifying, with its hundred-foot waves throwing boats and big fish into the treetops. A tsunami in 1896 killed twenty-seven thousand people in Japan. Now that a system has been set up to warn that the killer wave is on its way, very few lives will be lost.

We are living in wonderful times. Take, for instance, how the navy has trained sea lions to retrieve their dummy rockets, to be rewarded by the oldest sea lion delicacy, a raw fish! There are a great many almost unbelievable things being done in science now, and the inventions of the future will probably be even more amazing. But there is one thing that looking backward must teach us about the future: *natural resources will not last forever.* This is the only earth we have got, and we are the people who will care for it like a garden for the benefit of all — or neglect it, and pay with our own lives for our foolishness.

Consider the bison, more commonly known as the American buffalo. There was a time when the great buffalo herds spread from horizon to horizon and kept coming as though they would never stop. A whole culture, the life of the Plains Indian, was built around the buffalo. Then the white Americans came, and the buffalo were in the way. The railroad pushed out across the prairie, and more than one of the little old engines with the towering smokestacks was fought to a finish by some proud buffalo bull. Western Union pressed on West, putting up poles that the buffalo gladly used for scratching poles when their hides were itchy in the springtime. Hunters like Buffalo Bill Cody made it great sport to kill the beasts, and, gradually, they disappeared. All of a sudden, the millions of animals were gone forever; there were hardly enough animals left for someone to buy them up privately and try to save the breed from extinction. He was hardy, the old pioneer who surveyed all the railroads and highways across the plains; he survives. But the American buffalo, and the place where he was king, is gone. In the United States he now exists only in Yellowstone Park and on private preserves.

We must see that the redwoods, and the Grand Canyon, and our seashores, and our mountains do not follow him into oblivion.

> Can we carry through in an age where we will witness not only new breakthroughs in weapons of destruction, but also a race for mastery of the sky and the rain, the ocean and the tides, the far side of space and the inside of men's minds?
>
> *— President John F. Kennedy*

List of Things to Read, Do, See, and Discover

In the Days of Creation

BOOKS:

Our Continent, National Geographic Society Books.
Powers of Nature, National Geographic Society Books.
John Muir's Wild America, National Geographic Society Books.
Our National Parks, by Nelson Beecher Keyes.
The World of American Caves, by David L. Harrison.
Depths of the Earth, by William R. Halliday.
The Sea Around Us, by Rachel Carson.
The Age of Dinosaurs, by Kurten Björn.
Album of Dinosaurs, by Tom McGowen.
Monsters of the Ancient Seas, by William Wise.
Dinosaurs, by Herbert Zim.
Redwood Classic, Panorama of a Century, by Ralph J. Andrews.
There Stand the Giants, by Harriet E. Weaver.
Redwood Country, Sunset Magazine Publications.

NATIONAL GEOGRAPHIC MAGAZINE ARTICLES:

"Our Home-town Planet, Earth," by F. Barrows Colton (January 1952).

"Volcanic Fires of the 50th State," by Paul A. Zahl (June 1959).

"Craters of the Moon National Monument," by William Belknap, Jr. (October 1960).

"When Mt. Mazama Lost Its Top," by Lyman J. Briggs (July 1962).

"Our Living-giving Star, the Sun," by Herbert Friedman (November 1965).

"Our Changing Atlantic Coastline," by Nathaniel T. Kenney (December 1962).

"The Incredible Universe," by Kenneth F. Weaver (May 1974).

"Magnetic Clues Help Date the Past," by Kenneth F. Weaver (May 1967).

"Explorations in the Gobi Desert," by Roy Chapman Andrews (June 1933).

"Coal, Prodigious Worker for Man," by Albert W. Atwood (May 1944).

"This Changing Earth," by Samuel W. Matthews (January 1973).

"Lascaux, Cradle of World Art," by Norbert Casteret (December 1948).

"Carlsbad Caverns in Color," by Mason Sutherland (October 1953).

"Exploring America Underground," by Charles E. Mohr (June 1964).

"Among the Big Trees of California," by John R. White (August 1934).

"California Coastal Redwood Realm," by J. R. Hildebrand (February 1939).

"The Friendly Train Called Skunk," by Dean Jennings (May 1959).

"Giant Sequoias Draw Millions to California Parks," by John M. Kaufman (August 1959).

"A Park to Save the Tallest Trees," by Melville B. Grosvenor (June 1966).

SOURCES OF LITERATURE:

Save-the-Redwoods League
114 Sansome Street
San Francisco, California 94104

Dinosaurland
Vernal, Utah 84078

National Caves Association
1026 Balmoral Drive
Signal Mountain, Tennessee 37110

California Western Railroad
P.O. Box 907
Fort Bragg, California 95437

Roaring Camp & Big Trees R.R.
Felton, Santa Cruz County
California 95018

Very, Very Old Settlers

BOOKS:

Clues to America's Past, National Geographic Society Books.
Visiting Our Past: America's Historylands, National Geographic Society Books.
To the Pacific With Lewis and Clark, by Ralph K. Andrist.
The Lewis and Clark Expedition, by Richard L. Neuberger.
Mountain Men, Trappers of the Great Fur-trading Era, by Don Berry.

Beaver Skins and Mountain Men, by Carl Burger.
Seven Cities of Gold, by Mabel Farnum.
Coronado's Children, by J. Frank Dobie.
The Rocks Begin to Speak, by La Van Martineau.
Camels to California, by Harlan B. Fowler.
The Old Trails West, by Ralph Moody.
Maria, the Potter of San Ildefonso, by Alice Lee Marriott.
The Wilderness World of the Grand Canyon, by Ann and Myron Sutton.
The Sea Hunters, by Sonia Bleeker.

NATIONAL GEOGRAPHIC MAGAZINE ARTICLES:

"The Hohokam, First Masters of the American Desert," by Emil W. Haury (May 1967).
"Mounds: Riddles From the Indian Past," by George E. Stuart (December 1972).
"Pueblo Bonito the Ancient," by Neil M. Judd (July 1923).
"Exploring the Canyon of Death," by Earl W. Morris (September 1925).
"Surveying the Grand Canyon of the Colorado," by Lewis B. Freeman (May 1924).
"Everyday Life in Pueblo Bonito," by Neil M. Judd (September 1925).
"Secrets of the Southwest Solved by Talkative Tree Rings," by Andrew E. Douglas (December 1929).
"Utah's Arches of Stone," by Jack Breed (August 1947).
"Ancient Cliff Dwellers of Mesa Verde," by Don Watson (September 1948).
"Grand Canyon, Nature's Story of Creation," by Louis Schellenbach (May 1955).
"Solving the Riddles of Wetherill Mesa," by Douglas Osborne (February 1964).
"Down the Grand Canyon 100 Years After Powell," by Joseph Judge (May 1969).
"Santa Fe Trail, Path to Empire," by Frederick Simpich (August 1929).

"Down the Rio Grande," by Frederick Simpich (October 1939).

"The Romance of American Furs," by Wanda Burnett (March 1948).

"St. Augustine, Nation's Oldest City, Turns 400," by Robert L. Conly (February 1966).

"The Navajo Nation Looks Ahead," by Ralph Looney (December 1972).

"Exploring Frozen Fragments of American History," by Henry B. Collins, Jr. (May 1939).

"Alaska, the Big Land," by Robert W. Moore (June 1956).

SOURCES OF INDIAN INFORMATION:

Intertribal Dance Ceremonial
P.O. Box 1029
Gallup, New Mexico 87301

Indian City, U.S.A.
Box 695
Anadarko, Oklahoma 73005

Grand Canyon Scenic Rides
Box 520
Kanab, Utah 84741

Indian Travel Commission
10403 W. Colfax Avenue
Lakewood, Colorado 80215

Ute Mountain Tribal Park
Dept. WD
Towaoc, Colorado 81334

Roundup Association
Box 609
Pendleton, Oregon 97801

They Came by Sea

BOOKS:

Divers Voyages Touching the Discoverie of America, and the Ilands Adjacent Unto the Same; Made First of All by Our Englishmen, and Afterwards By the French and Britons (Imprinted at London for Thomas Woodcocke, Dwelling in Paules Church-Yard, at the Sign of the Black Beare, 1582). By Richard Hakluyt. (This book has recently been photocopied and printed just as it looked in the sixteenth century except for size.)

Vikings Bold, by Samuel Carter.
The Vikings, by Frank R. Donovan.
Westward From Vinland: America 1355-1364, by Hjalmar Holand.
Viking Expansion Westwards, by Magnus Magnusson.
Ferdinand Magellan, Master Mariner, by Gates Pond Seymour.
Drake, the Man They Called a Pirate, by Jean Lee Latham.
Francis Drake, Sailor of the Unknown Seas, by Ronald Syme.

NATIONAL GEOGRAPHIC MAGAZINE ARTICLES:

"The Voyage of Brendan," by Timothy Severin (December 1977).
"The Phoenicians, Sea Lords of Antiquity," by Samuel Matthews (August 1974).
"Vinland Ruins Prove Vikings Found the New World," by Helge Ingstad (November 1964).
"Spices, the Essence of Geography," by Stuart E. Jones (March 1949).
"Prince Henry, the Explorer Who Stayed Home," by Alan Villiers (November 1960).
"Henry Hudson's River," by Willard Price (March 1962).
"Captain Cook, the Man Who Mapped the Pacific," by Alan Villiers (September 1971).

"Christopher Columbus and the New World He Found," by John Scofield (November 1975).

"Columbus of the Pacific [Captain Cook]," by J. R. Hildebrand (January 1927).

"Vasco da Gama, Pathfinder of the East," by J. R. Hildebrand (November 1927).

"Ferdinand Magellan, Greatest Voyage in the Annals of the Sea," by J. R. Hildebrand (December 1932).

"Henry Hudson, Magnificent Failure," by Frederick G. Vosburgh (April 1939).

"Drowned Galleons Yield Spanish Gold," by Kip Wagner (January 1965).

"Sir Francis Drake," by Alan Villiers (February 1975).

"Reach for the New World," by Mendel Peterson (December 1977).

"Ships, From Dugouts to Dreadnaughts," by Dudley W. Knox (January 1938).

"How We Sailed the New Mayflower to America," by Alan Villiers (November 1957).

"Cape Horn Grain Ship Race," by A. J. Villiers (January 1933).

"Where the Sailing Ship Survives," by A. J. Villiers (January 1935).

"Under Canvas in the Atomic Age," by A. J. Villiers (July 1955).

"The Age of Sail Lives on at Mystic," by A. J. Villiers (August 1968).

"By Square-rigger From Baltic to Bicentennial," by Kenneth Garrett (December 1976).

"Navigating the Norge," by General Umberto Nobile (August 1927).

"Triton Follows Magellan's Wake," by Captain Edward L. Beach, U.S.N. (November 1960).

"Submarine Through the North Pole [Nautilus]," by Lieutenant William G. Lalor, U.S.N. (January 1959).

"Up Through the Ice of the North Pole," by Commander James F. Calvert, U.S.N. (July 1959).

"The Arctic As a Sea Route of the Future," by Commander William R. Anderson, U.S.N. (January 1959).

"North for Oil: Manhattan Makes the Historic Northwest Passage," by Bern Keating (March 1970).

"International Ice Patrol," by William S. Ellis (June 1968).

BOOKS ABOUT SAILING SHIPS:

History of American Sailing Ships, by H. I. Chapelle.
The Twilight of Sailing Ships, by Robert Carse.
Running Her Easting Down, by William F. Baker.
America Sails the Seas, by J. O. Cosgrove.
Pacific Graveyard, by James Gibbs, Jr.
West Coast Windjammers, by James Gibbs, Jr.
Old Ironsides, by Thomas Horgan.
Clipper Ship Days, by John Jennings.
Clipper Ship Men, by Alexander Laing.
The Charles W. Morgan, by John P. Leavitt.
Ships That Made U.S. History, by Helen Mitchell.
Men, Ships, and the Sea, National Geographic Society Books.
America Spreads Her Sails, Naval Institute Press (Annapolis).

MUSEUMS AND HISTORIC SHIPS ON DISPLAY:

Old Ironsides, berthed at Charlestown, Massachusetts.
Mayflower (replica): Plymouth, Massachusetts.
Golden Hinde (Drake, replica): Fisherman's Wharf, San Francisco.
Charles W. Morgan: Mystic Seaport, Connecticut (Maritime Museum, and courses in seamanship training for young people).
Star of India, Buccaneer Queen, and barkentine *California:* at Maritime Museum, San Diego, California (U.S. Navy also has days of open house for fighting ships that are berthed there temporarily).

Maritime Museum: Nantucket, Massachusetts.
Mariner's Museum: Newport News, Virginia.
Whaling Museums: at New Bedford, Massachusetts, and Sag Harbor, New York.
Windjammer cruises are available at most of the old shipping and whaling ports on the New England coast.

Tomorrow Is Here Today

BOOKS:

The Story of Maps, by Lloyd A. Brown.
Powers of Nature, National Geographic Society Books.
Antarctica, the Worst Place in the World, by Allyn Baum.
Heroes of Polar Exploration, by Ralph K. Andrist.
The Ocean Realm, National Geographic Society Books.

NATIONAL GEOGRAPHIC MAGAZINE ARTICLES:

"Men Who Measure the Earth," by Robert L. Conly (March 1956).
"How Soon Will We Measure in Metric?," by Kenneth F. Weaver (August 1977).
"The Pilot's Story," by Alan B. Shepherd, Jr. (September 1961).
"The Earth From Orbit," by Paul D. Lowman, Jr. (November 1966).
"First Explorers on the Moon," by Edwin E. Aldrin, Jr. (December 1969).
"What the Moon Rocks Tell Us," by Kenneth F. Weaver (December 1969).
"Journey to Mars [Mariner 9]," by Kenneth F. Weaver (February 1973).
"The Coming Revolution in Transportation," by Frederic C. Appel (September 1969).
"The Atomic Age: Its Problems and Promises," by Frank Friedel (January 1966).

"The Search for Tomorrow's Powers," by Kenneth F. Weaver (November 1972).

"Chemists Make a New World," by Frederick Simpich (November 1939).

"Crystals, Magical Servants of the Space Age," by Kenneth F. Weaver (August 1968).

"Arctic Research Laboratory," by Lowell Thomas, Jr. (November 1965).

"Antarctica, Icy Testing-ground for Space," by Samuel W. Matthews (October 1968).

"Conquest of Antarctica by Air," by Rear Admiral Richard E. Byrd (August 1930).

"Antarctica's Most Interesting Citizens," by Worth E. Shoults (February 1932).

"How the Sun Gives Its Life to the Sea," by Paul A. Zahl (February 1961).

"At Home in the Sea," by Captain Jacques Cousteau (April 1964).

"Tomorrow on the Deep Frontier," by Edwin A. Link (June 1964).

"Outpost Under the Ocean," by Edwin A. Link (April 1965).

"Fish Men Explore a New World Under the Sea," by Captain Jacques Cousteau (October 1952).

"International Geophysical Year," by Hugh L. Dryden (February 1956).

"Can the World Feed Its People?," by Thomas Y. Canby (July 1975).

"Can We Harness the Wind?," by Roger Hamilton (December 1975).

"Can We Predict Quakes?," by Thomas Y. Canby (June 1976).

"The Air Safety Challenge," by Michael E. Long (August 1977).

"The Power of Letting Off Steam," by Kenneth F. Weaver (October 1977).

"Man's New Frontier, the Continental Shelf," by Luis Marden (April 1978).

"Satellites Gave Warning of Midwest Floods," by Peter T. White (October 1969).

"We're Doing Something About the Weather," by Walter Orr Roberts (April 1972).

"Toilers of the Sky [Clouds]," by McFall Kerbey (August 1925).

"The Fire of Heaven [Electricity]," by Albert W. Atwood (November 1948).

"Measuring the Sun's Heat and Forecasting the Weather," by C.G. Abbot (January 1926).

PLACES TO SEE:

Smithsonian National Air and Space Museum, Washington, D.C.

Exploratorium: San Francisco (the management expects you to tinker with its far-out exhibits).

Museum of Science and Industry, Chicago.

TELEVISION SHOWS TO WATCH:

Don't miss the TV specials of Captain Jacques Cousteau.

Index

• A •

Alabama — 15
Alaska — 54, 68f, 136f, 179, 191ff, 200f, 217, 224, 234f
Allosaurus — 28
Ankylosauria — 31
Arizona — 44f, 70, 75, 77f, 94ff, 103, 127, 164, 175, 203, 207, 226, 231
Arkansas — 15
Armstrong, Neil — 36
Atlantic Ocean — 33, 88, 112f, 137, 139, 148, 165, 216, 218, 220, 234

• B •

Bandelier National Monument — 96, 100
Basket Makers — 70
Bering Sea — 43, 69
Bering Strait — 52, 70, 124
Black Hills — 22
Blue Lake Rhino — 20
Brachiosaurus — 27
Bridger, James — 19
Brontosaurus — 27f
Bryce Canyon National Park — 95

• C •

California — 19, 54, 56ff, 108, 122, 149, 152f, 160, 191, 196f, 199ff, 205, 207f, 211f, 219, 226
Canyon de Chelly National Monument — 95, 103f
Carlsbad Caverns — 20ff, 96
Carson, Christopher "Kit" — 104, 208
Cliff Dwellers — 14, 16, 76, 103
Clovis man — 51, 68
Cochise — 204f
Cody, William "Buffalo Bill" — 236
coelacanth — 25, 31f, 34
Coelophysis — 28
Colorado — 33, 43, 94ff, 103, 105, 204, 208, 211
Colorado River — 15f, 59, 94ff, 108, 226
Columbia River — 137, 160, 199f, 226f
Connecticut — 223
continental drift theory — 40f, 52
Coronado, Francisco Vásquez de — 47, 59, 126, 164ff, 169ff
Cowper, William — 36
Coxon, William — 78f
Craighead Caverns — 23

• D •

Davis, Jefferson — 203
Delaware — 228
Devil's Milhopper State Geological Site — 23
Dimetrodon — 28
Dinosaur National Monument — 33f, 44
Diplodocus — 27
Drake, Sir Francis — 141ff, 155ff, 196f

• E •

Elasmosaurus — 28
Endless Caverns — 23

• F •

Florida — 23, 41, 66, 113, 153, 156, 164, 234
Florida Keys — 42, 124
Folsom man — 47, 51, 68
Ford, Henry — 92

• G •

gastrolith — 34
Gateway Arch — 68
geologist — 14
Geronimo — 16f, 164
glaciohydrologist — 234
Gondwanaland [and Laurasia] — 40
Grand Canyon — 15f, 94ff, 104ff, 172, 191, 236
Great Lakes — 76
Great Plains — 48, 229, 234
Gulf of Mexico — 42, 79, 169

• H •

Hawaii — 149, 196
hydrologist — 14

• I •

Idaho — 16, 212
Indian tribes:
    Apache — 19, 95ff, 166, 175, 204ff
    Cherokee — 56
    Comanche — 95f, 166
    Havasupai — 95, 104ff
    Hopi — 95, 106
    Hualapai — 95, 106
    Makah — 179ff
    Modoc — 19

Indian tribes — *continued*

    Mojave — 106
    Navajo — 69, 95ff, 106f, 204
    Papago — 70
    Pima — 70
    Zuñi — 164, 167

• J •

Jefferson National Expansion Memorial [Gateway Arch] — 68
Jefferson, Thomas — 31, 136f

• K •

Kamehameha — 196
Kansas — 171ff, 208
Kennedy, John F. — 236
Kensington Rune Stone — 118f
Kentucky — 15f, 22
Kings Canyon National Park — 65

• L •

Lake Superior — 82
Laurasia [and Gondwanaland] — 40
Lava Beds National Monument — 19
Lee, Robert E. — 203
Lewis and Clark Cave — 22
Lincoln, Abraham — 191, 212
Louisiana — 230
Luray Caverns — 21

• M •

Maine — 60, 89, 206
Mammoth Cave — 22f

Mangas Coloradas — 204ff
Massachusetts — 32, 88, 216
McJunkin, George — 47
Mesa Verde National Park — 103
Michigan — 206
Minnesota — 118ff
Missouri — 15, 69
Mojave Desert — 23
Montana — 22
moon rocks — 38f
Mound Builders — 76
Mount Rainier — 16, 55
Muir, John — 55, 63, 65, 191
Muir Woods National Monument — 65

• N •

Nebraska — 172
Nevada — 43, 94, 203, 219
New Hampshire — 88
New Jersey — 206, 228
New Mexico — 16, 20f, 46ff, 54, 68, 75, 77, 89f, 94, 96, 98, 103, 124f, 164ff, 170ff, 202f, 206ff
New York — 48, 206, 219
Northwest Passage — 128ff, 137, 142, 160, 192, 195

• O •

Ohman, Olof — 118ff
Oregon — 20, 32, 58, 67, 69, 159f, 184, 212, 224

• P •

Pacific Ocean — 39, 114, 134f, 137, 139, 148, 156, 179, 220
Painted Desert — 44, 95
paleontologist — 14
Petrified Forest National Park — 44, 95

Pioneer 10 — 36
plesiosaur — 32f

• R •

Revere, Paul — 217
Rhode Island — 66, 88f
Rio Grande — 47, 52, 70, 168ff, 204, 211
Rocky Mountains — 20, 33, 43, 52, 76, 137, 212
Roosevelt, Theodore — 104, 226

• S •

Sandia Cave — 47, 51
Sandia man — 47, 51, 68
Sandia Mountains — 20, 46
Sequoyah — 56
Seward, William H. — 191
Sheridan, Philip H. — 203
Sherman, William T. — 203
Smilodon — 51
South Dakota — 22, 66
Spanish Cave — 23
speleologist — 14, 23
spelunker — 14, 23
stalactite — 15, 22
stalagmite — 15, 22
Stegocephalia — 28
stegosaur — 32
Stegosaurus — 28
Superstition Mountains — 175

• T •

Tennessee — 15
Texas — 32, 68, 164, 202f, 208, 211, 230
Triceratops — 28

Twain, Mark [Samuel Langhorne Clemens] — 233
Tyrannosaurus — 28

• U •

Utah — 33f, 43, 96, 103, 107

• V •

Valley of Fire — 43
Virginia — 15, 21, 206
Voyager — 36

• W •

Washington — 16ff, 48, 55, 68, 159f, 179, 212
Washington (D.C.) — 118, 208
Washington, George — 197, 216f
Wisconsin — 48, 55, 60, 176
Wright Brothers — 215

• Y •

Yellowstone National Park — 166, 236
Yosemite National Park — 58, 65

• Z •

Zion National Park — 95